S0-ABJ-972

Bill,
San Francisco
Our experience . . .
Here we have grown together,
. . . our love,
. . . our home,
. . . our children,
Our lives together!

All My Love,
Karin Lee

Happy Anniversary!

Happy

Jan. 10, 1974

THE SAN FRANCISCO EXPERIENCE

ALSO BY HAROLD GILLIAM

San Francisco Bay
San Francisco: City at the Golden Gate
The Face of San Francisco
Weather of the San Francisco Bay Region
Island in Time: The Point Reyes Peninsula
The Natural World of San Francisco
Between the Devil and the Deep Blue Bay

THE
SAN FRANCISCO
EXPERIENCE

HAROLD GILLIAM

Edited by Ann Gilliam

Doubleday & Company, Inc.
Garden City, New York
1972

Material incorporated in Chapters 5 and
6 of PART Two originally appeared in *True*
magazine, Copyright © 1959 by
Fawcett Publications, Inc.

Library of Congress Catalog Card Number 76–171292
Copyright © 1972 by Harold Gilliam
All Rights Reserved
Printed in the United States of America
First Edition

*Dedicated to two San Franciscans
whose good works for their city will be felt
for generations to come:
Dorothy Erskine and Augustin C. Keane.*

Preface

THE SAN FRANCISCO EXPERIENCE is not an encounter you can enjoy in an hour or a day or at a particular time or location. It is a composite of innumerable experiences over long periods of time in the entire region around the bay. San Francisco as a social and cultural entity long ago spilled over the political boundaries that were drawn up a century ago for another era. Nearly one-third of the people who during the day work and shop within the city limits go home at night beyond the bay or down the Peninsula. Nearly all of the tourists and visitors who come to the city also visit the far shores. Even the relatively few who do not venture across the bridges experience something of the far shores when they gaze across the bay from Nob Hill or Russian Hill or through the big windows at the Top of the Mark or the Crown Room of the Fairmont.

Although the experience of San Francisco necessarily involves Telegraph Hill and Twin Peaks, the Palace of Fine Arts and the Golden Gate Bridge, it also includes such diverse places as Angel Island, Berkeley, Oakland's Lake Merritt, and Mount Diablo. It embraces Tamalpais to the north, Skyline to the south, and the Pacific shoreline to the west. It includes not only Sunny Jim Rolph, Willis Polk, Adolph Sutro, and Joseph Strauss, who spent most of their time within "the city" proper, but among others John Muir of Martinez, William Kent of Marin, and Robert Gordon Sproul of Berkeley.

Perhaps this book should have been entitled *Tales About a Representative Cross-Section of Places and People Essential to Full Enjoyment of the San Francisco Experience*. But book titles being what they are these days, we were obliged to settle for the short form.

Some time after the title was selected, a multimedia show, *The San Francisco Experience,* opened at Ghirardelli Square. There is no connection, but it is an excellent show and we highly recommend it.

Pre-eminent among the dozens of people who helped make this book possible are two quintessential San Franciscans, men of culture, humor, broad sympathies, and cosmopolitan outlook. One is Chesley Bonestell, an artist whose long career has involved work for Willis Polk, Arthur Brown, Jr., and Joseph Strauss; in recent years he has achieved new fame as one of the world's foremost illustrators of space exploration. The other is his good friend since the prefire era, Augustin C. Keane, attorney, scholar of the classics, raconteur, civic leader, cultivator of roses, and Renaissance man. The first part of this book had its inception in leisurely lunch-time conversations over a period of years as I listened to their recollections around the tables at the Press Club, Bardelli's, and the Redwood Room.

Among others who generously gave time and information for this book were Mrs. Arthur Brown, Jr.; William Wilson Wurster; the late Mrs. Alfred McLaughlin; James Abajian; Clifford Paine; Mrs. Irving Morrow; Mrs. Olive Cowell; Director Richard Trudeau and naturalist Chris Nelson of the East Bay Regional Park District; State Park Director William Penn Mott and his valiant rangers; Newton B. Drury and the Save-the-Redwoods League; Alan Galloway and Edward Ross of the California Academy of Sciences; Robert Langner of the Marine Exchange; author-walker Margot Patterson Doss of just about everywhere around here; Mel Scott of the University of California, author of *The San Francisco Bay Area;* Eleanor D. Breed; Mrs. Max Stern.

Portions of the material in this book originally appeared in different form in *This World,* Sunday magazine of the San Francisco *Chronicle,* and I am grateful to the *Chronicle* for permission to use it here. I owe particular thanks to *Chronicle* colleagues Richard Demorest, Nancy Griffin, Suzanne Caster, Virginia Radenzel, Stanleigh Arnold, and Gordon Pates; to former editor Scott Newhall and publisher Charles de Young Thieriot.

My thanks to *True, Image,* and *Audubon* magazines and to the San Francisco *Examiner* for material that originally appeared in those publications; to the diligent librarians of the *Chronicle,* the Mechanics' Institute, and the San Francisco Public Library; to Julianne Thompson, artist, musician, and typist, for her work on the manuscript; to Luther Nichols and Walter Bradbury of Doubleday.

My final thanks and gratitude, as always, to Ann Lawrence Gilliam, editor this time as well as collaborator and co-worker in this and all my other projects.

Contents

Prologue

THE MORNING AFTER the first autumn rain, you get up before sunrise and walk to the northernmost summit of the long ridge west of Twin Peaks. The concrete steps rising at the end of Moraga Street are still damp from yesterday's storm. The wet hillside chaparral glistens in the predawn light, and you can smell the damp aromas of sage and coyote brush.

At the summit you face full into a cold northwest breeze. Four miles west of this ridge the early light illuminates the breaking surf along Ocean Beach. As you watch through the binoculars, a big swell curls, crashes silently into white roaring water and charges toward the shore. Out over the ocean are colossal explosions of pink and white—cumulus clouds following the storm.

At this hour the sea is still as wine-dark as Homer's Aegean, except where large zones of the surface glow with the reflected light from the masses of cumulus above. Off the Golden Gate the water is flecked with whitecaps, where an ebbing current from the bay runs counter to the wind. Due west, ten miles offshore, you can discern a flashing white light on the big red San Francisco Approach Buoy, which in 1971 replaced the historic San Francisco Lightship.

Swinging your glasses slowly around to the north, you spot a sailing vessel—the pilot boat *California*. Several miles farther north a black freighter approaches, doubtless preparing to take on a pilot for the narrow passage through the bar channel and the Golden Gate. On the horizon far out beyond the lightship four points of rock protrude darkly from the ocean surface. These are the northwest Farallones—barren eroded remnants of an ancient offshore land mass. To the left is the Southeast Farallon, largest of the chain, a mile-square mass of rock rising to a point from which an automatic light flashes. Masses of white appear rhythmically along the base of the island's cliffs as the ocean attacks this final bastion of the disintegrated land.

Scattered here and there across the glowing surface of the sea are small fishing boats, like water insects swimming in and out of the broad oceanic stripes where the clouds are reflected. On the northwest horizon a headland projects into the ocean like an elongated whale—the Point Reyes peninsula, a remnant of the same granitic land mass to which the Farallones belonged. On the nose of the "whale" you can see a recurrent flash, and through the glasses you make out the white buildings of the Point Reyes lighthouse.

At Point Reyes a Coast Guardsman leaves his living quarters and descends a nine-hundred foot stairway leading along the steep ridge to the lighthouse. He shivers slightly in the perennial sea breeze and zips his jacket up to the neck. Alongside the steps, the ground drops off to cliffs plunging to the churning surf, where a dozen sea lions roar.

At the lighthouse the seaman opens the door to the lamp room, glad to be out of the wind. After a few words with the night crewman going off duty, he looks out to sea to check the usual three points: the approach buoy, twenty-five miles to the southeast; the Farallon light, eighteen miles due south; and the Drakes Bay buoy, four miles to the east. The seaman notes that the ocean surface has a pink cast as the top rim of the sun emerges from behind Bolinas ridge. He flips a series of switches turning off the beacon and goes up a dozen steps to the lamp itself, a six-foot revolving lens built in Paris more than a century ago. He pulls a white curtain around the lens to shield it from the sun, then steps to the deck outside, picks up a hose, and turns it on the windows, washing off a thin layer of salt deposited by fine spray from the surf three hundred feet below.

As you watch Point Reyes in the northwest, the first direct sunlight strikes the white cliffs behind it, throwing into sharp relief the ridges, indentations, and projections of the wave-cut escarpment curving for a dozen miles along the shore of the peninsula. Southward down the coast you can see Point San Pedro, the other promontory enclosing the fifty-mile Gulf of the Farallones. Looking at these two headlands, you are swept back into time several centuries.

The bluffs of Point Reyes reminded Francis Drake of the white chalk cliffs of the English Channel during his month-long California landing in 1579. He named this wild land Nova Albion and claimed it in the name of Her Imperial Majesty, Queen Elizabeth.

Two centuries later, on a clear fall day much like this one, the first Europeans to arrive by land wearily climbed over Montara Mountain behind Point San Pedro and camped at its northern base. The next day Captain Gasper de Portolá sent Lieutenant José Moraga and some men north along the coast, where they discovered the Golden Gate. From where you stand on this ridge you can follow their route along the coastal shelf and across the miles of dunes stretching westward between this ridge and the ocean. The hills and swales of sand through which Moraga and his men trudged are still there in front of you, covered by the streets and houses and gently rolling contours of the Sunset and Richmond districts.

As you trace their steps, there is a roar in the sky. To your left a big jet plane rises from San Francisco International Airport, gains elevation, and swings overhead above Moraga's trail in a long right curve.

At an altitude of three thousand feet over Daly City, the pilot of the United Air Lines DC-8 orders: "Flaps up." The first officer, sitting to his right, reaches for a big lever on the right edge of the center console, moves it to the zero position, and the plane immediately begins to gain speed. The needle on the dial moves steadily from 200 knots to 250. Ahead and below, the pilot can see the waves breaking along the beaches for ten miles down the San Francisco Peninsula.

"Climb thrust," he says. As the flight engineer, sitting to his rear, changes the throttle setting, the pilot turns the wheel to the right, and the big aircraft goes into a shallow banking turn, curving over the beach, right wing low.

In seat 4D of the first-class compartment, a businessman returning to New York looks up from his Wall Street Journal and gazes out the window, past the dipping wing, at the long green swath of Golden Gate Park stretching halfway across the city, then at the downtown district, where several new skyscrapers are rising. The passenger reflects that San Francisco bears an increasing resemblance to Manhattan. Suddenly he is momentarily blinded as the

*rising sun flashes in the window. He draws the curtain and returns
to his paper.*

Up in the cockpit, the pilot turns the wheel slowly back to the
left as the needle on the magnetic direction indicator swings toward
040 degrees. By this time the plane is 4000 feet over Nob Hill. On
the horizon, 150 miles ahead, the pilot can see a jagged line of
white—the summit peaks of the Sierra Nevada.

Halfway between the Golden Gate and Point Reyes, you can see
Duxbury Point protruding into the ocean. Its long tide-level reef,
where the Gold Rush ship *Duxbury* went aground, is boiling white
as the tide drops and exposes the rocks to the surf. Behind Duxbury
reef, on top of the long row of dun-colored cliffs and in the clefts
between, are the white buildings of the village of Bolinas. Back of
the town you can see a wide flat mesa, an ancient sea terrace;
beyond is Inverness Ridge, with open rolling hills and groves of
Douglas fir.

*At the edge of the forest, on Inverness Ridge, a big blacktail
doe peers out of the woods, surveys the meadow for breakfast
possibilities, and steps out into the grassy area, followed by another
doe and three fawns. The five deer sample the sage and coyote
brush, fanning out over the meadow.*

*As they do so, fifty yards away at the edge of the woods, a
mottled tan bobcat creeps slowly through the brush. When he
reaches the edge of the long morning shadow cast by the trees,
within twenty yards of one of the fawns, he abandons concealment
and charges.*

*Instantly all five of the deer race across the meadow and down
the hillside in great bounding leaps. The cat follows for a hundred
yards, but the fawns are large enough to keep up with the does,
and within ten seconds it becomes clear that the cat is outdistanced.
He abandons the chase and walks off to try his luck in another
direction.*

Along the north shore of the Golden Gate from Point Bonita to
Point Diablo to Kirby Cove to the bridge, you can see the white
waves assaulting the base of the dark red Franciscan cliffs. The
Gate is a rare piece of geology, a gap in the Coast Range allowing
the ocean to penetrate deep into the continent. If you had stood on
such a hilltop as this during the late Pleistocene, the view would
have been quite different. Sea level was lower then; the ocean was

far to the west; and San Francisco Bay did not yet exist. This gap in the range was being carved by the combined waters of the Sacramento and San Joaquin rivers, which maintained their course as the mountains rose, through the millenniums, deepening the canyon. At the end of the Ice Age, rising sea level flooded the river-carved gorge and occupied the Golden Gate and the valley which became San Francisco Bay.

On top of the first ridge north of the Gate you can see the white bulbs of several Air Force radar domes. Beyond a second ridge rises the long crest of Mount Tamalpais, 2600 feet high. The early light throws its ridges, forests, and canyons into sharp relief.

Carrying a glass cup half full of water, Peter Rogney, the Tamalpais fire lookout, steps out the door on the east side of the small observation building on the summit. Turning up his jacket collar against the wind, he glances northward to flat-topped Mount St. Helena, fifty miles to the north, and double-peaked Mount Diablo, forty miles east. Both summits are brilliantly clear in the early light.

Rogney walks around the building to the southwest corner, where he opens a large white wooden box and peers inside at two thermometers. Both of them read forty-seven degrees. He holds the cup under the wet-bulb thermometer, dampening the wick, then switches on a small battery-powered fan. Within two minutes the moving air has cooled the wet wick until the mercury drops to forty-three. He notes both figures and returns to the lookout room, where his wife is cooking bacon and eggs. There he consults an arithmetical table posted on the wall, converting the two temperature figures to dew point and humidity.

Then he gazes out again at the Marin hills below, habitually scanning the landscape for smoke. A few minutes later the phone rings.

"Hi, Pete. This is Ken." The call is from the United States Weather Bureau office in Redwood City, where meteorologists make a daily forecast of the fire danger resulting from atmospheric conditions. "Did I wake you up, like yesterday?"

"Nope," Rogney says, grinning. "Got up early this morning. That cold wind did it. Let's see, now . . . Dry bulb temperature forty-seven. Wet bulb forty-three. Dewpoint thirty-nine. Humidity seventy-four . . ."

"Roger," replies the weather man. "How's the view today?"

"Clearest all year," Rogney replies. *"I can see the jackrabbits on the Farallones."*

Not all of the spectacle visible from your hilltop is on the far horizon. The near and middle distances have their own shows, equally intriguing. To the north you spot through the glasses a magnificent red-tailed hawk, hovering against a backdrop of the waters of the Gate. He seems to hold something in his talons, perhaps a mouse or gopher. You can see clearly his fan-shaped, maroon-colored tail, his dappled breast and brown wings, dipping as he maneuvers on the air currents. He rises a short distance on an updraft, and the backdrop is now the ridge north of the Gate. At that moment your eye is caught by a quick gleam of light reflecting from the windshield of a car emerging from the Waldo Tunnel, north of the bridge.

Traffic coming into the city is still light at this time of morning, and broker Alexander Mazour of Belvedere has the speedometer at sixty-five as he pilots his Volkswagen squareback over the Waldo grade into the tunnel. Over the car radio comes a stream of popular music from FM station KLOL, but he hears it only sporadically. His mind is on the day's work ahead in his office at Merrill Lynch on California Street. He wonders about the General Motors Acceptance Corporation debenture issue of one hundred million dollars coming on the market this morning. No doubt the price will be affected by yesterday's late announcement from New York that the Federal Reserve Board is lowering the reserve requirements.

As the car emerges from the tunnel, the broker whistles softly. This panorama, bursting suddenly on the vision after the tunnel's blackness, is always impressive, but this morning, after the autumn mists have been cleared away by the rain, the prospect has an impact reaching all the way from the optic nerve to the spinal column. Directly ahead, dominating the view, is the north tower of the bridge, a bright red colossus in the early light. Beyond is the bay, glowing with gold from the reflected cumulus above. Silhouetted against the glare in the east is the downtown skyline, upthrust towers rising from the city's hills and valleys, clean and sharp and vital.

This almost makes it worth getting up at five every morning, Mazour reflects. But by the time the car is on the bridge he is remembering GMAC and wondering which of the banks and insurance companies among his clients might want to buy in at a probable 8.75 per cent. As he crosses the mile-long span, the ebb tide is moving vast masses of water, and a fishing boat slides rapidly along the six-knot current 250 feet directly below Mazour's car.

By the time the sun is an hour above Twin Peaks, you notice that the poststorm cumulus clouds seem to be thinning out, but there is still a large white mass to the northeast, inside the Gate. It throws a dark shadow on the center of the bay, on Angel Island, Raccoon Strait and the Tiburon Peninsula, about ten miles away from where you stand.

On the northeast horizon, beyond Tiburon and the far reaches of San Pablo Bay, another cloud mass casts patterns of light and shadow on the rolling Sonoma Mountains, forty miles away, and on the parallel Mayacamas, bounding Sonoma Valley on the east. Beyond the Mayacamas is Napa County. These are the valleys of the vineyards, Jack London country, Robert Louis Stevenson country, wine country.

On a knoll above the century-old Buena Vista winery, two miles northeast of Sonoma, the vineyard foreman steps from the door of his white farmhouse and peers up at the sky. He is glad to see the early sunlight shining from the wet leaves of the tall eucalyptus trees and a clearing sky beyond. Too much rain before the harvest is finished can ruin the grapes on the vine; yesterday's storm was mercifully brief. Within a few minutes several cars arrive with the crew of pickers—pensioners, teen-agers, housewives.

"We'll be picking down by the gatehouse today," he tells them. "No hurry, though. We'll have to wait for 'em to dry."

The pickers get their buckets and knives from the shed and pieces of chalk to mark their boxes. Then the foreman starts his pickup and the members of the crew follow in their own cars, down the hill to the vineyard by the gatehouse. He looks over the four-foot-high trellised vines, where big clusters of ripe red cabernet sauvignon grapes, wet from the rain, glisten in the morning sun. Several years from now their juice will go out to stores and restaurants across the country in bottles with the Buena Vista label.

"Let's give 'em about half an hour. They should be dry enough by then," the foreman says. Then he adds, with a grin: "Dry enough to make some good dry wine."

Over the bay, masses of cumulus continue to drift eastward on the wind, throwing moving patterns of light on the land and water below. Alcatraz is suddenly bright against a dark expanse of water; the next moment it looms black on a brilliant surface. Light and shade follow each other up the chaparral-clad slopes of Angel Island. Through Raccoon Strait you can see a glimpse of the broad bay surface beyond and the gleam of the Richmond-San Rafael Bridge like an elongated silver spider web. At the end of the bridge, the long hill of Potrero San Pablo extends from Point Richmond to Point San Pablo, and you can see the big flat tanks at the Standard Oil refinery planted on the slope like giant steppingstones.

At Tank Number 922, on the hill above the Richmond refinery, a gauger, clipboard in hand, climbs the long steel stairway spiraling around the tank. At the top he stoops down and flips back the lid of the gauge well. The odor of gasoline spreads up from the opening. With a steel tape, he measures the depth of the fuel, then drops a thermometer down the well on a wire. While he waits for the temperature to register, he looks over the panorama before him— down the hill past the cluster of silver tanks to the freeway, beyond it to the long company wharf where three tankers are moored, and beyond that to the blue bay sweeping to the white towers of the city.

Pulling the thermometer back up, he records the reading, and calculates that the tank contains 97,284 barrels of gasoline. He goes down the long stairway again and phones the wharf where the tanker SS Hillyer Brown *is waiting. He reports the number of barrels in the tank.*

"Okay," says the dockman, "we're all set. Let 'er come."

The gauger turns the tank valve and the gasoline begins to flow through the pipe down to the ship. In Seattle, the tanker's destination, the fuel will provide tankfuls of gas for about three hundred thousand automobiles.

The freighter you saw on the horizon earlier has now taken on a pilot and entered the Golden Gate. Passing it outward bound on the far side is a gray aircraft carrier, twice the size of the freighter. Inside the Gate, on the surface of the bay, you spot an Army Corps of Engineers dredge, a white "sugar boat" distributing sugar from the C&H refinery at Carquinez, the early ferry from Sausalito, and three Redstack tugs headed for separate destinations. Anchored off Treasure Island is the long low shape of a giant tanker, most of it submerged like an iceberg. Nearby, headed north from the Embarcadero, is a towboat lashed to a long barge loaded with railroad cars.

Captain Hans Hansen, of the northbound Santa Fe tugboat John R. Hayden, *keeps his eye on a patch of rough water ahead. The meeting of the currents and the west wind from the Gate sets up a tide rip—a stretch of white water two hundred yards long. Lashed to the* Hayden *on the port side is a three-hundred-foot barge bearing four refrigerator cars, six boxcars and two tri-level cars, each with racks carrying eighteen Datsun automobiles just off a ship from Japan.*

As the bow of the barge hits the turbulent water, the captain swings his wheel to the starboard, then picks up the bullhorn and calls across to the wheelhouse of the barge.

"Give me some starboard rudder, Joe," he calls. "Easy, not too much . . . Okay, hold 'er there."

The bow, which had drifted slightly to the west, veers back slowly until it heads directly toward Point Richmond. A few minutes later, having passed through the rip, the captain gazes out across the water. After months of peering at the bay and its shores through fogs and mists, he welcomes the first sharp, chill weather of fall, when he can see every detail of the panorama across which he navigates every day. Eastward the sunlight blazes up from the water. Behind the cities of the eastern shore, the near slopes of the Berkeley Hills are beginning to be touched with light. The ridges are illuminated; the canyons are still in deep shadow; the eucalyptus and Monterey pines along the summits are brilliantly etched against the sky in the clear morning light.

One hour and ten minutes after leaving San Francisco, the captain pulls the two craft into the dock at Ferry Point, Richmond, the Santa Fe terminal. This afternoon the Datsuns will be delivered by rail down the San Joaquin Valley for distribution to dealers in Bakersfield.

The sea breeze continues to blow cold and salty from the northwest, but as the sun climbs higher in the eastern sky, you can feel the welcome warmth on your back. Slowly the sun dries the rain-dampened sage and coyote brush on the eastern slopes below. The currents of the bay and the currents of the metropolis are both beginning to move on the flood tide. Four lanes of cars flow out of the Waldo Tunnel in a continuous stream toward the bridge. Along the arterials below this hill—Nineteenth Avenue and Lincoln and

Crossover Drive through the park—traffic moves in nervous rhythms, dammed temporarily at the stop lights, spilling over onto the secondary streets.

Out on the bay, tugs, barges, fishing boats, freighters, and ferries move from the Embarcadero across the blue surface. Jet planes drone overhead every few minutes. From the yard of Columbus School, four blocks down the hill, rises the ebullient clamor of several hundred shrill voices; from the streets comes the occasional blare of car horns; from the bay you can hear the bass tones of an outbound freighter.

In the city, on the bay, in the satellites and suburbs around these shores, millions of people are going to work, and their sounds seem to rise to this hill like the roar of a far-off surf. To the north along the cliffs and headlands of the Golden Gate, the breakers continue to rise in white geysers of spray. To the west, the swells from the storm curl over and break on a four-mile front. Above the ocean the sky is clear now; over the eastern mountains the decks of cumulus linger and rise into castellated towers of vapor, soon to be demolished by the warmth of the morning sun.

PART ONE

---◆---

THE CITY

1

The Pleasure Palace of Sunny Jim

SAN FRANCISCO is a city of surprises at the ends of the streets. From North Beach you can look down busy Columbus Avenue to a quick view of the blue bay and passing ships, Sausalito rising on its hillside on the far shore, Tamalpais towering half a mile into the sky. You may round a corner on Cervantes in the tightly built Marina District and suddenly, there beyond the wall-to-wall apartment houses, confront the north tower of the Golden Gate Bridge, rising at the street's end on a colossal scale totally unrelated to that of the buildings around you.

Perhaps the most impressive street-end experience of all occurs as you turn off Market at Fulton and enter the Civic Center. The clutter and clamor of the downtown commercial districts are gone and you confront another dimension of time.

Looming across the Civic Center Plaza is the massive dome of the City Hall, surmounting a structure of Renaissance splendor. Entering this building and standing in the richly ornate rotunda, you can feel the weight of history—both the history of Western culture and the history of this city. This building was the last grand architectural gesture of San Francisco's youth, a product of the same age of exuberance that produced the Victorian mansions of the Nabobs, Ralston's fabulous Palace Hotel, and the fantastic Panama-Pacific International Exposition of 1915.

Appropriately, the man largely responsible for this palace—and its first occupant—was himself the final representative of that same age of exuberance, James Rolph, Jr. That was the era of the great showmen in American life—the Great Ziegfeld, the Sultan of Swat, the Manassa Mauler, Sister Aimee, Mayor Jimmy Walker; but there are innumerable San Franciscans who will aver with a lifted glass and a misty eye that the greatest showman of all was Sunny Jim Rolph, Mayor of San Francisco for nearly two dazzling decades and Governor of California for one term that ended in tragedy.

THE BIGGEST DOME

Picture the rotunda of the City Hall with its ceiling ten stories high and crowds lining the galleries and banks of flowers massed below the glittering gilt lanterns and scrolls and statues. The band plays "Smiles"; the crowd cheers; and there at the top of the grand staircase appears Sunny Jim, smiling and resplendent in morning coat and striped pants.

There are smiles that make you happy,
There are smiles that make you blue;
There are smiles that steal away the tear drops,
As the sunshine steals away the dew . . .

Sunny Jim built the City Hall (with some help from the architects and assorted contractors and workmen), and its classic opulence reflected the mayor's modest tastes. It was his proudest boast— repeated on innumerable occasions—that the City Hall dome was thirty-seven feet higher than the dome of the Capitol in Washington "and built without a nickel of graft." Actually, Sunny Jim's figures were a little off. The nickel may be accurate, but the City Hall dome is not thirty-seven feet higher than the Capitol dome. It is forty-six feet lower.

Fortunately for the city's pride, however, the mayor was not totally wrong. The top of the lantern spire above the City Hall dome attains a height of 301 feet five and a half inches above Polk Street, outreaching the Statue of Freedom on top of the Capitol dome by fourteen feet. This comparison is valid, however, only if you measure the Capitol from the East Front, where it rises 287 feet five and a half inches above the street. Capitol Hill slopes down to the west, however, making the West Front higher above ground level, and it is possible to add twenty feet or so to the Capitol's measured height—and surpass the City Hall—by resorting to what Sunny Jim would doubtless regard as unscrupulous tactics.

In any case San Francisco indisputably comes out on top in the inside dimensions. Our rotunda ceiling is 183 feet above the floor, surpassing the Capitol's rotunda by three feet.

THE FLOWERY MAYOR

Sunny Jim loved flowers, in the City Hall as elsewhere. His Mission District home on San Jose Avenue was surrounded by brilliant gardens, and there was an inevitable carnation in his buttonhole. Once while campaigning for governor, he stopped his car on a mountain road and had his chauffeur scramble over a barbed wire fence to pick a wild flower so that he would have a boutonniere for his appearance at the county seat.

In those days spring came to San Francisco not at the equinox but on April 15, when the mayor each year appeared at the City Hall in gleaming white suit and straw hat. The only undeviating aspect of his costume was his footgear—leather boots burnished to a high glitter. Anyone wanting to give the mayor a present could count on his being pleased with a new pair of handmade boots, and he was particularly delighted with a pair presented to him on his fifty-fifth birthday by the laundresses of the City Hall.

In keeping with the tradition that a politician should have humble origins, Rolph seldom lost an opportunity to remark that he was just a boy from the Mission District, and he declared with pride at the august Pacific Union Club that he was the only member of the organization who was also a member of the garbage men's union. He was equally proud of his ancestry; whenever he met an American Indian he would solemnly announce that he was a descendant of Pocahontas.

With all his love of ceremony (he marched, refusing to ride, in every major parade in the state) he still had time for the serious business of his office. His gift for the theatrical even entered into such normally grim affairs as settling strikes. He sometimes would call a meeting of the adversaries in his office at 5:30 P.M., continue through the dinner hour (presumably having stoked himself up in advance) and announce his intention of getting a settlement before adjourning the meeting. Before midnight, the famished negotiators usually were able to work out a compromise settlement.

Besides the City Hall, his proudest achievement was the 1915 Panama-Pacific International Exposition, which included the Palace of Fine Arts (preserved after the exposition through his efforts) and several hundred acres of other palaces almost as impressive. The closing of the exposition in November was a sad occasion, which

he made even sadder by reciting verse after verse of an ode to the
city:

> *I've collected souvenirs*
> *From Alaska to Algiers,*
> *From Cuba to the beach of Waikiki;*
> *But no matter where I am*
> *Be it Sydney or Siam,*
> *San Francisco, you are Home Sweet Home to me.*

The poem was chiefly notable for being the only instance on record
of a versifier successfully finding a rhyme for "Waikiki."

SHADOWS IN THE ROTUNDA

Most of the city's achievements during his era had more enduring
results than the exposition: the Civic Center, including, besides the
City Hall, the Library, and the Civic Auditorium; the observation
road on Twin Peaks; the Hetch Hetchy aqueduct; the yacht harbor
and Aquatic Park; the city airport and the successful campaign to
build the Bay Bridge.

As Republican candidate for governor in 1930 Rolph smiled and
shook hands in each of the state's fifty-eight counties and so impressed the electorate that he defeated incumbent Governor C. C.
Young in the primary.

Rolph's genuine love for people is illustrated in a story told by
marine biologist Joel Hedgpeth, whose family had been Mission
District neighbors of the Rolphs on San Jose Avenue. When Hedgpeth was to receive his degree at commencement ceremonies at the
University of California, Rolph as governor, marching with President
Robert Gordon Sproul into the Greek Theater, spotted Hedgpeth's
mother in the crowd. Although he had not seen her for many years,
he stopped the academic procession to greet the beaming lady, pulled
her by the elbow up to the platform and found a seat for her between Sproul and himself.

As Depression governor he anticipated the New Deal with a big
program of public works and a youth conservation corps, and he
later campaigned mightily for the colossal Central Valley Project,
Cailfornia's counterpart of TVA.

Then he made a fatal blunder. An outbreak of kidnapings had
outraged the nation, and after a young boy was abducted and
murdered in San Jose in November 1933, a mob broke into the
county jail there and lynched the confessed kidnapers on the oaks of

St. James Square. Rolph, echoing the first sentiments of many an American, made the statement that was heard around the world: ". . . The might of the people was aroused to serve notice that kidnaping and murder will not be tolerated in California . . . If anyone is arrested for this job, I will pardon him."

The reaction was swift and violent. Whatever he might have felt in the heat of the moment, it was unforgivable for a high public official to condone a lynching. The storm of wrath that descended on Rolph was quite possibly a mortal blow. His health had been steadily declining, but, disregarding his doctor's orders, he was strenuously campaigning for re-election a few months after the lynching when he was stricken in Marysville. He was driven back to San Francisco in great pain, but as his car passed through each town en route he straightened himself up and rode down the main street with all his old smiling splendor, like Sarah Bernhardt playing her final scene. After his death, his body lay in state in the rotunda of his City Hall as thousands of people filed by for their last look at Sunny Jim.

Today on the rotunda wall opposite the grand staircase, are inscribed in letters two feet high the words "JAMES ROLPH JR." And at times after business hours when the crowds are gone and the light filtering down from the high clerestory windows invests the chamber with ghostly shadows, the visitor who listens carefully may hear the far-off strains of the municipal band playing "Smiles" and see in recollection a beaming figure in a cutaway at the top of the stairs, a vanished symbol of an expansive, reckless, dazzling era that has gone out of American life forever.

THE TRIUMPH OF THE BEAUX ARTS

The story of the City Hall, however, is only partly the story of Sunny Jim. It is also the story of a man who was Rolph's opposite in temperament. Arthur Brown, Jr., the building's designer, was quiet and unassuming, with no talent for showmanship and no desire for the limelight. He merely had what his teacher, Bernard Maybeck, called with admiration "perfect taste."

Maybeck, creator of the Palace of Fine Arts and the precursor of the architectural style known as "Bay Area modern," was in the 1890's an instructor in architecture at the University of California and one of the most brilliant stars in the Berkeley firmament of those years. Among the undergraduates who met at Maybeck's home regularly for informal discussions and study was young Brown, an engineering student whose father had been principal bridge engineer in the construction of the transcontinental railroad. Another was Brown's fraternity brother, John Bakewell, Jr., student of the classics. Maybeck, who had an eye for talent as well as for buildings, encouraged both of them to go into architecture and to attend that artistic mecca, the Ecole des Beaux Arts in Paris. Brown's father had hoped that his son would follow in his own footsteps as an engineer, but at the urging of Maybeck he finally agreed to send the young man to the Beaux Arts.

Bakewell, the son of an Episcopal clergyman, told Maybeck that he hadn't the financial resources to attend the Paris school. The professor sagely arranged for him to meet Phoebe Apperson Hearst, wife of Senator George Hearst and patron of the arts. Mrs. Hearst was so impressed with Bakewell's talents that she offered to finance his Beaux Arts education.

Bakewell gratefully accepted the money as a loan and passed the entrance examination easily. But Brown, who had been a model student at Berkeley, was so nervous that he flunked his first attempt and had to take the test again. Once in Paris, however, he succeeded in winning more Beaux Arts architectural prizes than had ever been received by an American. According to legend, the school's authorities were so taken aback that they thereafter barred Americans from the competitions.

After their return to San Francisco from Paris, the two Beaux Arts graduates set up the architectural firm of Bakewell and Brown. Bakewell ran the business while Brown concentrated on design. Brown's habit of winning competitions carried over: His design won a contest for a city hall in Berkeley, a building that was finished in 1908 and was still in use sixty-three years later.

The Berkeley success encouraged the two to compete for a greater prize—the design for a San Francisco city hall to replace the building destroyed in the earthquake of 1906. In the face of competition from prestigious firms, the two young architects felt that their chances of winning were slight, so they decided to disregard practical limitations and design an ideal building in the best Beaux Arts classic tradition.

With the dome of the Invalides in Paris—housing the tomb of Napoleon—as their inspiration and starting point, they conceived a spectacular structure that lacked nothing in lavishness or taste. In many another era—including our own—such an entry would have been rejected as exorbitant in design and expense. But in the flush of optimism and opulence that followed San Francisco's recovery from the 1906 disaster and the expectation of prosperity arising from the opening of the Panama Canal, the times were ripe for exactly the kind of Beaux Arts grandeur expressed in the Bakewell-Brown design. To everyone's surprise, the drawings by the two young architects won out over impressive entries by the established luminaries in the field of architecture.

"THE GREATEST ARCHITECTURAL ENSEMBLE"

Sunny Jim, of course, was delighted with the drawings, and when it appeared that budget restrictions would hamper the design, he made prodigious and ultimately successful efforts to find additional funds. With philosophical roots still in Paris, Brown sent for several of his friends of Beaux Arts days, who worked out details of the design. One was Jean-Louis Bourgeois, who made suggestions for changing the scale of the building and enlarging the dome, and who designed many of the sculptured effects of the rotunda. (Before the building was completed, World War I broke out, and Bourgeois was called back to France, where he was killed in the "taxicab army" defending Paris).

The building, completed in 1915, is a triumph of Renaissance styles. A Roman Doric colonnade sets off the wings, and over the east and west entrances high columned porches are surmounted by pediments containing traditional sculptured figures. Over the Van Ness entrance are figures representing Wisdom, the Arts, Learning, Truth, Industry, and Labor, and on Polk Street are the figures of San Francisco, the riches of California, Commerce, and Navigation— all the work of another Beaux Arts colleague of Bakewell and Brown, Henri Crenier.

Impressive as is the dome from the exterior, its full impact comes on viewing the vast rotunda inside. The marble staircase seems to flow down from the main gallery, spreading as it reaches the main floor. Above it in every direction is a wealth of architectural detail worth hours of study—walls and columns of cut granite, lanterns, arches, vaults, bas-relief figures, sculpture groups, bronze and iron work, and gallery after gallery rising toward the opulently ornamented interior of the dome.

Brown's design for the City Hall catapulted him to the front rank of American architects. His subsequent career spanned a remarkable era; he was on the boards of architects for both the 1915 and 1939 world's fairs and for the Bay Bridge. His contribution to the 1939 fair on Treasure Island was the four-hundred-foot Tower of the Sun, the dominating feature of the exposition.

Not only was he architect for two world's fairs, but, what is perhaps even more remarkable, for two rival universities: Stanford and California. On the Stanford campus his contributions (also in partnership with John Bakewell) covered a period of a quarter of a century, including both gymnasiums, Stanford Union, the University Library, the Art Gallery, the Stanford Theater, and the Hoover Tower, developed in collaboration with his good friend, Herbert Hoover. The ex-President once commented: "Arthur saw to it that all the campus buildings held to the Romanesque as long as he was University architect. There have been sad desecrations since."

Brown's contributions to the campus at Berkeley include Cowell Hospital, Sproul Hall, and in 1949 the last building he ever designed, the Library Annex. His most famous achievement was the War Memorial Opera House (1932), birthplace of the United Nations. Embellished in Brown's classic style, the building is a structure of compelling beauty. The Opera House, his adjacent Veterans Building, and the City Hall, across Van Ness Avenue, together constitute what Henry Hope Reed, Jr., in his book *The Golden City,* has called "the greatest architectural ensemble in America."

Other Brown designs in the city include Coit Tower; Temple Emanu-El, at Arguello and Lake; the California School of Fine Arts on Russian Hill; the old Federal Office Building in the Civic Center; and the PG&E building on lower Market Street, his only commercial structure.

"DIGNITY, COUNTERPOINT, AND BALANCE"

In 1933 Brown designed one of the most noted groups in Washington, D.C., the Department of Labor building, the Interstate Commerce Commission building, and the connecting Interdepartmental Auditorium. In recognition of his achievements both in Washington and San Francisco, he was called to Washington in 1956, at the age of 82, as a member of the board of three architects to give advice on the rebuilding of the East Front of the Capitol, the historic scene of presidential inaugurations.

His conclusion was that the building could not be rebuilt as planned without destroying its architectural harmony.

"The dome and its columns," he said, "come down in a harmonious flow. This is very rare in domes, and very beautiful. It has a certain quality which would be lost if anything basic is changed."

The two other architects agreed with him, but they pointed out that Congress had not asked whether the job should be done; they were simply instructed to find a way to do it. Brown was adamant. Usually calm and amiable, on this occasion he protested vigorously: "The building is very satisfying. . . . The trouble is there are a lot of fellows with itchy fingers who want to monkey with it all . . . bumbling milliners who think architecture is a fashion and want to change it every year."

Brown stood his ground but did not prevail. Against his advice, plans were completed to rebuild the Capitol, and it was finished in time for the inauguration of President Kennedy in 1961. Early in 1957, a few months after Brown had made his report on the Capitol, he died at the Hillsborough home, Le Verger, which he had designed for himself and his wife.

Brown's words of praise of the original design of the Capitol are revealing. He had spoken of the structure's "dignity, counterpoint, and balance"—qualities eminently characteristic of Brown's own life and works. His finest buildings, particularly the City Hall, embody these values in a superb expression of a great civilized tradition. The City Hall is San Francisco's link with the civic magnificence of earlier ages—the Florence of the Medicis, the London of Sir Christopher Wren, the Paris of the Bonapartes and Haussmann.

It is an illuminating reflection on the spirit of our own times to compare the City Hall with some of the more functional structures of recent years, such as the gigantic slab of the Federal Building overshadowing the Civic Center two blocks away. Evidently our era has less respect for the arts, which symbolize the purposes of life, than for technical efficiency. In our preoccupation with the means, we lose sight of the ends. In an age more concerned with technics and speed than with broad human purposes, San Francisco would do well to cherish its City Hall. Nothing like it will be built again in our time.

2

Farewell to the Hill

TELEGRAPH HILL must be seen slowly. Stroll and gaze and listen and savor the essence of these heights above the bay. Wander among the old houses on the gentle western slope where you will hear the accents of Genoa mingle with those of Canton. Go down the precipitous eastern hillside, where Greenwich and Filbert streets become stairways and glassy modern apartments stand opposite century-old cottages in the trees. Walk along pathways once frequented by Robert Louis Stevenson, Jack London, George Sterling. On the steps below Montgomery Street look for Darrell Place and Napier Lane and the rambling gardens on the public right of way planted and tended by residents.

Have lunch or dinner at Julius Castle or the Shadows, if you can find them among the old houses. At the bottom of the hill you will see the clattering Belt Line Railroad and the ships that unload their cargoes from around the world. Beyond the waterfront are the changing colors of the bay, the flowing currents, the encircling shores, the far mountains.

Come to the hill, if you can, many times, in different weathers, in sun and mist and rain. Come early in the morning, before the city is awake; as the sun comes up from behind the Berkeley Hills across the bay, it illuminates first the tops of the highest downtown towers; and as the light descends the city appears to rise from a pool of shadow as this peninsula once rose, in an Indian legend, from the waters around it. Come on a summer afternoon; see the fog flowing through the Gate and over the bay like a flood tide.

Feel the force of the west wind and watch the leaves of the eucalyptus trees vibrate in the light like Japanese wind chimes. Watch the sun go down behind the Gate in a blaze of ocher and crimson as if the ocean were on fire. In the early evening gaze south and west, where the inner-lighted towers of downtown, Nob Hill, and Russian Hill rise like a wall of jewels in the twilight sky. On the north and east the bay spreads out like a black mirror to the glowing constellations of cities along the far shores.

THE PASSING OF THE LURLINE

To anyone who has lived or lingered here overlooking the bay, the most dramatic aspect of the panorama is the procession of ships that come from around the world and pass below the hill to unload at the docks along the Embarcadero. Many a hillside resident develops a personal relation to the ships, keeping track of their comings and going, following their schedules in the daily papers or in the *Pacific Shipper* as avidly as a horse buff studies the racing form, developing his own favorites among the hundreds of vessels that make this bay a regular port of call.

In our years of living on the hill, long ago, we regarded the ships out the window as regular visitors and noted with satisfaction the return of a vessel after a long absence. When someone we knew was arriving on a particular ship, we waved a sheet from our balcony in greeting or flashed our lights after dark.

Our favorite in those years, the queen of the bay, was the *Lurline,* the latest in a line of vessels by that name that had sailed between here and Honolulu since 1887. That was the year Captain William Matson bought *Lurline I,* a spread-sailed brigantine yacht, from San Francisco's Spreckels family. The yacht had been named for a contemporary operetta, whose name, in turn, had been anglicized from the German "Lorelei." She became the forerunner and flagship of the Matson shipping empire, which still carries most of the cargoes bound for the islands.

The *Lurline III,* and later her successor, *Lurline IV,* docked at Pier 35, below our window, and the ship's arrivals and departures became a regular part of our pattern of living on the hill. Once, when we were newcomers on the hill, we were sure the *Lurline* was sinking. We heard her whistle give a series of short alarm blasts; water spouted from her hull as if she were leaking; and her crew was taking to the lifeboats. Then, as we gaped at the presumed disaster, expecting to see passengers leaping into the water as she went down by the bow, it occurred to us that this was not the way a ship leaked, that her fire hoses were being tested, that there were no passengers aboard, and that the crew was engaged in a routine boat drill.

We could never avoid watching her four-o'clock sailings as the tugs ushered her gingerly out of the dock, the band played "Aloha," and her sonorous whistle reverberated from the hills of the city. The slowness with which the ceremony took place gave it an air of ponderous majesty. The vessel's movement away from the pier was barely visible, and there was something elemental and planetary about her as she parted the strands that connected her to shore and moved almost imperceptibly out into the bay. Once out in the stream and headed west, she moved toward the Gate with increasing speed, white water rising at her bow and trailing off to stern, a floating city that diminished in size until she sailed under the bridge and disappeared behind Fort Point.

The sound of the old ship was as impressive as her appearance. Her blasts when she was about to depart would rattle our windows and cause momentary suspension of all conversation in the house. Her voice was unique on the bay—a resonant, musical bass whistle that seemed to be sounding simultaneously on two pitches. It was as unmistakably a San Francisco sound as the Ferry Building siren or the clang of the cables. It echoed among the downtown skyscrapers and hills as from a sounding board.

Now the voice of the *Lurline* is no longer heard in the city, and her old dock at Pier 35 below the hill is vacant much of the time. The growth of jet travel to Hawaii had taken most of her passengers, and in June of 1970 *Lurline IV* made her final voyage through the Golden Gate.

FAMILIES OF SHIPS

Matson, which in the 1920's and 30's operated as many as six liners to the islands, is entirely out of the passenger business now but still operates two dozen freighters to the islands, distinguished by the big blue "M" on the buff-colored funnels.

Sailing past the hill on the transpacific run to Yokohama, Hong Kong, and Manila are American President Lines' big gray liners *President Cleveland* and *President Wilson*. APL's freighters and passenger-cargo vessels, such as the *President Polk* and *President Monroe*, all carry the white presidential eagle on their red funnels. The third stack insignia on San Francisco-based vessels sailing below the hill is the Pacific Far East Lines' golden bear, visible on twenty-one freighters sailing to the Orient. The PFEL bear also appears on two passenger liners formerly owned by Matson—the *Mariposa* and the *Monterey,* operating to the South Pacific.

During our years on the hill we felt we had come to know certain families whose members took special pride in seeing their names emblazoned in huge letters on the hulls of their vessels. The Isbrandtsens and the Luckenbachs were among the American families enjoying this privilege. Japanese shipping families were well represented —among them the Daido, Iino, Mitsui, and Mitsubishi families. (The Mitsuis and Mitsubishis are two of the eight "ruling families" of Japan, known before World War II as the Zaibatsu.)

Most freighters were painted in dark colors, but the Mitsui family evidently had a fondness for brilliance. Its ships were a bright green. They were outshone only by the more brilliant blue of the Danish Maersk line. The Maersk vessels were further distinguished by being emblazoned not only with the family name but with the given names of the family members—sisters, cousins, aunts, and great grandfathers. Sally Maersk, Jeppesen Maersk, Susan Maersk, Chastine Maersk and several others were among the members of the Maersk family whose names can be spotted a mile away on the hulls of ships in most of the ports of the world.

P & O

The parade of vessels goes by day and night—the tankers, the container ships with their cargoes in big aluminum boxes visible above decks, the colossal aircraft carriers, and the P & O liners, doubtless the most distinguished of all the ships that float below the windows of Telegraph Hill. Every two weeks, on the average, they sail in through the Gate like a symbol of the British Empire— panoplied in dignity, swank as the Savoy, elegant as Claridge's, global as Lloyd's, traditional as *The Times,* a remnant of that magnificent century when Britannia's rule of the waves was undisputed from London to Calcutta. The sun never sets on them, and they are the embodiment of imperial Britain in fifty world ports from San Francisco to Yokohama and Port Said to Hong Kong.

These are the largest liners in the Pacific, and in a time when passenger ships are on the decline worldwide, supplanted by jet planes, the P & O is carrying more travellers each year. One of them—the *Canberra*—accommodates more passengers than any other vessel afloat on any of the seven seas. If she were to be upended on her stern at the dock, her bow would not only look down on Telegraph Hill, it would rise several hundred feet higher than the tallest buildings in the city.

P & O is not only the largest but the oldest steamship line in the world. There are abundant references to it in English literature; "P & O" is the title of a short story by Somerset Maugham and stands along with Cunard as a symbol of the shipping establishment in *The Pirates of Penzance*. Gilbert and Sullivan's pirate king boasted: "A keener hand at scuttling a Cunarder or cutting out a P & O never shipped a handspike."

The venerable company traces its ancestry to 1815, when the armies of Wellington repulsed the final charge of Bonaparte's troops on the field at Waterloo. Its name—abbreviated from Peninsular and Orient Steam Navigation Company—dates back to 1840, when it began to serve not only the Iberian Peninsula but India. In the pre-Suez days India-bound passengers had a grueling camel-back or carriage trip across Egypt to the Red Sea, and many a passenger who had weathered Atlantic and Mediterranean storms without missing a meal turned green after an hour on the swaying hump of a "ship of the desert." On the hot trip through the Red Sea to India, VIP's were given special accommodations, including staterooms on the cool side of the ship—the port side on the way out, the starboard side on the return trip. Their tickets were stamped "P.O.S.H." for "Port Out; Starboard Home," and thus, according to P & O tradition, a new word for special treatment and luxury service entered the language.

Telegraph Hill ship watchers have another reason for being especially fond of the P & O liners. As representatives of Her Majesty Queen Elizabeth II, these ships are successors of the first British vessel to visit the Bay Area. It was Drake's *Golden Hind,* representing Queen Elizabeth I, and four centuries ago it pioneered the transpacific route now used by its descendants.

If you happen to be on the hill on departure day of one of the big liners, listen carefully as she sails away, and you might hear, far off, a regular rhythmic beat that could be the throb of her engines or perhaps the drum of Drake or the tolling of Big Ben. You might even see, in imagination, a stout figure with a big cigar clenched firmly in a bulldog jaw, standing on the bridge, gazing out to sea, contemplating with satisfaction this magnificent vestige of the imperial tradition.

TO NIAGARA IN A SLEEPER . . .

If the ships were a vital part of the pattern of our lives on Telegraph Hill, equally so was the Belt Line Railroad, which carried cargoes to and from the docks along the Embarcadero. Its clang and clatter on the tracks below the hill were as familiar as the whistles of ships and the drone of the foghorns. Like the ships, the freight cars came as symbols of far places. They were emblazoned with the escutcheons of all the major railroad lines of the United States and Canada. Here the rhythms of the names on the American land encountered those of the world's great ports. London and Liverpool, Marseilles and Bombay and Hong Kong met St. Louis and Sauk Center, Grand Rapids and Keokuk.

Most of the freight cars below the hill were the traditional dull red, but here and there bright colors stood out, such as the green-and-white of the New York Central (The Water Level Route—You Can Sleep), a car that had doubtless rumbled on many a trip up the storied Hudson from Yonkers to Poughkeepsie to Albany and across upstate New York to Utica and Syracuse and Buffalo and Niagara Falls. (*To Niagara in a sleeper. There's no honeymoon that's cheaper. And away we go . . . shuffle off to Buffalo.*)

And there the yellow cars of the Great Northern, with its painted symbol of the Rocky Mountain sheep atop a continental crag—the line that rolls through Lewis and Clark country on the upper Missouri, through the land of the Sioux and Crow and Blackfoot, land of aboriginal names—Lakota and Oswego, Wiota and Chinook.

Clanking along a track beneath the Embarcadero Freeway one day was a bright red boxcar of the Burlington (Route of the Zephyrs), which had doubtless made many a trip over the bridge across the Missouri between those cities whose names conjure up a summit conference of the feathered chieftains, Council Bluffs and Omaha, and had rolled along the upper Mississippi past places named by and for the French trappers and explorers—Dubuque, Des Moines, La Crosse, Prairie du Chien.

Alongside Pier 31, where the stern of a black freighter from Yokohama loomed above the dock, was a bright green car of the Maine Central (The Pine Tree Route) and not far away a gray tank car of the St. Louis Southwestern (the Cotton Belt Route)—East St. Louis to Hickory Ridge to Little Rock to Pine Bluff to Texarkana.

Side by side below the hill were the dull red cars of the Rock Island (*Oh that Rock Island Line it is a mighty fine line. Oh that Rock Island Line it is the road to ride*) and the Pennsylvania Railroad, running from Manhattan (*. . . the Pennsylvania Station at a quarter to four . . .*), across to Jersey and down the Delaware

River to Philadelphia and across the Susquehanna to Baltimore and the white city on the winding Potomac.

CHATTANOOGA CHOO-CHOO

In the strings of cars near Fisherman's Wharf we often saw one which unabashedly proclaimed in big letters across the door the single word: FRISCO—a contraction for the St. Louis and San Francisco Railroad Company, a name that may be a symbol of unfulfilled ambition, for its closest track to San Francisco ended at Floydada, Texas.

Most numerous along the Embarcadero were the boxcars of the mighty Southern Pacific and the orange-colored refrigerator cars of the Pacific Fruit Express, operated by SP and Union Pacific, hauling fresh lettuce and green vegetables and frozen foods from the fields and packing plants of California and the Southwest to refrigerator ships bound for ports around the Pacific. Mingled with the PFE cars was an occasional reefer of the Bangor and Aroostook, which had come across the continent after hauling tubers from the potato country of Maine.

Almost in the shadow of Coit Tower the clanging electric locomotive of the Belt Line shunted back and forth long strings of cars with reverberating bangs and rumbles that echoed from the cliffs of the hill, cars bearing such evocative names as Missouri Pacific (Route of the Eagles), Southern (*Pardon me, boys, is this the Chattanooga choo-choo? . . .*), Western Pacific (Feather River Route), Northern Pacific (Main Street of the Northwest) and Wabash (*Oh the moonlight's shining down upon the Wabash. From the fields there comes the scent of new mown hay . . .*).

Cars of the Canadian Pacific brought newsprint from the mills in the northern forests, and Canadian National cars were loaded with coffee destined for breakfast tables in Vancouver.

The most motto-conscious of the railroads had cars proclaiming: Route of the Texas Chief or Route of El Capitan or The Grand Canyon Line or Route of the Super Chief or Santa Fe all the way (. . . *All aboard for Califor-nye-ay, On the Atchison, Topeka and Santa Fe*).

Along the northern waterfront where the spars of the old windjammer *Balclutha* rose above the bay we spotted one day a car of the Illinois Central (The Main Line of Mid-America), running from Chicago down the Great Plains where the cold Canadian winds in winter whistle across the prairie, and in the towns the lights glisten on the frosty streets and the snow piles up in drifts along the white picket fences.

Since our years on Telegraph Hill, the railroads have largely gone out of the passenger business, and their slogans these days are more likely to deal with the advantages of handling goods than of hauling people. (*Hydra-Cushion for Fragile Freight . . . Be Specific—Ship Union Pacific.*) Yet the Embarcadero is still a crossroads of the continent, and the names on its boxcars bring to anyone who has ever crossed the country on a railroad the sounds and sights and smells of the American landscape, memories of the deep rhythmic rumble of the big passenger trains, the hypnotic click of the wheels on the tracks, the streets of a hundred towns flashing past the windows, the lonely wailing whistle of a steam locomotive in the night (*. . . from Natchez to Mobile, from Memphis to Saint Joe, wherever the four winds blow . . .*).

RING OUT THE OLD

Sadly, the Belt Line below the hill is evidently doomed. Condemned also are most of the cargo piers below the hill. They are old and outmoded. Plans for the port call for the freighters to dock at new efficient terminals to be built in the industrial zone south of the Bay Bridge. The strip of flat land between Telegraph Hill and the waterfront is too "valuable," with rising land prices, to be devoted to an industry even as glamorous as shipping. It is steadily going into apartment houses and profitable business buildings. One proposed commercial center would in effect fence in the lower third of the hill on the north and east. This most historic and picturesque part of the hill, on the lower Greenwich and Filbert steps, and along Napier Lane, would no longer look out to the bay but into a wall of buildings.

The view from the hill will change, and the hill itself will not be immune to the forces of progress. Taxes continue to climb, and property which could pay off handsomely by being used for apartments will not much longer be devoted to century-old cottages and exotic pathways among rambling gardens. With rising rents, the hill's diverse peoples will move to less expensive areas and will be supplanted here by a homogeneous high-income population.

Cities grow and change and mature, as do people, and Telegraph Hill, as we have known it, evidently must disappear. A well-organized, mature city could not indefinitely tolerate the inefficiency of the hill's brilliant but haphazard diversity—a place where many peoples, many varieties of buildings, many kinds of residential and commercial and industrial activity are as hopelessly jumbled together as they are on and around this hill. Diversity must be replaced by standardization, efficiency, uniformity.

So we are thankful to have known this high enclave before its character has changed irrevocably. For the rest of our lives we will see in recollection its ancient cottages, its reflected light welling up through the trees from the bay, its steep paths looking down on the harbor. We will smell in memory the fragrance of its hillside gardens, its flowing fogs, its salt winds, the rich odors of the ravioli factories, the Neapolitan bakeries, the coffee shops. We will listen to its medley of languages and accents and hear again the haunting orchestration of sounds of ships, warehouses, foghorns, and railroad cars. We will remember and savor these vanished sights and smells and sounds as an incomparable experience of the city's earlier years—and of our own.

3

The Glass Wall
and Willis Polk

OF ALL THE pyrotechnic personalities who blazed across the skies
of San Francisco in the early years of the century—Jack London,
George Sterling, Gelett Burgess, Bruce Porter, Arnold Genthe—
none was more brilliant, eccentric, or talented than architect Willis
Polk. And none made a more enduring contribution to American
culture. Just as Jack London overturned the tables in the literary
world, so Polk did in the field of architecture. His most significant
work was a structure of revolutionary design that was at least
forty years ahead of its time—the progenitor of all modern glass-
and-steel skyscrapers.

You can see it on Sutter Street near Montgomery—a shining
jewel of a building to delight the eye amid the humdrum structures of the downtown district. It is hard to believe now that
Polk's building was originally greeted with shock, incredulity, and
disapproval.

He designed it for a piece of income property then owned by
the University of California—a site the university originally intended for a hotel. When the building was completed in 1918,
it hit the city with the impact of an architectural explosion—as
the irreverent designer doubtless intended. The front "curtain wall"
is glass, reflecting the sky, nearby buildings, clouds, and wraiths of
fog like a seven-story mirror framed in elaborate ironwork.

The building was named for another San Francisco innovator—
Andrew Hallidie, a regent of the university and the inventor of

the cable car. Subsequent owners, however, apparently unaware of the building's historic value, dropped the name, referring to it only as "150 Sutter," and permitted considerable violence to Polk's design in remodeling the first floor for a clothing store.

Polk had evidently not anticipated one eventuality. The building faced south, and on a warm day the sun, pouring through the glass wall, heated up the interior like an oven. The occupants— in the days before air conditioning—found it necessary to devise elaborate systems of blinds as a sun shield.

THE REDISCOVERY OF A MASTERPIECE

The glass curtain wall was a radical innovation in an era when walls were supposed to be solid and substantial. A few other American architects had experimented with glass but none had gone this far. Theoretically the glass wall had been possible ever since the Eiffel Tower in 1889 had demonstrated that a steel framework could rise to great heights and that heavy bearing walls were no longer necessary. But tradition dictated that the walls still should be massive, as if they, and not the steel frame, were holding up the building. With this structure, Polk opened the door to new and imaginative designs not bound to stone and masonry.

Yet no one went through the door. The concept was too advanced. The building was regarded as a freak, and several decades passed before architects began to catch up with it. It was rediscovered at mid-century, when big photographs of it were hung at the Harvard Graduate School of Design and in other architectural halls of fame. The first major building to follow Polk's lead was the United Nations Secretariat in New York in 1950, designed by an architectural team headed by Wallace Harrison and based on concepts of Le Corbusier. By mid-century, Polk's glass wall was an idea whose time had belatedly arrived. In New York the United Nations Building was followed by the Lever Brothers Building on Park Avenue, designed by Skidmore, Owings and Merrill, and the House of Seagram nearby, a work of Mies van der Rohe. The Lever design inspired San Francisco's second glass-walled building, Crown-Zellerbach (also by Skidmore, Owings and Merrill) on Market Street two blocks away from its ancestor on Sutter—and forty-two years later.

MAN OF THE SIXTEENTH CENTURY

The Hallidie Building had jolted even many of Polk's admirers, familiar with his tasteful designs in classic styles. Although it was a startling departure from his previous work, the innovation itself was consistent with his personal life as an unpredictable iconoclast and an implacable foe of staidness and pomposity. Some San Franciscans regarded him as a near genius with irresistible personal charm and others saw him as an intolerable egomaniac. Quite possibly he was both.

There is a story that he once stood on his head in the lobby of the St. Francis Hotel to collect on a bet. He often wore a French silk hat on Market Street, twirled a Malacca cane, and cultivated an extravagantly courtly manner. ("He belonged to the sixteenth century," said one of his friends.) But he also took great pleasure in insulting dignitaries. Legend holds that he was expelled from the august Bohemian Club for pulling a chair out from under a particularly starchy millionaire.

Although he was small in stature, he somehow was able to give the impression of looking down from a great height. On one occasion he was approached by an Eastern businessman, who wanted him to design a major building. The industrialist told the architect that he had greatly admired his work. Polk's response was an Olympian stare. "I would feel complimented," he said, "if I thought you knew anything about art." The rebuffed industrialist took his business elsewhere.

At a banquet in Tait's restaurant on O'Farrell Street, artist Charles Rollo Peters made a long-winded speech attacking architects for designing art galleries improperly. The next speaker was Polk, who immediately declared, "I have always known that there were more horses' asses than horses."

The outraged Peters rushed up onto the stage, shouting, "Willis, you called me a horse's ass!" Members of the audience intervened to prevent bloodshed.

Polk's monumental self-esteem and his propensity for antagonizing important people frequently had him in court. He once refused jury service because of his bitter antagonism to Prohibition, which he regarded as a personal affront and which he violated as conspicuously as possible. During one court battle he was called to the stand to testify as to his own character and reputation. "When it comes to originality," he affirmed, "Michelangelo had nothing on me."

THE GIRALDA TOWER

His remarkable self-assurance (or perhaps self-reassurance) may have been rooted in his early life in Kentucky and Missouri. His father, also an architect, was a disabled Civil War veteran who found it hard to earn a living, and young Willis helped to support the family from age six. When the boy was fourteen, the family moved to San Francisco, and he was apprenticed to an architect. In the early 1890's he became a designer in the office of Arthur Page Brown (no relation to Arthur Brown, Jr., the City Hall architect). Brown at that time had the job of designing San Francisco's Ferry Building to replace an outmoded earlier ferry terminal at the foot of Market Street.

When Brown was killed in a runaway horse accident in 1896, Polk, as chief designer, completed the job. Like most monumental buildings of that era, the Ferry Building was modeled after an ancient structure in Europe. The tower was an adaptation of the Giralda Tower of the Cathedral of Seville, which itself had been originally built as a Moorish minaret. Polk had never been to Seville, but he had pored through the architecture books in search of good designs—a custom of virtually all architects at a time when Americans still had little self-confidence regarding architectural design. Europe, particularly Paris, was the mecca of the arts; and after completing the Ferry Building Polk took a job in Chicago in the offices of Burnham and Root, one of the top American architectural firms of that era. There, Polk fell under the spell of Daniel Burnham, who later, with Polk's help, developed the Burnham Plan for San Francisco. (See Part One, Chapter 6.)

Burnham in turn was so impressed by Polk that he sent him back to San Francisco to open a branch office. Polk later set up his own firm. His largest building of that period—the tallest downtown structure at the time of the disaster of 1906—was the Merchants Exchange, center of the business life of that time. The building, at 465 California Street, restored by Polk after the fire, is now a bank office, but its great hall, where ship arrivals were once posted in the manner of Lloyds of London, still shows signs of Polk's opulent décor.

REBUILDER OF THE CITY

As the city's leading architect after the earthquake and fire of 1906, Polk redesigned and reconstructed more major buildings than any other architect. In later years, Polk asked Bonestell to draw up a composite picture of the large buildings he had worked on. The drawing was published in the newspapers with Polk's own heading: "The Man Who Rebuilt San Francisco."

The structures pictured included the Mills Building on Bush, the de Young Building at Market and Kearny, and the brand-new

Hobart Building on Market at Second, then the tallest structure in the city. The detail for the Hobart Building's elaborate flaring tower was worked out by artist Chesley Bonestell, Polk's designer. When he tried to follow Polk's instructions, he noticed that the straight roof line appeared incongruous with the tower's curving side walls. He tried to convince Polk that the roof line should be curved, but his objections were unheeded. One morning after the building was finished, Polk called Bonestell into his office and complained, "I was walking down Market Street and I noticed how badly that straight line on the roof of the Hobart Building looks."

"I protested at the time we were designing it," Bonestell replied. "I told you it should be curved."

Polk, who could never admit he had been wrong, retorted, "You didn't protest hard enough!"

The same building caused other problems. The City Building Department claimed during construction that he was not properly fireproofing the building, and Polk retaliated with his usual acerbity. He placed a large sign on the Market Street fence enclosing the site, denouncing the city officials as incompetent bureaucrats and declaring in large letters that their requirements were unnecessary and ridiculous. It was during this controversy that there took place the well-known altercation between Polk and a city inspector, who accosted the architect on the site. Polk told him to talk to the construction superintendent, who at that moment was on the top of the steel framework. The official laboriously hauled himself up to the twelfth floor only to be informed by the superintendent that he was simply following the architect's design. The inspector clambered down again and strode up to Polk with blood in his eye, whereupon the architect airily declared with a wave of his cane that he did not wish to discuss the matter, hopped on a girder that was about to be raised to the upper stories, and was transported into the heavens. The dispute was settled only when Mr. Hobart, the building's owner, intervened, ordered Polk to remove the sign on the fence, and worked out a satisfactory settlement on the fireproofing.

TO REMEMBER R.L.S. . . .

It was about this time that the disgruntled architect, fed up with bureaucratic interference, decided to become a candidate for mayor, evidently in order to run the city more to his liking. He called a press conference to announce his plans, but nobody showed up—possibly because the press refused to take his candidacy seriously. His opponent would have been the overwhelmingly popular Sunny Jim Rolph. In any case, Polk faced the facts and promptly announced that he would have nothing more to do with the sordid business of politics.

One of Polk's proudest accomplishments was restoration of the oldest and most revered building in the city—Mission Dolores. He meticulously studied the Franciscan missions and their traditions, following the original plans in every detail of construction. When it was necessary to replace some of the original tiles, he ordered them made in exactly the same way they had been fashioned by Indians under the padres. He shored up the old adobe with steel beams so inconspicuously that visitors declared they could not see what he had done on the building—a reaction he accepted as the highest compliment.

Polk also developed the original plan for the Opera House. It was under the inspiration of his design that a fund-raising campaign was held to build the nation's first municipal opera house as part of a World War I memorial. He died before the plans came to fruition, however, and the Opera House and Veterans Building were ultimately designed by Arthur Brown, Jr.

Another structure not entirely designed by Polk but bearing his influence is the Robert Louis Stevenson Memorial in Portsmouth Plaza. Polk was dining at the Palace Hotel with three companions— Bruce Porter, sculptor and architect; poet Gelett Burgess, author of the *Purple Cow* ditty; and designer Porter Garnett—when a ship arrived in the harbor with word of the death of their friend Stevenson in Samoa.

The warm presence of Robert Louis Stevenson was still felt in this city, and when his friends had recovered from the shock, they reminisced late into the night about the colorful Scot. Together they drew up plans for a Stevenson memorial, sketching their ideas on the tablecloth. So inspired was Polk that when he left the hotel he swept up the tablecloth and walked off with it. From the sketches on the tablecloth came the present Stevenson Memorial in Portsmouth Plaza. Polk designed the pedestal, with its inscription from Stevenson's *Christmas Sermon*. Above it is Bruce Porter's design of a galleon under full sail, symbol of the author's tales of adventure.

THE HOUSE ON RUSSIAN HILL

The Vallejo Street summit of Russian Hill is another location carrying the signature of Polk. As part of the beautification of the city for the Panama-Pacific International Exposition of 1915, Polk designed in the classic manner a pair of ramps leading up from Jones Street to the summit block of Vallejo. Immediately north of the ramps, on a cul-de-sac named Russian Hill Place, are three of Polk's Mediterranean style villas. The nineteenth-century redwood shingle houses on both sides of Vallejo were saved from the fire of 1906 because they were above the city's reservoirs and had their own water supply. The quake had broken the city water mains, but these houses had sufficient water in their cisterns to fight off the flames. One of them is Polk's own house. Vallejo Street ends in a classic balustrade he designed as part of the 1915 landscaping, and the house is immediately to the right at the top of the long stairs descending the steep eastern slope of the hill.

When Mrs. Virgil Williams asked Polk to design a house for her on that site, he agreed, but his price was a stiff one—the eastern one-third of the lot. This portion consisted principally of a nearly vertical slope, so Mrs. Williams consented. Polk's ingenious design combined both houses as a single building. His portion was draped down the hill for seven stories in a curious vertical room arrangement. From each room in the house Polk could look to the east and take pride in gazing on his first great triumph, the Ferry Building. The house has since been divided into several separate apartments, but much of Polk's elaborate woodwork remains. The upper room is two stories high with a broad mezzanine. Alongside the fireplace is a hidden panel which opens to a steep stairway leading to the lower stories and an outside exit. There are several explanations for the architect's "secret door." One was that that he needed a quick escape when creditors appeared. Another story maintains that he kept the secret from his wife and sometimes found it convenient to disappear suddenly. She was the former Christine Bareda, an ambassador's daughter of Spanish descent. The hot-blooded young lady and the tempestuous architect made a volcanic couple, and the neighbors told stories of seeing plates sailing through the windows of the big house and down the hillside. Despite their battles—and Polk's frequent affairs with other women —his wife was so devoted to him that she compiled clippings of every newspaper item referring to her illustrious husband, even those in which his name was merely mentioned in a list.

A SKYSCRAPER GIRALDA

So great was Polk's pride in the Ferry Building and his admiration for the Giralda Tower (on a trip to Spain he purloined a piece of its tile as a souvenir) that it became his strange ambition to reproduce the same tower on a colossal scale. Had he been successful, San Francisco would have had not one Ferry tower but two or three. He first tried to convince Chronicle publisher M. H. de Young to allow him to build a Giralda tower on the de Young Building at Kearny and Market when it was being redone after the fire. De Young could not be persuaded, and Polk designed for him instead an annex to the structure, which has again been rebuilt in recent years as the San Francisco Federal Savings Building.

Later he tried the same idea on the Crocker family, for whom he had designed the original Crocker Building still standing (although refaced) at 1 Montgomery Street. The Crockers liked the idea and told him to go ahead on a design. Polk built a four-foot model for a Giralda-style skyscraper eight hundred feet high, higher than the tallest buildings in the city today. Sadly for Polk, the building was so large that it would have required the entire triangular block behind the Crocker property at Market and Post; and the Mechanics Institute, owner of the building in the middle of the block, refused to sell. Polk died in 1924 without having achieved his ambition to build a skyscraper Giralda.

Probably it is just as well. It is ironic that his ambition lay in that direction rather than in carrying on in the modern style he pioneered with the Hallidie Building. Bonestell regrets that Polk did not live a few decades later. "All we did in those days was to go through the architecture books and adapt the classic styles. It is a pity that Polk, with all his great flair for the art, didn't live into the modern era, when architecture began to develop new styles to suit the times. But at least we have the Hallidie Building."

DESIGN WITH NATURE

And it is doubtless for his "glass building" on Sutter that Polk will chiefly be remembered—a thrust forward into a promised architectural land to which Polk pointed the way but himself could not enter. In one respect, however, Polk may still be ahead of the times. He designed the Hallidie Building's decorative ironwork—with curving lines and leafy frills—in the Venetian style of the Doges' Palace in Venice. In this respect, Polk was still indulging in his taste for ancient European styles. But the early years of this century were also the period of the *art nouveau*, a time when artists and architects were turning to "natural" forms in revolt against the harsh technology of industrialism—the same natural leafy shapes found on the Hallidie Building. If Polk's glass wall is now universally admired, his ironwork, including the imaginatively integrated balconies and fire escapes, is often regarded as hopelessly old-fashioned. Yet fashions change, and cycles bring back varying tastes. Our own era is again a time of cultural revolt, particularly among the young, and the results are apparent in natural styles of dress, poster art, and colorful decoration. A contemporary taste for lively décor is evident in San Francisco in the widespread restoration of old buildings remaining from a more imaginative era—such as Victorian houses, Ghirardelli Square, and Jackson Square. Polk's ironwork on the Hallidie façade, now painted a pallid green, was originally the bright blue and gold of the University of California—not precisely psychedelic but perhaps an indication of an affinity between the architect and the present avant-garde taste for brilliant color.

The current revolt against drabness and regimentation has not yet found major expression in commercial architecture. The city's new buildings, with a few exceptions, are mostly stark and unadorned; some resemble colossal filing cabinets. It may be time for architects again to look at the Hallidie Building and wonder if Polk had perhaps found the proper balance of sheer surface with playful decoration, of straight lines with flowing forms, of technological precision with curvaceous natural contours.

In early 1971 a new owner, who evidently cared nothing for the building's historic significance, proposed to tear it down and replace it with a high-rise structure. Its demolition was delayed under a city ordinance providing for a one-year moratorium on the razing of buildings designated as historic landmarks. Beyond that period, however, there were evidently no legal means to prevent its destruction. Clearly San Francisco urgently needs methods of permanently protecting its few architectural treasures.

4

The Wild Animals
of Arthur Putnam

THE COVERED WAGONS roll along Market Street by the hundreds,
but hardly anyone notices them. Like Keats's figures on a Grecian
urn, they move interminably around the bases of the light standards.
The oxen that pull them and the pioneer and dog walking alongside
are immortal, placed there by the hand of a San Francisco sculptor
who achieved international fame, then dimmed and was forgotten,
as ignored by the present generation as his sculptured wagons.

Arthur Putnam was one of the group of brilliant young rebels
who kept artistic life in the city in an uproar around the turn
of the century—among them Jack London; Gelett Burgess, editor
of the *Lark;* Willis Polk; and Bruce Porter, artist and sculptor.
Of all the group Putnam most resembled Jack London in background and temperament, drive and originality. Like London,
Putnam was propelled by a compulsive artistic energy that made
up in power what it lacked in discipline.

London learned his art along the waterfronts of San Francisco
Bay. Putnam learned his in the rugged California mountains, where
as a boy he herded cattle and took long hikes to watch for wild
animals, particularly his favorite, the puma, or mountain lion. Both
men brought to their work a crude vitality that broke all the neat
Victorian rules of the academies and helped launch the movement
toward realism in modern American art and literature.

Some of the same irreverent fatalism and verve found in London's
books were indicated in a remark Putnam once made in a letter

to his fiancée expressing his affection: "Life is a sea of cactus, and if you can get a partner to walk with you and help you cuss—you're in luck."

FURY AT THE BEACH

Grace Storey Putnam was herself an artist, but most of her life with her husband, who had little regard for money, was spent trying to make ends meet. Coming across the bay on the ferry to live in San Francisco, they discovered that they had only a nickel left between them. With a typical gesture to fate, Putnam grinned and flipped the coin into the water.

In a small North Beach hotel, while Putnam tried to get work as a sculptor, the two lived on coffee, doughnuts, and beans, and occasionally banqueted on a piece of meat which Grace cooked by holding it over the fire on a hatpin. Through the efforts of Porter, Polk, and other architects who admired his work, Putnam gradually began to get jobs doing ornamental work for new buildings.

At the urging of friends and with the help of Mrs. W. H. Crocker, who commissioned several pieces of work from him, the Putnams went to Europe to study. There he and his work created a sensation. Fresh from the "wilds" of the New World, Putnam's powerful animal figures contrasted sharply with the pallid, academic art of the Continent. After an exhibition in Rome, one critic wrote: "Putnam's bronzes made all other animal casts in the show look as though they had been stuffed with hay."

Back in San Francisco after the disaster of 1906, he found plenty of work in the postfire reconstruction, and the next few years were the most productive of his life. He built a house on an isolated sand dune at Ocean Beach and found the pounding surf and roaring wind more congenial to his own temperament than the salons of Europe. With a drive and energy that often kept him going until he dropped from exhaustion, he modeled the animal figures that are still visible around the city.

In the palatial Bank of California at Sansome and California streets, two of Putnam's pumas rear on either side of the big clock, an odd note of wildness in the bank's atmosphere of classic elegance—symbolic of the sculptor's own personality. On a drinking fountain in the St. Francis Hotel are two small but superb bronze mountain lions, signed "A. Putnam, '07."

For the windows of the bank at Post and Montgomery (now Crocker-Citizens), Putnam designed a figure that was one of his few departures from realism—a winged mammal that is presumed to be a griffin, a grotesquely graceful figure on the razor's edge between whimsey and nightmare. Across the window frames is a procession of his more familiar animals. The Bohemian Club, of which Putnam was a member, has some of his works, including *The Cave Man,* a powerful figure of dawning intelligence, reminiscent of Rodin's *The Thinker.*

PATH OF GOLD

When Willis Polk was designing the standards for the postfire Market Street lights, to be known as the "Path of Gold," he asked Putnam to do the sculptured art work for the base of the standards, on the theme: "The Winning of the West." The designs, while far from Putnam's greatest work, nevertheless embody the same realism that distinguished most of his art. The pioneer walking alongside the wagons does not have the chin-up-and-light-in-the-eyes pose characteristic of most such pictures; his shoulders are stooped and, like the oxen themselves, he is obviously begrimed and bone-weary. In the upper panel are other familiar Western figures, a prospector and a mounted Indian. The sculptor's sense of humor is expressed in the lower panel, where a puma and a bear stare quizzically at a scared jackrabbit and an Indian looks on from above.

The same kind of whimsey is visible in the dance-hall figures on the façade of the old Barbary Coast building at 560 Pacific. The plaster female figures once adorned the vanished Moulin Rouge, and there is a legend that public protests forced the artist to modify discreetly their original nudity. In contrast are Putnam's angels over the organ of the First Unitarian Church and his immensely vital figure of Padre Junípero Serra in the garden at Mission Dolores.

By 1911, the creative frenzy that had caused Putnam to drive himself relentlessly began to erode his health. He was thirty-eight then, at the height of his powers and jubilant at having been appointed director of sculpture for the Panama-Pacific Exposition to be opened in 1915—his chance, finally, to work on a grand scale. The appointment came from Polk, the exposition's architectural director. At the same time, Polk was rebuilding the gutted Flood mansion on Nob Hill as a clubhouse for the Pacific Union Club, and asked Putnam to do the carved ceiling. During this arduous work, Putnam began to feel pains in the head and neck, but he forced himself to finish the job.

Gradually, to his dismay, his left arm became numb and paralyzed. The trouble was diagnosed as a brain tumor and required surgery. The operation was successful, but the paralysis remained. His efforts at sculpture or drawing resulted only in clumsy distortions. Doubtless partly out of frustration, he was possessed by frequent rages in which he lashed out at his wife, friends, or anyone within reach. Grace Putnam was driven from the house, and for a time he lived alone at the beach, his rages matching the winds and storms that roared off the ocean.

INTO THE DEPTHS

He divorced his wife, later remarried, and lived on for two decades as a near invalid. The lion had been cut down at the peak of his strength. He was kept from starvation mainly by the generosity of his friends and his fellow members of the Bohemian Club.

In later years Mrs. Adolph Spreckels met Putnam, admired his work, and bought some of his plaster originals. She sent them to Paris for casting by Rodin's foundryman and presented them to the Palace of the Legion of Honor, which she and her husband had given the city. There, together with some of his drawings, are the bronzes of restless pumas and other animals he loved to model —although they are seldom on display nowadays. Putnam died in Europe in 1930; many of his works are preserved in a series of striking photographs by Ansel Adams, some of which appear in the Putnam biography by his friend and fellow artist, Julie Helen Heyneman.

In many of his animal and human figures there is an almost terrifying quality of depth, of dark primitive power, reminiscent not only of Jack London's more savage tales but of Hawthorne and Melville—a quality which has finally been reflected in modern art. It is as if the sculptor throughout his life had been able to see clearly not only the tragic element in all human life but the personal tragedy of his own later years. Yet the Arthur Putnam his friends remembered fondly was the rangy, handsome young man with a grin and shaggy black hair, tilted back in a chair at North Beach parties, strumming a banjo and singing spirituals.

Sixty years after Putnam's covered wagons first appeared on Market Street, the ornate lamp standards were taken down for the reconstruction of the thoroughfare during work on the Bay Area Rapid Transit subway. Rather than replace them with the modern standards that flood many boulevards with glaring light, city authorities carefully stored the old lampposts in a warehouse, scoffed at rumors that they had been destroyed or lost, and put them up again after the street was finished. As has happened more than once in San Francisco, sentiment and art had triumphed over progress.

5

Mountain Lake, Outpost of Empire

ON PARK-PRESIDIO BOULEVARD, a short distance before you enter
the tunnel leading to the Golden Gate Bridge, you can look to the
right through the trees and catch a glimpse of Mountain Lake,
a body of water small in size but very large in history. This lake,
now part of a city park, was the site of the most important camp
of what may be the most remarkable expedition in North American
history.

The commander was Captain Juan Bautista de Anza, a brilliant frontiersman as hard as the rocks of his native Sonora in
northern Mexico. After an exploration of the Southwest that involved five thousand miles in the saddle, he had organized an
expedition of 240 men, women, and children in Mexico (then
New Spain) and led them 1600 incredibly arduous miles to the
outpost of Monterey—a feat unmatched by Lewis and Clark or
any other expedition in pioneer annals.

Leaving most of his exhausted charges temporarily in Monterey,
he led a small party on up the coast to find a site on which
to plant the northernmost colony of New Spain. Accompanying
him were Lieutenant José Joaquín Moraga and sharp-eyed Padre
Pedro Font, whose detailed diary of the expedition offers the best
available description of San Francisco in the days of exploration.
Shortly after eleven o'clock on the morning of Wednesday, March
27, 1776, the party approached Mountain Lake from the south
and set up camp on its shores.

Leaving some of his men at the lake to finish making camp, Anza, Moraga, Font, and four of the soldiers quickly set out for their first look at the Golden Gate. They headed west across the sand dunes of the Richmond District to Point Lobos, above the site of the Cliff House, where they had a breath-taking view of the outer Golden Gate, the entire coast from Point Reyes to Point San Pedro, and the Farallon Islands on the horizon—altogether, Font wrote, "a prodigy of nature which it is not easy to describe."

THE CONTROVERSIAL CROSS

After exploring Ocean Beach, then Bakers Beach, "where the sea is very quiet, to which runs the arroyo of the port" (Lobos Creek, draining Mountain Lake), they crossed the hills of the Presidio to the narrows of the Golden Gate. There they stood on the top of a white cliff (which was later leveled in the 1850's for the construction of Fort Point) and gazed in awe at the rushing waters of the strait.

"The cliff is very high and perpendicular," wrote the padre, "so that from it one can spit into the sea . . . From here we saw the pushing and resistance which the outgoing water of the estuary makes against that of the sea, forming there a sort of a ridge like a wave in the middle . . . We saw the spouting of whales, a shoal of dolphins or tunny fish, sea otter and sea lions.

"On this elevation," Font continued, "the commander decided to erect a cross . . . ordering it made at once so that he might set it up the next day."

Then the party returned to Mountain Lake, where there occurred an episode indicating that even the heroic commander and the devout priest were both very human individuals.

"As soon as we returned from the reconnaissance," wrote Font, "I said to Señor Anza: 'Señor, now that you wish to erect a cross at the point tomorrow, order it made right off, so that in the morning after Mass I may bless it, if you think well, before going to erect it.'

"He replied: 'All right, that shall be done, Father.'

"Then, turning his back to me, he went into his tent, snorting and saying between his teeth: 'You always come with "if you think it well, if you think it well!'"

"The fact is," the padre continued, "that he could not bear to have me give my opinion about anything . . . I note this down in order to show the tact with which it is necessary to conduct oneself with persons of sensitive nature and satisfied with themselves."

Anza's version of the episode is not recorded.

In a different vein, Font went on: "This place and its vicinity has abundant pasturage, plenty of firewood, and fine water, all good advantages for establishing here the presidio or fort which is planned. It lacks only timber, for there is not a tree on all these hills, though the oaks and other trees along the road are not very far away.

"The soldiers chased some deer, of which we saw many today, but got none of them. We also found antlers of the large elk . . . Here near the lake there are yerba buena and so many lilies that I had them almost inside my tent." It is not clear what "lilies" the padre may have seen, unless they were California poppies, but the *yerba buena* ("good herb," an aromatic creeper whose leaves made good tea) later gave its name to a cove and the town that became San Francisco.

THE PRESIDIO ON THE MESA

The next morning the cross was constructed without further acrimony, blessed by the padre, and hauled to the Golden Gate, where it was erected on the edge of the white cliff. From there the party climbed to a flower-covered mesa behind the point.

"This mesa," Font wrote, "affords a most delightful view, for from it one sees a large part of the port and its islands, as far as the other side, the mouth of the harbor, and of the sea all that the sight can take in as far as beyond the Farallones.

"This mesa the commander selected as the site for the new settlement and fort which were to be established on this harbor; for being on a height, it is so commanding that with muskets it can defend the entrance to the mouth of the harbor, while a gunshot away it has water to supply the people, namely the spring or lake where we halted."

The padre had a good eye for possibilities. Lobos Creek, flowing from Mountain Lake, actually did become the water supply of the Presidio and later of San Francisco itself. Having selected a home for his settlers and the presidio that was to protect them and extend the domain of New Spain to its northernmost point, Anza and his men rode eastward along the shore of the Golden Gate to a beach near the present Marina. There they found a hut and four Indians who "were very gentle and obliging."

Not far away was a small lake formed at a place where creeks running down from Pacific Heights were blocked by sand dunes along the bay shore. This was probably the body of water the Yankees later called Washerwoman's Lagoon. The practical-minded padre felt that the lagoon should be drained and the area used for planting crops. He noted that the canyons at the foot of Pacific Heights were "very green and shady, with plentiful small trees . . ."

THE MISSION AND THE WATERFALL

The explorers climbed to another high spot, probably Russian Hill, and "entered a very thick grove of scrubby live oak and other small trees and brush," which continued across Nob and Telegraph hills.

The padre returned to Mountain Lake to make observations of the latitude, while Anza and Moraga explored farther. The next morning the party headed east, probably on about the line of California Street, then circled to the south in the lee of the ridge running from Buena Vista to Twin Peaks.

"Passing through wooded hills, and over flats with good land in which we encountered two lagoons and some springs of good water, with plentiful grass, fennel, and other useful herbs, we arrived at a beautiful arroyo which, because it was Friday of Sorrows, we called the Arroyo de los Dolores.

"On its banks we found much and very fragrant manzanita and other plants and many wild violets. Near it the lieutenant planted a little maize and chickpeas to test the soil, which to us appeared very good, and I concluded that this place was very pretty and the best for the establishment of one of the two missions."

Thus was designated the site of Mission Dolores. (The second mission was eventually established in the Santa Clara Valley.) The padre felt that the Arroyo de los Dolores could be put to practical use. The creek "enters the plain by a fall which it makes on emerging from the hills, and with it everything can be irrigated, and at the same fall a mill can be erected. . . ." Dolores Creek descended from Twin Peaks along the present line of Eighteenth Street, and the waterfall was probably near the intersection of Eighteenth and Market.

Having sown the seeds of San Francisco, the party continued on to the south, deeply impressed by the vast potentialities of this imperial location above the great bay. In his diary Font had written a prophetic passage:

". . . Although in my travels I saw very good sites and beautiful country, I saw none which pleased me so much as this. And I think that if it could be well settled like Europe, there would not be anything more beautiful in all the world, for it has the best advantages for founding in it a most beautiful city . . ."

6

Twin Peaks and the
Vision of Daniel Burnham

IT WAS Sunny Jim Rolph's idea to build a road up Twin Peaks overlooking what is perhaps the world's most awe-inspiring metropolitan panorama. The view might remind travelers of the sight of Hong Kong from the heights behind that city or the long curve of Rio de Janeiro from the pinnacles near Sugar Loaf. Yet it is doubtful that either can equal in scope, diversity, or magnitude the breath-taking sweep of this white city, the blue bay, and the cities and mountains around the far shores.

Since the road was finished during Mayor Rolph's regime in 1927, millions of residents and visitors have experienced the mixed sensation of dominion and vertigo that comes from standing on these heights and gazing down into what historian Hubert Howe Bancroft called "the throne room of an imperial city." If the sightseers were able to divert their gaze long enough from the far horizons, they would see, on the slopes below, a grove of Monterey cypresses hovering over a cluster of houses near the Twin Peaks School. A cottage under these trees played a vital part in one magnificent unfulfilled episode in the city's history.

If you can imagine yourself standing here seventy years ago, when most of the hills and valleys visible from here were still in their natural state, you might be able to project yourself into the mind of a man who stood on this height, gazed into the future, and designed for this peninsula the ultimate City Beautiful. His name was Daniel H. Burnham, and the story of his plan for San Francisco is a brilliant chapter in the history of the city.

THE OLYMPIAN PROSPECT

By the turn of the century, some leading citizens had begun to realize that man-made San Francisco was an ugly city. The city's famed beauty had always been a credit to nature rather than to man. James D. Phelan, former mayor, millionaire attorney, *bon vivant*, and patron of the arts, had been inspired, as had many of his contemporaries, by the design of the monumental Chicago Columbian Exposition of 1893, and he took the initiative in inviting to San Francisco Daniel Burnham, the fair's chief designer, to discuss a plan for this city.

Burnham was a renowned architect, the nation's leading city planner, a visionary who knew how to put foundations under his dream castles, a man of action with a highly developed aesthetic sense, a scholar with a businessman's aggressiveness and a politician's know-how. Doubtless an influence on Burnham's decision to come West was one of his assistants, the ebullient young Willis Polk, who after leaving San Francisco joined Burnham's staff in Chicago.

During 1901 Burnham was deeply involved in Washington, D.C., along with landscape architect Frederick Law Olmsted, developing a plan for the nation's capital. However, early in 1902 Burnham and Polk arrived in San Francisco to talk to Phelan and a committee of the Merchants Exchange. The opportunities offered by San Francisco's natural setting exceeded anything Burnham had yet attempted. He was so enthusiastic about the proposal for a planned city here that he agreed to donate his services, accepting only expenses. He did make one further stipulation. It was his habit in making city plans to find a high point from which to look down on the planning area. In making his plan for Washington, he frequented the Anacostia heights and went across the Potomac to gaze at the capital from the Custis-Lee mansion in Arlington. When he was working on a plan for Chicago, he found an office on the top floor of one of the city's tallest buildings. In San Francisco, Twin Peaks is the obviously supreme vantage point. Although it lacks a few feet of being the highest point in the city (nearby Mount Davidson, at 938 feet, is slightly higher, Twin Peaks is more central and commands the best view. Phelan and his associates agreed to provide Burnham with an office-lookout near the summit. The location selected was a few hundred feet down an eastern spur from the windy, foggy ridge. Willis Polk eagerly accepted the job of designing a cottage for the site.

PHELAN'S DOUBTS

Owing to Burnham's other obligations, it was September of 1904 before he arrived in San Francisco with his assistant, Edward Bennett, to go to work on the plan. Polk proudly escorted the two to the newly completed cottage and Burnham was delighted with the eagle's eye view it afforded him. He never afterward forgot his first experience on Twin Peaks. The commanding view of the city below and the prospect of shaping the future of this "Emporium of a New World on the Pacific" fired the planner's imagination.

"The afternoon and evening of surpassing beauty," Burnham wrote in his diary, "our shanty a charmer . . . Polk cooked. Had soup, steak, salad, and omelet, with good red wine; the best dinner we ever had. We all three sat on the east porch until ten o'clock and saw the moon rise over Diablo in the distance and shine on the China basin far below us. We reluctantly retired at last, each on his cot, without sheets or pillows."

During the following two weeks Burnham and Bennett paced over the peaks, studying the city from various angles, making preliminary drawings, occasionally entertaining at the cottage such friends as artist William Keith. Burnham's first interest was in extending the Panhandle of Golden Gate Park eastward across the city to the shore of the bay as a long boulevard and parkway. At the end of the two weeks, however, Burnham sailed for Manila; he had been engaged by the United States Government to prepare a plan for that city. Bennett remained in San Francisco to do the detailed drawings until Burnham's scheduled return in February.

From time to time Phelan chugged up the hill to the cottage in his new automobile (one of the few in the city) to look over Bennett's shoulder. He became increasingly concerned about what seemed to be the grandiose picture Bennett was laying out in detail. He began to doubt that such sweeping plans were practical. As mayor, he had been forced to meet the hard realities of municipal budgets, and he now feared that this plan would be far beyond the city's power to finance. But when Burnham returned from Manila, he invited Phelan up to the cottage on Twin Peaks and gave the former mayor a table-thumping lecture that fully justified his reputation as a spellbinder. In effect he told his chief sponsor: The plan should have scope and splendor commensurate with the magnificence of this panorama below. It should not be limited to what the city could then pay for. "You would not have called me in had it been to plan for the small expenditure of the present," he emphasized. "The plan for your city must be framed in accord with your needs in the distant future—for all time!"

In the face of such enthusiasm Phelan found himself nodding his assent and finally told Burnham to go ahead.

PARIS WITH HILLS

In September of 1905, the Burnham Plan was presented by its author in a banquet at the St. Francis Hotel. The audience was enthralled by the boldness of the plan. It combined the gardens of Babylon with the order of ancient Rome and the parklike beauty of modern Paris. At Market and Van Ness was a classic Civic Center laid out around an equivalent of the Place de la Concorde, the site of a city hall, a railway depot, an opera house, theaters, and museums. Eight broad boulevards radiated outward from the center, one of them the Panhandle extension. A scenic outer boulevard with unobstructed views of the bay and ocean would ring the city at its perimeter.

Burnham was generations ahead of his time in recommending such innovations as one-way streets, downtown subways, and superblocks in which back yards would be merged into a common park in the center of the block. The plan gave special attention to the city's hills. Their crests, he noted, should be "preserved in a state of nature, while their slopes below should be clothed with trees. . . ." Streets would not be imposed on the hills in the conventional gridiron pattern but would follow the contours; houses would be prohibited for a sufficient distance below the streets to preserve the views—a quality of openness regrettably absent in the present-day city. From their hilltop vantage point, Burnham and Bennett naturally developed a special interest in Twin Peaks. Burnham's penchant for formal parks and classic design reached a climax in his ideas for a huge park covering the peaks and the broad hilly region extending from there for several miles southwest to Lake Merced. The slopes of the peaks would be elaborately landscaped with terraces, colonnades, trees, gardens, grand staircases, and a spectacular watercourse where the city's water supply would spill down from the heights in a series of lakes, fountains, and cascades.

The city was dazzled by the classic splendor of this vision of its future. The Board of Supervisors immediately appropriated funds for a book elaborately reproducing the plan, with photographs and drawings. The book was printed and ready for distribution. But early on the morning of April 18, 1906, the San Andreas Fault gave a mighty lurch, and the City Hall collapsed in a few seconds, burying the books.

It did not, however, bury the Burnham Plan. Burnham, who had been traveling in Europe, rushed to San Francisco and met Phelan, Polk, Benjamin Ide Wheeler, Rudolph Spreckels, John McLaren and others of the newly formed "Committee of Forty," who realized that San Francisco had now a supreme opportunity to build "the city beautiful" on the ruins of the old. Willis Polk's house on Russian Hill was one of the few that survived the fire, and Burnham and his supporters met there to plan the campaign to rebuild the city, as they looked out across miles of ruins.

THE FALL OF BOSS RUEF

Burnham and the committee proposed as the first installment of the plan the widening of a number of streets into one-hundred-foot boulevards—Montgomery Avenue (now Columbus Avenue), Golden Gate Avenue, Pacific, Powell, and Pine Streets. Nob and Russian hills would be encircled by entirely new streets following the contours and replacing the gridiron pattern. The Panhandle would be extended to Market Street, and a number of diagonal streets, similar to the radial boulevards in Washington, would cut across the city for quicker transportation.

Acquisition of the necessary property would be paid for by a long-term bond issue. The committee's support and Burnham's vigorous presentation convinced the supervisors, and the measure passed unanimously. Burnham was delighted, but his optimism proved premature. He reckoned without a series of political earthquakes which centered around boss Abe Ruef, his associate, Mayor Eugene Schmitz, a number of Ruef's supervisors. Also involved were several business leaders who had bribed Ruef. Ruef had embraced the Burnham Plan (perhaps because he saw in it the opportunity for controlling lucrative construction projects), but his principal political opponents were Phelan, Spreckels, and others of Burnham's backers. In the graft prosecutions that followed, Phelan, Spreckels, and company succeeded in sending Ruef to San Quentin, but the Burnham Plan was shelved by default. Meantime the city was being rebuilt along the old lines.

By 1909, when the political front was quiet again, Burnham returned to meet with Phelan and Polk and salvage at least part of his plan. He urged first a monumental civic center at Van Ness and Market. With Phelan's help, Burnham convinced the supervisors to submit a bond issue to finance the plan. Polk prepared an elaborate drawing of the proposed civic center, which appeared in the newspapers, and subsequently various parks proposed in the original Burnham Plan were added. But in the campaign that followed, the plan was again attacked as impractical and extravagant. In a heartbreaking outcome for Burnham and his supporters, a majority of the voters approved the bonds, but the proposition failed by a few votes to get the necessary two-thirds.

THE SITING OF THE CIVIC CENTER

Burnham died in 1912, but his vision of the future San Francisco had made a mighty impact. Some years later, Phelan, then United States senator, summarized the results of that critical chapter in the city's history:

"The destruction of San Francisco by fire in 1906 temporarily threw the people on their immediate resources, and as their resources were slender and their business condition precarious they dropped the ideal plan in order to house themselves and rehabilitate their affairs. It was the worst time to talk about beautification. The people were thrown back to a consideration as to how again they would live and thrive. Burnham revisited San Francisco and made a good impression and helped to check this recession from the artistic. As a result of his educational influence and the Plan, we now have a beautiful civic center . . . and . . . the parkway connecting Golden Gate Park and the Presidio."

Willis Polk assessed the Burnham impact in a similar vein:

". . . The plan was not intended to be limited in availability only to the immediate present. It was primarily intended as a record of things to be done, and the order in which they should be done even through a distant future. It presents a path of logical progress whereby a city destined to be important may also become convenient and beautiful."

Burnham's civic center plans had languished for several years, but the idea was revived and the center laid out as the city prepared for the exposition of 1915. The location was two blocks away from the Market-Van Ness intersection Burnham had designated, and both Phelan and Polk were highly critical of this departure from the plan. However, the reason for the change was sound. One of the proponents of the new location was an eloquent young attorney named Augustin C. Keane, who persuaded the Bar Association to support his views. A scholar of the classics, Keane argued from his knowledge of the great cities of Europe that a civic center should not be located at a major crossroads of traffic. Foreseeing the impact of the automobile far better than Phelan or Polk did, Keane argued that the increasing traffic and resulting congestion would preclude the proper atmosphere of dignity and serenity and beauty that a civic center should have. His arguments were persuasive, and sixty years later, Keane, still practicing law in San Francisco, could contemplate with satisfaction the fact that the city had taken his advice. Partly as a consequence, the Civic Center has often been called the finest in the nation.

NO LITTLE PLANS

Stand on Twin Peaks now, near the site of Burnham's cottage, and contemplate the city as he did. If his plan had been carried out in more than a few details (the Civic Center, Park-Presidio, Marina, and Sunset boulevards) this would be a very different city, for better or for worse. The years have eliminated the open spaces that remained at the time Burnham looked down from here, and surely the record must show the loss of a magnificent opportunity to plan a spacious, parklike city. In its details the Burnham Plan is outmoded. But in concept and principle it has great contemporary value.

In 1971 the City Planning Commission presented San Francisco with a new Urban Design Plan, setting forth a number of commendable principles. However, it was in large measure tailored to short-term political possibilities (as official documents almost inevitably must be) and seemed not so much a plan as an expression of amiable generalities. It is a good guess that Burnham would denounce such timidity with a resounding thump of the table.

"We should develop a picture of what kind of a city and region we want this to be in the centuries to come," he would argue, "and plan now for posterity."

Willis Polk at one time compiled passages from various Burnham speeches and writings, including his most famous piece of advice, which San Franciscans now badly need to ponder and apply. Perhaps it should be engraved on a plaque and placed at the lookout point on Twin Peaks:

"Make no little plans. They have no magic to stir men's blood and probably themselves will not be realized. Make big plans. Aim high in hope and work, remembering that a noble, logical diagram once recorded will never die, but long after we are gone will be a living thing asserting itself with ever-growing insistency. Remember that our sons and grandsons are going to do things that would stagger us. Let your watchword be order and your beacon, beauty."

7

The Roman Baths
of Adolph Sutro

EXPLORING THE ROCKY SHORELINE near the Cliff House during an extraordinarily low tide, I clambered over a boulder just in time to escape an incoming breaker and found myself in a hidden cove facing what appeared to be the ruins of an ancient palace. It was Sutro Baths, for half a century one of San Francisco's prime recreation spots. Winds, waves, and vandals had broken nearly every one of the hundreds of panes of glass that faced the ocean. I walked across a beach left bare by the minus tide, scrambled up the sea wall, and peered inside.

The floor of the hangar-sized room was terraced back up the hillside, and on the lower levels were five empty swimming pools of various sizes and shapes. The long pool nearest the window was partly filled with sand where storm breakers had swept inside the building. In a sudden flashback, there came to me a recollection of the last time I had swum here many years earlier. The vast pavilion was filled with the shouts of hundreds of bathers and the music of Strauss waltzes. On the upper terraces, behind seats where thousands of spectators had once watched Duke Kahanamoku slice through the water for one-hundred yards to set a new world's record, were acres of tropical vegetation, palms, big-leaved vines, exotic flowers, classic plaster statues and huge stuffed animals—all in delightful Victorian array.

The pools themselves were a wonder. You could plummet into

the water from diving platforms up in the rafters; rocket into the pools down giddy slides that seemed to come down from the roof; whirl into the water from a carousel; swing out over the pools on trapeze-like rings attached to the ceiling. In memory, at least, these were pools to surpass the fabled spas of Europe and the Lucullan baths of the Roman emperors.

KING OF THE COMSTOCK

This aquatic magnificence was the final achievement of Adolph Sutro, an indomitable pioneer and early mayor who left his mark in this vast natatorium; on the heights above, where he lived; and elsewhere in the city. In 1860, young Sutro, an immigrant from Europe, was a San Francisco storekeeper with a mighty dream. He wanted to build one of the greatest engineering projects ever attempted up to that time—a four-mile-long tunnel through a mountain to drain and provide better access to the fabulous silver mines of the Comstock Lode in Nevada.

But, to do so, he had to take on the Goliaths of the Comstock, William C. Ralston and William Sharon, whose Bank of California controlled the mines. His tunnel, they realized, would threaten their domination of the lode, and through their influence with Eastern banks they blocked his attempt to raise capital.

The turning point came when a disastrous fire swept through the mines and killed forty-five men. During a two-hour oration to the embittered survivors in a mass meeting at the Virginia City Opera House, Sutro thundered his denunciation of Ralston and Sharon and their bank—"the vampires that have nearly sucked you dry." The tunnel, he asserted, would have provided escape for the trapped miners, and he asked his audience to buy stock in the enterprise, "a cause," he roared, "which will make you the power of this land, make powerless your oppressors, and break up your arch enemy, the California Bank."

The miners shook the opera house with their roars of approval and lined up behind Sutro like the children of Israel behind Joshua at Jericho. With pledges from the miners as a beginning, later buttressed by British capital, Sutro was able to start work on the tunnel in 1869—a grueling struggle of man against mountain that culminated successfully, after innumerable setbacks, a decade later. Before he was finished, the Bank of California had collapsed; Ralston was dead; and Sutro himself was "King of the Comstock," builder of one of the engineering wonders of the age.

SPA FOR THE MASSES

Then, the job done, Sutro sold his interest in the tunnel and returned to San Francisco to look for new outlets for his gargantuan energies. He invested the profits from the tunnel in land until he owned one-twelfth of the city, including the the old Rancho San Miguel, around Twin Peaks. He planted thousands of trees on San Francisco's barren hills; the largest remnant is Sutro Forest on Mount Parnassus, now Mount Sutro.

His favorite piece of land was this northwest corner of the peninsula, where the Golden Gate opens into the Pacific and you can see for miles down the long white strand of Ocean Beach to the Santa Cruz Mountains rising abruptly from the sea. He bought a house on top of the headlands (now called Sutro Heights) —a cottage belonging to a settler named Tetlow, rebuilt it to suit his own purposes, and over the years indulged his lifelong penchant for tree planting by raising a forest of well-spaced Monterey pines, cypresses, and eucalyptus trees on the acres surrounding the house.

Unlike many a frontier millionaire, Sutro, a native of Aix-la-Chapelle, brought with him the traditions of a cultivated European. In the spirit of *noblesse oblige,* one of his perennial ambitions was to enlighten and elevate the masses. He opened his gardens to the public, and the families of workingmen could stroll on lawns under the trees and along flower-bordered paths, gaze at the ocean, and stare at the statues he erected there in the style of the Louvre gardens—Greek gods and goddesses, heroic lions and stags, even characters from the novels of Dickens.

With the same benevolence that caused him to put the unemployed to work planting trees on his property around Mount Sutro, in the Nineties he conceived for this place at the ocean's edge a spa that would be built not for the leisure classes, like the baths of Europe, but for the masses. On the bluff below his gardens was an old resort of bad repute, the Cliff House; he bought it, converted it into a respectable restaurant, and made it San Francisco's favorite gathering place.

THE HARNESSING OF THE TIDES

Walking over the rocks and beaches north of the Cliff House, he was fascinated by the sea life in the tidal basins and decided to construct a big pool, to be filled by spray from waves at high tide, where his patrons could find easy access to the wonders of the life of the intertidal zone. He built a stone wall across the big cove just north of the Cliff House and extended the wall seaward to an acre-sized rock, where people could fish and explore in the crevices for sea life.

In the fertile imagination of the self-taught engineer, the idea grew rapidly. If there were to be pool, why limit the activity to passive gazing? Why shouldn't the public enjoy the health-giving benefits of bathing and swimming? (With Sutro, bathing was almost a fetish. In a time when the Saturday-night bath was an institution, he was considered somewhat eccentric for bathing daily. He took a collapsible tub on his travels and even sent portable bathtubs to his children when they went away to college.) Early designs for the baths show simply an open air "swimming pond" at the cove, next to his tide-pool "aquarium," but it soon became obvious that few swimmers would be attracted to the windy, foggy ocean front. However, the man who had built the Sutro Tunnel could not be deterred by adverse weather. He decided to create his own climate. The result was "Tropic Baths," this glass palace where the masses could bathe in a man-made tropical atmosphere under the palms.

Sutro's water system was typically ingenious. Salt water from his aquarium and from another wave-filled pool below the cliffs flowed through a system of tunnels and canals into the swimming pools, so that his patrons could almost literally bathe in the waves of the Pacific in perfect comfort. Sunlight streamed through the colored-glass roof, and while swimming you could watch the waves breaking outside. In a superb gesture of fantasy, Sutro built some miniature "Sutro Tunnels" which extended back into the cliffs, where awed patrons could gaze at the churning waves in the coves and caverns below.

If the completion of the Sutro Tunnel was the triumph of Sutro's early years, the opening of the Tropic Baths in 1896 was the supreme achievement of his later life. One writer noted in rhapsodic Victorian prose:

"The baths rival in magnitude, utility and beauty the famous abluvion resorts of Titus, Caracalla, Nero or Diocletian . . . these wonderful expressions of architectural skill—airy, graceful yet substantial—are located in a wave-worn cove at the foot of the cliffs, and brought to utilitarian perfection by a triumph of engineering invention . . . Thus have the tides been harnessed and made subservient to the multitudes."

THE BURNING OF THE BATHS

To provide the multitudes with inexpensive transportation to the baths, Sutro did his best to induce the Southern Pacific to reduce the rail fare to five cents on the steam line that ran out along the cliff tops to his beach resort. When the Southern Pacific refused, he was undaunted; he proceeded to build a competing electric line of his own out Clement Street and transported the multitudes for a nickel.

Meantime he had run for mayor on an anti-Southern Pacific ticket and won. But it was his last victory. The hard-driving tycoon had none of the tact required of a politician. He was past his prime; his health declined; and one year after he left office at the end of a single term, he was dead—one of the last of San Francisco's titans.

Sutro Baths continued to attract the multitudes for more than half a century after his death. Eventually part of the biggest pool was turned into an ice rink. By World War II, Tropic Baths fell into disrepair. The pools were finally closed in the early 1950's, and abandoned to the elements. For another dozen years San Franciscans and visitors were still drawn to the mammoth building to skate or wander through Sutro's museum, full of antique music boxes and other Victorian oddities. But both the rink and the museum were closed in the late 1960's when new owners decided to demolish the building for an apartment-house complex.

A short time after my last visit to the ruin, it burned to the ground, perhaps the victim of arson. A New York *Times* editorial mourned the passing of the old showplace, and quite properly chastised San Francisco for failing to preserve the historic structure.

You can still stroll through Sutro's Gardens on the heights above, presented to the city as a park after his death. His house is gone, and like the baths themselves in their later years, the park is poorly maintained. Most of the statues have been broken or hauled away. Many of Sutro's trees remain, but are seldom replaced when they fall. The present Cliff House, rusting on its laurels, is but a shrunken vestige of Sutro's huge hostel, which burned in 1907.

As this is written, you can still walk along the cove north of the Cliff House and see the crumbling remains of the pools, the stone wall, the wave-filled tide pools Sutro built, his tunnels, and his system of canals carrying water for the swimmers. But San Francisco voters in 1968 failed to pass a bond issue to buy the property, and it seems only a matter of time until the area is occupied by multistory dwellings for the wealthy. And so ends a dream, Sutro's vision of an aquatic pleasure dome for the common man.

8

The Reborn Ruin
of Bernard Maybeck

DESIGNER CHESLEY BONESTELL tells a dramatic story of the origin
of the Palace of Fine Arts—the classic temple whose beauty so
haunted San Franciscans that they rebuilt it in permanent concrete half a century after it had been erected as a temporary exposition building.

In 1911 Bonestell was working for Willis Polk, who had been
chosen chairman of the board of architects for the forthcoming
Panama-Pacific International Exposition of 1915. (The tempestuous
Polk had been appointed at the urging of Daniel Burnham, although
several older architects, including John Galen Howard, refused to
serve under him.) Before the location for the exposition had been
selected, Polk sent Bonestell out to inspect Harbor View, a resort
on a small promontory on the shore of the Golden Gate just inside
the narrows. Although there was powerful pressure to locate the
exposition in Golden Gate Park, Superintendent John McLaren
was adamantly opposed. Polk felt that the site near the Gate would
offer a spectacular location and avoid disrupting the natural setting
of the park.

From Harbor View, Bonestell looked eastward past a broad slough
to Fort Mason at Black Point, two miles away. If the marshy area
could be filled, Bonestell felt, it would make an ideal site for the
exposition. He reported favorably to Polk, who later persuaded
the city fathers to adopt the Harbor View site, and Golden Gate

Park was spared. (Perhaps as a consequence, there is a small plaque in the park: "To Willis Polk, lover of trees.")

THE WITHDRAWAL OF WILLIS POLK

As his own personal project, Polk chose the job of designing the building that would house the fair's art exhibits—the Palace of Fine Arts, to be located on the point where young Bonestell stood that day in 1911. Polk later assigned Bonestell and his colleague Harry Stearns to develop a design for the palace. Nothing the two designers came up with satisfied Polk, and he tried his own hand at several possibilities. But he remained dissatisfied and began to despair of ever developing a structure that would sum up the ideals and aspirations of the arts. Then one morning he strode into the office in triumph. "This is it!" he shouted, waving a charcoal sketch. "This is the Palace of Fine Arts!"

But the sketch he held was not his own. It had been drawn by the only man Polk ever acknowledged to be a greater architect than himself—Bernard Maybeck. At that time Polk was at the height of his fame as "the man who rebuilt San Francisco," but Maybeck was relatively unknown, although he had designed some imaginative houses and taught architecture at Berkeley. Two decades earlier Polk and Maybeck had worked together as designers in the office of Arthur Page Brown, architect of the Ferry Building, and Maybeck's fertile imagination had been made visible in the Swedenborgian Church on Lyon Street near the Presidio, still one of the city's architectural landmarks.

The two architects had remained friends over the years, but they were at opposite poles of character and temperament. Maybeck was as shy and introverted as Polk was aggressive, social, and flamboyant. Polk, who had whiskey for breakfast and had corresponding tastes in other areas, died in his fifties, while the bearded, ascetic Maybeck continued a creative career until he died in 1957 at the age of ninety-five. He had submitted his sketch of the Palace of Fine Arts to Polk as a suggestion to his friend, but Polk immediately saw it as the answer to the problem that had been plaguing him for months. Bonestell and the rest of the staff were equally impressed and agreed that this was an inspired design.

To his credit, Polk then performed what may have been the only act of renunciation in his entire career. He immediately went to the directors of the exposition with the announcement that he was withdrawing as architect of the building in favor of Maybeck. However, the directors, who evidently knew less about art than business and had already been ruffled several times by Polk's arrogance, evidently felt that he was trying to push them around.

"We hired you to do that job," one of them scolded, "and we insist that you do it."

"Very well," Polk replied. "I'll do it. But I'll hire Maybeck as my designer."

Alhough Polk remained the official architect, he turned over the entire job, the fee, and the glory to Maybeck.

MAYBECK IN MUNICH

Maybeck's own account of his conception of the Palace of Fine Arts reveals a man of a simple, naïve, semimystical temperament, yet basically progressive in his approach. He anticipated the modern architects by beginning his work on the palace with a consideration of the building's function. The purpose of the building, Maybeck believed, was to provide an appropriate transition from the noise and color and clamor of the fairgrounds to the contemplative atmosphere of the galleries inside. The building should put the observer in the mood for the illusions of art just as an overture to an opera provides a transition from everyday activities into the world of music. If the building was to be a prelude to art, Maybeck was faced next with an even more profound question: What is the nature and purpose of art?

"In every good painting," Maybeck wrote, "there is a quality which makes you feel that years of experience have preceded it. The artist began his work a long time ago in a nebulous haze of whys . . . and a great deal of hard work and disappointment must come before he suspects that it is not the object nor the likeness to the object that he is working for, but a portrayal of the life that is behind the visible. Here he comes face to face with the real things of this life. He is alone before his problem and drifts away from superficial portrayals. After this he strives to find the spiritual meaning of things and to transmit that secret to the layman."

Maybeck recalled a visit to an art gallery in Munich, where he had seen Madonnas, crucified Christs, and such paintings as Bocklin's *Isle of the Dead,* a portrayal of a boat carrying dead across a dark lagoon to an island where there was a columbarium half hidden in tall trees. He had watched the solemn faces of the people looking at the pictures and "realized right there that an art gallery was a sad and serious matter. . . . The keynote of a Fine Arts Palace," he concluded, "should be that of sadness modified by the feeling that beauty has a soothing influence."

THE IRRETRIEVABLE MOMENT

Beyond Maybeck's simple account of the Munich experience seems to lie a deeper intuition. It involves a perception of life that should be more evident in our own time—after mankind has experienced two world wars and sometimes seems on the brink of a third—than it was in 1915. Art should interpret life, Maybeck seems to be saying, and life is basically a tragic matter. Man's tragic fate is made noble by art and beauty, which give life purpose and meaning.

The sadness that Maybeck noted in art also arises, perhaps, from the knowledge that each moment of life is infinitely valuable and utterly irretrievable. The "soothing influence" he observed may be found in the capacity of art to elevate such moments to immortality. The artist attempts to capture the essence of one particular moment and make it eternal, to stop the flow of time in order to express and preserve the meaning and value of the fleeting instant.

The next question Maybeck faced was how to portray this mood in architecture. He played with various ideas. "An old Roman ruin," he wrote, "away from civilization, which two thousand years before was the center of action and full of life, and now is partly overgrown with bushes and trees—such ruins give the mind a sense of sadness."

He also gave more thought to the painting *Isle of the Dead,* which had made a great impression on him. The painting is sometimes erroneously believed to be the inspiration for the design of the palace, but actually Maybeck rejected it as "overdone in sadness." A better example, he believed, were the islands of Clear Lake, California, "where the trees and bushes seem to rise out of the water," giving an impression of sadness—yet one tempered by beauty.

THE RUINED TEMPLE

And so the elements of the design began to take form: a Roman ruin, an island, bushes and tall trees, "a note of vanished grandeur." Maybeck did not elaborate on the question as to why a ruin would convey an atmosphere of sadness or tragedy, but it may be that in contemplating the vanished grandeur of an earlier age the observer is impressed, perhaps subconsciously, with the mortality of his own life and culture. In looking at the ruin he confronts the fact of death and the certainty that his own civilization will someday meet the same fate, leaving other ruins to be gazed upon by observers in some remote future.

Another statement of Maybeck's is revealing. If a Greek temple, "pure and beautiful in lines and color, were placed on the face of a placid lake, surrounded by high trees and lit up by a glorious full moon, you would recall the days when your mother pressed you to her bosom . . . a protecting spirit hovering over you warm and large. You have there the point of transition from sadness to content which comes pretty near to the total impression of the Fine Arts Palace and lake."

The mother image and the ruined temple, a sense of tragic sadness for a lost parent or for the bygone glory of a great civilization, a feeling of the relation of life to death—these were the elements that went into the conception of the palace. Perhaps here in Maybeck's philosophy is the beginning of an explanation for the compelling fascination that this building has exerted on observers, for the fact that San Franciscans could not bring themselves to tear it down for fifty years after it was supposed to be demolished. Through a gift of philanthropist Walter Johnson and public funds, it was rebuilt in permanent form.

See the palace at twilight, or at times when wisps of fog drift past the colonnade and through the slowly stirring limbs of the eucalyptus around it, and you are transported into another dimension of time and space. The trivia of everyday life fall away, and you confront the ultimates of human existence. This was the purpose and the vision of Bernard Maybeck.

9

The Specter of
Grand View Peak

GRAND VIEW PEAK, which has a resident ghost, is virtually unknown except to people who live nearby, yet it is in some ways the most remarkable of all the hills of San Francisco.

It lies about a mile west of Twin Peaks and is the northernmost high point of the north-south ridge known as Sunset Heights or Golden Gate Heights. It commands a sweeping panorama including Montara Mountain down the peninsula, immense expanses of the ocean, the Farallones, Point Reyes, Tamalpais, the Golden Gate, and large parts of downtown San Francisco and the East Bay.

Owing to its strategic location between the ocean and the bay, it is sometimes a meeting place of inland and marine weather conditions, and it was under these circumstances that I have occasionally seen the colossal spook. But more of that in a moment.

The hill itself is a rare phenomenon geologically. It is the highest point in the great sand drift that swept in from the ocean, blanketed the western portions of the city, and flowed through the passes to the bay over a period of several thousand years. This drift, unparalleled elsewhere in the United States, rose here some seven hundred feet above its origin at Ocean Beach and flowed around outcrops of Franciscan bedrock, the tops of which are still visible—dark red chert in opulently sculptured layers and volcanic greenstone that erupted millions of years ago when this region was the bottom of an ancient sea.

Botanically, too, this hill is extraordinary. It is the last sizable location where you can see native dune plants of the kind that once covered the land on which the city was built. In early spring there are fragrant beds of sweet alyssum and luminous stalks of Franciscan wallflower, a cream-colored blossom that grows only here and in southern Marin, across the Golden Gate. Later you can begin to see the bright gold of California poppies, followed in turn by blue lupine and then by the spectacular tree lupine with its immense stalks of yellow bloom. In early fall will come goldenrod, Indian paintbrush and dozens of other varieties, spreading color down these slopes.

NATURE AND THE BULLDOZERS

Wildlife driven from other areas by the advance of the subdivisions has found refuge here and on the slopes below. Often in the early morning you can see intricate tracings on the damp sand, indicating the presence of small animals. The mellifluous meadowlarks, almost unknown elsewhere in the city, can be heard here. There are quail, red-shafted flickers, woodpeckers, and white-crowned sparrows. Doves and a pair of red-tailed hawks roost in the eucalyptus and Monterey cypresses at the summit.

Perhaps the most remarkable aspect of this hill is the fact that it has survived as a natural enclave in this densely populated urban area. But its days, apparently, are numbered.

Some years ago power shovels and bulldozers arrived and began to cut into the southern side of the hill from an old quarry site. They clawed their way into the slopes, destroying trees and plant life. New houses rose below the big gash, which can serve as another classic example of landscape butchery.

The earth-eating machines stopped, temporarily, leaving most of the hill intact. But from time to time they begin roaring again and hack out more pads for houses. "For Sale" signs appear around the northern, eastern, and western slopes, in locations so steep that it will be impossible to build without cutting down virtually all of the hill that is left. Whether houses can be built here safely is questionable, owing to the steepness of the slopes and the danger of sand landslides, particularly during earthquakes or heavy rains.

The San Francisco Recreation and Park Department owns about an acre at the top of the hill, known officially as Grand View Park, where John McLaren years ago planted the Monterey cypresses and eucalyptus. If the slopes below it are destroyed, this publicly owned piece of land will become an isolated patch with little value.

The entire hill and the slopes below would be an ideal location for a natural park. The city's other parks are all man-made, and there is now no place in the park system set aside as an example of the native landscape. It is possible to envision here a nature preserve where school children could be brought to see what the tip of this peninsula looked like in the days of the first settlers, to learn about the native plant and animal life, to hear the story of the creation of this peninsula with all the elements in plain view—the ocean, the islands, the bay, the central ridge of the city from Mount Davidson to the Presidio. And if they came at the right time, they might see the ghost.

APPARITION OVER THE SUNSET

I first saw it early one winter morning. The air was clear overhead and the sun was about to come up just south of Twin Peaks, but an impenetrable bank of tule fog was drifting from east to west throught the valley occupied by Golden Gate Park. As I walked around the north end of the ridge I could see that the rest of the city, except for the highest hilltops, was wrapped in the fog, and the area where I was standing was clear only because it was in the lee of Twin Peaks and Mount Sutro.

I looked west and was surprised to see the shadow of the peak on which I was standing outlined clearly on the fog bank over the Sunset District. As I climbed to the summit, the scene began to change. The fog was not only flowing west; it was rising like a tide and soon began to wash against the lower slopes of the peak where I was standing. The air turned cold, and I realized I would soon be enveloped in the fog masses. Then, suddenly, as I was about to leave, I saw the ghost. It appeared to the northwest, a shadowy human form of incredible size. Its legs seemed more than a mile long. They stretched from the hilltop to the point on the fog bank a mile west where the shadow of the peak was projected. Above that point the giant form—trunk, head, and arms—seemed to extend out toward the ocean for a couple of more miles.

Startled, I jumped back. At the same instant the ghost jumped. Then, as I moved again, I grasped the truth: I was looking at my own shadow projected on the fog. I pulled off my sweater and waved it back and forth over my head. Incredulously I watched as the shadow seemed to sweep across the top of the fog in a vast arc over half the city, from the Sunset District, across Golden Gate Park and the outer Richmond District to the vicinity of the Cliff House. With a euphoric feeling of omnipotence I jumped and waved my arms, enjoying myself immensely for about five minutes. Then the rising fog bank enveloped the peak completely, and the stupendous show dissolved into the cold mists.

WITCHES' SABBATH

The experience stirred a vague memory, and when I got home I thumbed through the writings of John Muir until I found his description of a similar incident. In November of 1875, after a fresh snowfall, Muir made his first ascent of Half Dome. As he stood on the summit looking down on the valley nearly a mile below, a flock of small clouds gathered below him.

"Then the sun shone free," he wrote, "lighting the pearly gray surface of the cloud-like sea and making it glow. Gazing, admiring, I was startled to see for the first time the rare optical phenomenon of the 'Specter of the Brocken.' My shadow, clearly outlined, about half a mile long, lay upon this glorious white surface with startling effect. I walked back and forth, waved my arms and struck all sorts of attitudes, to see every slightest movement enormously exaggerated. Considering that I have looked down so many times from mountain tops on seas of all sorts of clouds, it seems strange that I should have seen the 'Brocken Specter' only this once."

Clearly it was the Specter of the Brocken I had seen on Grand View Peak. Turning to the encyclopedia, I learned that the Brocken is a peak in the Harz Mountains of northern Germany where this phenomenon was first observed. The peasants attributed the ghostly figures in the sky to supernatural causes, and it may be for this reason that the Brocken is a mountain of ancient legend.

It is the site of Walpurgis Night in German folklore, when the witches gleefully hold their saturnalian sabbath. The scene appears in Goethe's *Faust* and has raised the hackles of several generations of movie-goers in Disney's *Fantasia* to the diabolic music of Moussorgsky's *Night on Bald Mountain*.

If there are any witches on Grand View Peak, I have failed to see them, perhaps because I have never arrived at the right moment. But I have seen the Specter of the Brocken a few more times, in various forms, when weather conditions were precisely right. And I have learned that the giant ghost has occasionally been observed at other points in the Bay Area—from the summit of Mount Diablo and from the ridge east of Muir Woods, when a summer fog bank in the canyon below creates a similar screen at sunrise. At the latter location, the shadows were surrounded by rainbow-like haloes, known as Brocken bows.

The scientific explanation for the Specter of the Brocken, I find, is that the phenomenon is the result of what artists call a *trompe-l'oeil*. It is an illusion caused by the eye's error in estimating the distance of the fog or cloud screen. But I find this explanation highly unsatisfactory. I prefer to believe that for a few unforgettable moments I was a giant three miles tall.

10

The Fort at the Narrows

On foggy nights the thick billows of vapor roll in past the old brick fort at the Golden Gate, blotting out the colossus above and enveloping the building in shrouds of mist. There is only the sound of the wind, the deep-throated moans of the foghorns, and the rhythmic rise and fall of the roar of the waves against the old sea wall below.

At such times the moving mists give rise to odd illusions. The billowed darkness seems to be more than darkness. Shadowy forms appear and disappear around corners of the abandoned bastion.

There, perhaps, pacing the ramparts high in the fog, standing behind an iron pillar of the dark courtyard inside, flitting furtively among the deserted gun galleries, stalking the top of the bluffs behind the fort are the ghosts of men who knew this place long ago: Anza, Vancouver, Rezanov, von Kotzebue; Frémont the Pathfinder and Kit Carson the Scout; Richard Henry Dana and General Custis Lee, son of Robert E. Lee.

On that clear day in March of 1776 when Captain Juan Bautista de Anza, Lieutenant José Joaquín Moraga, and Padre Pedro Font stood on the cliff at the point on the south shore of the Golden Gate, Font wrote in his diary: "The port of San Francisco is a marvel of nature, and might well be called the harbor of harbors. . . . This mesa the commander designated as the site for the new settlement and fort which were to be established on this harbor."

Anza's successors were in no hurry to build the planned fort. Sixteen years later, energetic young Captain George Vancouver, emissary of the burgeoning British Empire, sailed past the point into

San Francisco Bay and noted its lack of fortification. Later he went ashore and observed the strategic location on the point, writing to his superiors about the vast potentialities of this place, possibly envisioning a new outpost of the British Empire.

Two years later the Spaniards built a brick and adobe structure they called El Castillo de San Joaquín. Fortunately the fort was never attacked by a hostile force. It was not even strong enough to withstand the assaults of the elements and had to be repaired and rebuilt several times.

When the representative of another empire, the Russian explorer von Kotzebue, appeared on the scene in 1824, he noted the decrepitude of the fort: "I found St. Joachim on his rocky throne, truly a very peaceful and well disposed saint; no one of his cannon in condition to fire a single shot."

FRÉMONT'S RAID

The Russians, like the British, looked covetously at the weakly defended prize of San Francisco Bay, but they were not in a position to seize the bastion and incorporate it into their own empire. That job remained for yet another "empire," the new nation spreading westward from the east coast of the continent under the spur of Manifest Destiny. Its harbinger was the empire builder and man of destiny Captain John Charles Frémont, who had pushed west across the continent with his scout, Kit Carson, and had given to the strait at the bay's entrance the inspired name, Chrysopolae, Golden Gate.

Although he could easily have seized San Francisco without encountering much resistance, Frémont was obliged to follow President Polk's policy for "peaceful" acquisition of California. In order to achieve his purpose, he quietly encouraged a revolt of a group of Americans at Sonoma. They tore down the Mexican flag and proclaimed the Bear Flag Republic. On the excuse of "protecting" the Americans, Frémont organized the settlers into the California Battalion and routed the Mexican forces in a skirmish at San Rafael. He continued south to Sausalito and peered across the Golden Gate at the cannons of the old Spanish fortress. He had no means of crossing, but luckily found an American merchant windjammer, the *Moscow,* anchored at Sausalito, commanded by Captain William D. Phelps. Meanwhile Frémont had received word that American and Mexican forces were engaged in battle near the Rio Grande. He persuaded Phelps that the United States had declared war on Mexico and secured the captain's help in a plan to "capture" San Francisco (then called Yerba Buena). In the dark hour before dawn, Phelps piloted Frémont, Carson, and a party of Frémont's men across the Golden Gate in his launch toward El Castillo de San Joaquín. The attackers waded ashore and stormed up the white cliff to the fort. It was deserted. With some rat-tailed files borrowed from the stores of the *Moscow,* Frémont's men spiked the fort's cannon. The only casualty was one of the attackers who accidentally shot himself in the arm. Then the Americans, still without resistance, stalked into the village of Yerba Buena in daylight, captured the captain of the port, and returned to Sonoma. One of the Castillo's cannons now stands in front of the Officers' Club at the Presidio.

(Captain Phelps later sued the United States Government for one hundred thousand dollars for his services to Frémont in the "conquest" of San Francisco. He was awarded fifty dollars.)

SENTINEL OF THE GATE

The conquering Americans, realizing that the Castillo de San Joaquín was the key to a defense of the harbor, made plans to rebuild it. One of the weaknesses of the old fort was that it stood on sand and crumbling rock. In order to obtain a secure foothold for a large, modern fortification, the Americans decided to level the cliff and built the fort on solid ground at the water's edge. They scraped the cliff down to a few feet above sea level, dumping the rocks and soil along the beach to the southeast. However, owing to a lack of appropriations, the work on the new fort stretched over nearly a decade.

In a postscript to *Two Years Before the Mast* Richard Henry Dana records his return to San Francisco in 1859, twenty-four years after his original voyage: ". . . I rode to the fort, now nearly finished, on the southern shore of the Gate, and made an inspection of it. It is very expensive and of the latest style. One of the engineers here is Custis Lee, who had just left West Point at the head of his class—a son of Colonel Robert E. Lee."

It was ironic that young Lee should have been one of the builders of the fort. Two years later he joined his father in the Confederate forces, and the fort he helped construct became the keystone of San Francisco Bay's defenses against any possible Confederate raids. An additional purpose of the fort was for defense against the British, who were believed to be hoping to take advantage of the Civil War to seize San Francisco. The attacks never came, but the very existence of this formidable bastion at the entrance to the bay may have discouraged any contemplated raids and helped prevent California from going either to the Confederacy or to the British. It was the strongest fort west of the Mississippi.

The point of land on which it stood had been known as Fort Point since the days of the Spanish *castillo,* and the new structure was referred to simply as "the fort at Fort Point," finally abbreviated to Fort Point, a term designating either the building or the promontory. In 1882 General William Tecumseh Sherman ordered that the name be changed to Fort Winfield Scott, in honor of Lincoln's first chief of staff, but in general usage the old building is still called Fort Point. Fort Winfield Scott now designates the entire northern section of the Presidio above the point.

THE VINDICATION OF JOSEPH STRAUSS

As the fort's cannons became outmoded, the building was used by the Army only occasionally, and it was assumed that it would be demolished for the construction of the Golden Gate Bridge in the 1930's. However, Chief Bridge Engineer Joseph B. Strauss had a well-developed sense of history and could see the potentially dramatic contrast between the old fort and his bridge. He decided to preserve the fort in the hope that it would become a museum and historic landmark. Clifford E. Paine, his assistant, designed the steel arch that overleaps the fort, contrasting with the concrete arch at the Marin end of the bridge.

During World War II, Fort Point housed an antiaircraft unit and antisubmarine guns. The only wartime casualty was a soldier who was walking across the courtyard and was knocked down by a falling glove dropped by a painter on the bridge, 250 feet above.

Joseph Strauss's dreams for the fort were finally realized when in 1968 it was opened to the public by the privately sponsored Fort Point Museum Association. Among the numerous exhibits is one of the old Spanish cannons spiked by Frémont—an ancient fieldpiece cast in Peru in 1684. In 1970 Congress passed a bill creating the Fort Point National Historic Site as part of the National Park System. To enter the fort today is to step back into history. You see it substantially as it looked when completed in 1860. The basic design is similar to that of the other great forts of the era— Sumter and Pulaski. You walk in through a massive pair of iron-studded doors to a corridor or "sally port" lined with menacing loopholes, then emerge into a big courtyard surrounded by galleries.

Here it becomes evident that the structure is an architectural masterpiece. Facing you across the courtyard are three tiers of can-

non galleries with rows of arches as rhythmic and pleasing to the
eye as a Romanesque arcade. The galleries are connected by finely
wrought granite staircases that seem to spiral upward without visible support. The granite was quarried and finished to size in China,
then set in place here, like triangular building blocks, in such a way
as to support their own weight—a fascinating piece of engineering.

CISTERNS FOR A SIEGE

On the opposite side of the courtyard are fluted iron columns
and wrought-iron balustrades now rusting in the sea air. A University
of California architectural expert writes: "There is probably no example of nineteenth-century cast iron work in the United States
more chaste in conception, elegant in proportion, refined in detail. . . . [The fort] is one of the finest examples of military architecture in the United States."

Oddly, the roof of Fort Point's top gallery, behind the cannon
tracks, was originally planted to turf, and for many years the remnant of that soil sprouted with wild weedy vegetation. Beneath the
fort's floor are two big cisterns storing rain water from the roof's
gutters for use during a siege. Although no siege ever took place,
the cisterns were found usable during another emergency—the 1906
earthquake and fire.

In clear weather the view from the old fort is one of the most
impressive in the city. The bridge arches across the sky directly
overhead, incredibly gigantic and intricately structured from this an-
gle. The waters of the Gate rush by at flood tide like a river, and on
occasion giant combers thunder against the old sea wall and send
up plumes of spray half the height of the fort itself. Across the
water to the southeast, the towers of the city rise from its hills,
reflecting the blaze of sunset or glowing from within after dark.
Eastward are the cities along the far shores of the bay; to the north,
the red cliffs and steep ridges of Marin; to the west, past the far
heads at Point Bonita and Point Lobos, the ocean and the Farallones.

But to see the fort at the most propitious time, go there when the
thick fogs are rolling in from the ocean, the great horns intone
their rhythmic chant like voices of the long-dead past, and elusive
shapes appear in the gray shifting billows. Are these phantoms of
history standing on the bluff, pacing the ramparts, striding along
the sea wall . . . or merely errant wraiths of vapor? The fog advances and recedes and advances again, and you cannot be sure.

PART TWO

---•---

THE BAY

1

---◆---

The Mystery of the Gate

"GOLDEN GATE IN '48!" we used to say hopefully during those dark years overseas when it seemed as if the war would go on forever. My own return to the United States was not through the Gate but past that other mighty symbol, the Statue of Liberty. However, one evening after the end of the Korean War, my wife and I were standing at Fort Point looking out under the bridge when an incoming troopship from the war zone was entering the bay. The vessel was half a mile away, but the moment it passed under the bridge we were startled to hear a shout that rose from hundreds of throats and echoed across the water from the cliffs beyond. This was the place and the symbol every man aboard had been dreaming of during the months and years of exile, and it resulted in a spontaneous upwelling of sentiment and sound—a soldiers' chorus of total exuberance.

Since the completion of the bridge in 1937, visitors to San Francisco have often assumed that the structure itself is the Golden Gate. But the strait is several miles long and was a symbol of wealth and fortune to the Argonauts nearly a century before it was spanned by steel. Although Frémont had named it Golden Gate as the Western Hemisphere's equivalent of the Golden Horn, the strait at Byzantium that joins Europe and Asia, neither the Golden Horn nor any of the other fabled straits of history—such as Gibraltar and Magellan —has a more dramatic natural setting. Along the north shore for four miles from Point Bonita to Point Cavallo the dark red cliffs rise abruptly from the roaring surf. Above them are high ridges culminating in 2600-foot Mount Tamalpais.

The southern shoreline is also precipitous in places but is broken at intervals by valleys and beaches, making it more accessible to the contemporary explorer. The cliffs of Land's End bear the full brunt of the oceanic combers that attack from the northwest, and the jagged offshore rocks here have punctured many a luckless ship. At low tide you can still see the remains of the *Ohioan,* which piled up off Point Lobos in 1936, the *Lyman Stewart,* which ran aground opposite Mile Rock in 1922, and the *Frank H. Buck,* which was pounded to pieces at the same spot in 1937. The sandstone cliffs are interrupted at intervals by dangerous landslides and a few hospitable coves, the largest of which is China Beach, now Phelan Beach State Park.

TRAGEDY AT BAKERS BEACH

Northeastward beyond another stretch of cliffs is half-mile-long Bakers Beach, at the mouth of a broad valley coming down through the Presidio. Here, on the stretch of sand named for the Baker family's old dairy ranch, is prime exploring and beachcombing territory. In 1776 Padre Font was delighted with this beach, felt it would make a fine harbor and that Lobos Creek, flowing across the beach to the ocean, would be a good source of water. The padre was wrong about the harbor. He saw the beach at a time of low surf; the colossal combers that often thunder ashore here would make landings impossible. But he was right about Lobos Creek. It afforded one of the city's first sources of water supply; in 1858 a redwood flume was built from here to carry water along the beach and around the cliffs to reservoirs on Russian Hill. Portions of the flume are still visible along the cliffs.

As a boy, poet Robert Frost, a native San Franciscan, came to this beach one day for a picnic with his family, but the weather was ill suited to picnics, and in later years he remembered the occasion as ominous:

> *The shattered water made a misty din.*
> *Great waves looked over others coming in,*
> *And thought of doing something to the shore*
> *That water never did to land before.*
> *The clouds were low and hairy in the skies . . .*
> *It looked as if a night of dark intent*
> *Was coming, and not only a night, an age . . .*

As if to confirm Frost's sense of dread, this beach has seen tragedy. On a foggy night in 1901, only a few years after Frost's visit, the steamer *Rio de Janeiro* ran aground at Fort Point and sank; the Coast Guard put out rescue boats from a station at this beach, and bodies of some of the victims were washed ashore here. In 1959 young Albert Kogler was attacked by a shark while swimming here and died despite a heroic rescue by his companion, Shirley O'Neill.

From Bakers Beach to Fort Point is a stretch of cliffs and coves that are sometimes passable in the summertime at low tide, although the depth of sand on the rocks at the foot of the cliffs varies as much as fifteen feet from season to season. The cliffs continue for a half mile east of Fort Point, where they are traversed by the road to the fort; then they end in a low-lying area that is chiefly man-made fill—the Presidio's Crissy Field (the first airfield in the Bay Area) and the Marina District. Evidently hidden by the fill are some valuable clues to the geologic story of the Gate itself.

THE CLUE OF THE STRANGE PEAT BOG

For centuries the origin of the Gate has been a matter for speculation. An Indian legend maintained that the Gate had been formed in a single shudder of the earth: The mountains were rent asunder in a cataclysmic earthquake, and the ocean rushed through to the interior valley, forming San Francisco Bay. San Francisco novelist Gertrude Atherton thought that the event might have taken place in historic times. Why had Drake and the Spanish explorers sailed along the coast in the sixteenth and early seventeenth centuries and anchored as close as Point Reyes without ever seeing this auspicious portal to the great bay?

They did not see it, she theorized, because it was not in existence at that time. Where the Gate now pierces the Coast Range, there was only a solid wall of mountains. If her theory were correct, the forming of the Gate would have occurred some time between 1604, when Vizcaíno sailed to Point Reyes, seeing no sign of the strait, and 1769, when Portolá's weary men, trudging up the coast from San Diego, stumbled across the Gate by accident, having overshot their goal of Monterey Bay.

There was no scientific evidence for the Atherton theory, although nineteenth-century geologists suspected that the Gate had been formed in geologically recent times. Some intriguing evidence for the latter assumption appears in an 1853 "Geologic Report on the Coast of California" by W. P. Blake. He described the shoreline as it then appeared between Fort Point and Point San Jose, or Black Point, the present location of Fort Mason, about three miles east.

"It is a curious and interesting fact," he wrote, "that the sand beach between Fort Point and Point San Jose has been thrown up by the surf upon an extensive alluvial deposit, which has the character of a peat bog or swamp. When the tide is very low the edge of this peat formation may be seen. Large masses of the peat are also broken out during storms, and thrown upon the sand of the beach.

"This sand and all the loose boulders rest upon a foundation of the peat; and the continuation of the peat is found in the swamp or flat meadow land which lies inside the belt of sand and between it and the sandstone hills. It is very difficult to account for the swamp under conditions like those at present existing. A strong current is constantly setting backward and forward through the channel and the action of the surf constantly undermines and encroaches upon the beach, so that the present action is destructive and the swamp could not possibly have been formed while the Golden Gate was open as we now find it."

THE SUBMARINE CANYON

Blake's implication is clear: The Golden Gate was opened some time after the peat bog was formed. Peat is created by the decomposition of mosses and marsh plants in a swamp over long periods of time in quiet water—conditions quite different from those Blake was describing. Nothing of Blake's peat bog is visible today. The remains of it were evidently covered when fills were made along the shoreline for Crissy Field and for the Panama-Pacific International Exposition of 1915, now the Marina District.

If the swamp was formed before the opening of the Golden Gate, how did the waters of this region in those days reach the ocean? The Golden Gate today drains not only the San Francisco Bay Area but, through the Sacramento and San Joaquin river systems, a region of sixty thousand square miles, including the five-hundred-mile-long Central Valley and most of the Sierra Nevada.

Here another speculative theory comes into the picture. Some nineteenth-century geologists believed that before the opening of the Gate these waters flowed out of the Bay Area to the south in a river, the combined waters of the Sacramento and San Joaquin, through the Santa Clara Valley to Gilroy and into the Pajaro River, which empties into Monterey Bay. The geologists cited an impressive piece of evidence for this theory—the existence at Monterey Bay of a deep submarine canyon, which might have been carved by this river at a time when sea level was lower and the present bottom of

Monterey Bay was dry land. No evidence of such a canyon has been found off the Golden Gate, indicating, under this theory, that the Sacramento and San Joaquin rivers began to reach the ocean through the Gate only after sea level rose to near its present height.

EXPLORERS' OVERSIGHT

Unfortunately for the older theories, most geologists nowadays believe that the Gate was open at least a million years ago when the present landscape was taking shape, and that the waters of this region never did drain out through Monterey Bay. The Monterey submarine canyon, they are convinced, was probably the result of other causes.

In the latest theory the Gate was carved by the river waters maintaining their course to the sea through the rising Coast Range. San Francisco Bay came into existence in its present form at the end of the last Ice Age, ten or fifteen thousand years ago, when rising sea level flooded the river gorge and inundated the valley inside.

If this theory is correct, in the age of the explorers the Gate appeared as it does today. Yet the question remains: why did they miss it? The usual answer is that it was hidden by fog. However, some of the navigators, notably Cermeño in 1595 and Vizcaíno in 1604, passed here not in the summer fog season but in the winter. The winter tule fogs form inland and rarely blanket the coast. Another consideration is that even in clear weather navigators heading up the coast would normally not hug the shoreline but would tend to steer for Point Reyes, which projects into the ocean thirty miles northwest of the Gate. From several miles offshore, the hills of Angel Island the East Bay loom as a backdrop to the Gate, obscuring the opening. Nevertheless, one would assume that the sharp-eyed explorers would have examined the shoreline quite carefully through telescopes.

It would not be consistent with any reasonable geologic explanation to assume that the Gate was opened suddenly in the past few hundred years. But there is still the mystery of Blake's peat bog, which he was certain "could not possibly have been formed while the Golden Gate was open as we now find it." Evidently the full story of the Gate's origin has not yet been told.

2

Angel Island and the
Voyage of the *San Carlos*

As THE EXCURSION BOAT pulls away from the wharf at Sausalito, you can see the sunlight gleaming from the water, from the wing of a circling gull, from the rolling green hills of Marin, from the long ridge of Mount Tamalpais—as it did on that clear summer morning nearly two centuries ago.

On the fifth of August 1775, the Spanish vessel San Carlos, *commanded by thirty-year-old Juan Manuel de Ayala, headed into the Golden Gate, but was swept back to sea by the powerful ebb currents. Finally, toward sundown the tide turned, and Ayala piloted the* San Carlos, *its sails full, through the narrows of the mile-wide strait in the twilight. He carefully guided the vessel along the north shore and dropped anchor in the dark, doubtless with high emotion. To his knowledge, the* San Carlos *was the first ship in history to enter this strait.*

At dawn the next morning, Ayala and his crew stood at the ship's rail and stared at the sight revealed by the rising sun: the blue bay spread out before them, the Marin hills, the peninsula where San Francisco would one day stand, the mountains encircling the far shores.

ENSENADA DE LA CARMELITA

From the excursion boat you can look into the cove where Ayala probably anchored. The morning light illuminates the masts of the boats at the docks; the clean white hull of the old ferryboat, *Berkeley;* the windows of houses climbing the hillside, half hidden in the trees. Then, looking north and east into Richardson Bay, you observe a half-dozen ungainly black cormorants perched on Cone Rock, which protrudes from the water a quarter-mile off Belvedere.

Gazing out across Richardson Bay early on that summer morning in 1775, Ayala spied Cone Rock. Its shape reminded him of the garb of a Carmelite friar, and he named the bay "Ensenada de la Carmelita." At seven o'clock he sent his pilot, Jose Cañizares, to probe the Ensenada de la Carmelita in a launch and find a good anchorage for the San Carlos. *While Cañizares and his men were sounding the bay, they were amazed to hear someone shouting at them from the high ridge of Belvedere. Peering eastward into the sunlight they could see groups of Indians gesture excitedly and run to the shore, beckoning for the boat to come closer. Cautiously, Cañizares edged the boat nearer to the island, proceeding with the soundings. In a gesture of greeting, the Indians raised a long pole tipped with feathers. Cañizares kept about his business, however, as he had no orders to go ashore. The Indians evidently assumed the Spaniards feared an attack. To demonstrate their peaceful intentions, they threw their bows down, waved their arrows in the air, and then stuck them into the sand.*

The excursion boat passes rocky, cliff-bound Belvedere Point, and suddenly you see a long black line on the water—thousands of cormorants and gulls bobbing and diving over a school of herring. Here off the point, where the current ebbing swiftly through Raccoon Strait meets the Richardson Bay ebb, the water is roiled into whitecaps and a clearly marked tide rip.

A WELCOME FROM THE NATIVES

Cañizares returned to the San Carlos *and reported to Ayala that Ensenada de la Carmelita—Richardson Bay—would not afford a satisfactory anchorage because the bottom was too soft to hold an anchor. The* San Carlos *then moved around past Belvedere Point, where the eager Indians were still shouting, and anchored in a cove Ayala called Ensenada del Santo Evangelio—Bay of the Holy Gospel —today's Belvedere Cove.*

Ayala was still not totally convinced the Indians were friendly, but he decided to take a chance. He sent the launch with Cañizares, the chaplain, and several armed sailors with orders to treat the natives well and offer them presents of beads and other trinkets. Once ashore, Cañizares and his men were overwhelmed with hospitality. With gestures and shouts the Indians tried to persuade the Spaniards to go to their village, where they were invited to eat and sleep. When Cañizares cautiously refused, the Indians prepared for them on the spot a meal of pinole, bread, and tamales. The natives proved to be adept at repeating Spanish words, but when they were invited to go aboard the San Carlos, they insisted that the Spaniards visit the village first. However, Cañizares declined with thanks and returned to the ship.

To the left of the excursion boat you can see Belvedere Cove, the fleet of small boats docked at the San Francisco Yacht Club, tiny Corinthian "Island," and the harbor of the Corinthian Yacht Club. Belvedere and Corinthian actually ceased to be islands long ago, when road fills across sand bars connected them to the Tiburon Peninsula. At the village of Tiburon are the dockside restaurants that are frequented by bay yachtsmen. To your right, across Raccoon Strait, Angel Island looms larger as you approach. Its hills are covered with chaparral, wild flowers, and groves of live oak and laurel. Slicing across the western part of the island from north to south is a long "dike" of serpentine rock, greenish outcrops eroded into grotesque shapes.

ISLA DE LOS ANGELES

On the thirteenth of August, Cañizares finally found an ideal permanent anchorage for the San Carlos. It was a sheltered cove on the north side of the island that Ayala had named for the Virgin— Isla de Nuestra Señora do Los Angeles—Island of Our Lady of the Angels. While the San Carlos was anchored in the cove, the persistent Indians approached in rafts and canoes. Ayala invited them on board and offered them food and entertainment. The Spaniards were delighted when the Indians quickly learned the Spanish word for "bread." Significantly, however, there is no indication that the Spaniards learned any Indian words.

As your boat rounds Point Ione, you get the first view of Ayala Cove—white sailboats at anchor in a placid bay, a curving beach, a wide expanse of green grass, palms and cypresses, a few white buildings, wooded encircling hills. You momentarily have the illusion that you are approaching one of those legendary South Pacific islands, half expecting to be welcomed by brown-skinned natives.

But this is Angel Island State Park, and instead of girls in sarongs there are rangers in khaki and picnic tables under the eucalyptus trees.

The month spent by the San Carlos *in the cove at Angel Island must have been a trying one for Ayala. He was nursing a foot injury and was unable to leave the ship. He sent Cañizares out in the launch to make a survey of the bay. Ayala was a young man with his first ship; he was full of the enthusiasms of youth. As he waited there in the cove at Angel Island, gazing over the rail of the* San Carlos, *he may have envisioned the future of this great bay—the ships coming from all the ports of the earth, cities rising from the surrounding shores. Cañizares returned every few days with growing amounts of data, completing a detailed map of the bay, and it soon became clear that this bay was the greatest natural harbor in the New World.*

Cañizares' early suspicion of the Indians was soon overcome, and wherever he visited them throughout the Bay Area he found them hospitable: "They presented us with exquisite fishes (amongst them salmon), seeds, and pinole. I had the opportunity of visiting them four times and found them always as friendly as the first time, noticing in them polite manners, and what is better, modesty and retirement in the women. They are not disposed to beg, but accept with good will what is given them. . . . This Indian village has some scows or canoes, made of tule, so well constructed and woven that they caused me great admiration. Four men get in them to go fishing, pushing with two-ended oars with such speed that I found they went faster than the launch."

ACCIDENT AT HORSESHOE COVE

On many a weekend, hundreds of people come to Ayala Cove on the excursion boats, picnic, play on the lawn, walk the beach, hike or bicycle or ride an "elephant train" on the five-mile loop road around the island. Aside from a plaque, there is nothing marking Ayala's visit, but visitors stare at the century-old Army buildings in the West Garrison, the abandoned overgrown barracks in the East Garrison, the remains of the old immigration station dating from the time this was the Ellis Island of the west. But the greatest attraction is the insular scenery. Aside from the few acres occupied by the old buildings, most of the island has changed little since Ayala's time. The chaparral-covered slopes, the wild flowers, the

groves of live oak, laurel, and madroño afford a view of what the
entire Bay Area was like when the *San Carlos* anchored here two
centuries ago.

The Indians are long gone, but some descendants of those who
welcomed the Spaniards may have been among the Indians who
occupied the neighboring island of Alcatraz in 1969. And doubtless
they had reason to regret their ancestors' cordial hospitality toward
the Europeans.

"On September 7," Ayala wrote in his report, *"I decided to
leave the Port of San Francisco, as I considered the reconnaissance
completed, and in doing this, having no wind, I was carried by the
strong current against some rocks (on the north shore of the Golden
Gate), injuring the rudder and breaking two female and one male
bolts. This obliged me to enter a cove (Horseshoe Cove at Fort
Baker), where I repaired as well as possible the accident, and again
sailed forth, a light breeze from the north . . . aiding the sailing."*

3

Treasure Island and the Dream That Died

FOR THREE DECADES man-made Treasure Island, belying its name, has been a navy base—"T.I." to thousands of navy men who spend a few months there in training schools and move on. Driving across the base on business one day, I came upon a large open space in the middle of the island, where big recumbent statues were grouped around what appeared to be the remains of a large fountain. Similarly recumbent navy men lounged on the lawns eating lunch. The statues at first seemed vaguely familiar. Then I recognized them. This was once the Court of Pacifica at the California Golden Gate International Exposition. And I was suddenly transported in flashback to an unforgettable day more than thirty years ago.

From the ferry bound for Treasure Island that summer morning in 1939 I watched the sunlight scintillate from the wind-riffled water below, from the colossal silver span of the new Bay Bridge overhead, from the city's skyscrapers rising like monoliths on its hills. It was one of those sharp clear mornings when every tree and building on the shores seemed resplendent in the brilliant light. I stood on the upper deck of the boat inhaling lungfuls of the brisk salt breeze from the Golden Gate, peering ahead with youthful anticipation at the white towers on the island rising out of the bay like some mirage from the Arabian Nights. In retrospect there seems a fabled quality about that voyage; it recalls the perennial legend of youth journeying toward a shining city that symbolizes hope and promise and the great world beyond.

I stepped off the ferry and wandered through the fair's massive portals into a world of wonder. There, above the cascading Fountain of Western Waters was the colossal figure of Pacifica, a woman with her hands raised in the benediction of peace. Behind her was a mobile metallic curtain, shimmering in the morning light. And in front of her, around the fountain, were the recumbent statues—all that now remain of the magic city in the bay.

OVER THE RAINBOW

I walked through the Court of the Seven Seas to the fountains and gardens of the Court of Honor, dominated by the four-hundred-foot Tower of the Sun. (So tall was the tower that one day someone looked up, saw a wisp of fog drifting past its top, had an illusion that the tower was falling, and screamed a warning that scattered the visitors in all directions.) I strolled through the Ford Building and watched an automobile being assembled before my eyes; gazed at the Botticellis and Raphaels and Michelangelos in the Fine Arts Palace (an attraction that outdrew Sally Rand's "Nude Ranch"); watched the history of America thunder across the acre-sized stage of the "Cavalcade"; smashed an imitation atom at the University of California's imitation cyclotron (little suspecting what atom-smashing would lead to); saw Johnny Weissmuller knife through the water at Billy Rose's "Aquacade"; stared at the steel colonnade of States in the huge Federal Building; watched Diego Rivera working on a gigantic fresco; and gaped at a woman being sawed in two in a sideshow.

I walked out of a fair building in late afternoon as a thousand windows on the Berkeley Hills were ablaze with the reflected light of the setting sun, and I climbed to the roof of the Administration Building to watch the lights come on in the towers of the city and on the incredible bridge arching across the sky overhead. At night the fair was transformed into a dazzling polychromatic display; indirect lighting turned buildings, fountains, reflecting pools, and courts into pastel blues, yellows and reds, purples and golds.

To all who saw the fair through the eyes of youth, it still retains the timeless quality of a dream. The Panama-Pacific International Exposition of 1915 held that role for our parents' generation, a time which seemed to us to be about as recent as the Middle Ages; and it requires a special effort of imagination to realize that the 1939 fair is equally remote for today's young people, including the sailors who eat lunch around the statues from the court of long-gone Pacifica.

One measure of the passage of time is afforded by a recollection of the entertainers who appeared at the fair. There was Morton Downey, crooning "Carolina Moon"; Kay Kyser, the corn-pone professor and his College of Musical Knowledge; the big bands of Benny Goodman and Eddy Duchin; Betty Grable; Alec Templeton; Lawrence Tibbett and Grace Moore. In a single show, on the final day of the exposition, George M. Cohan sang and danced "Yankee Doodle Dandy" and "Give My Regards to Broadway"; W. C. Handy trumpeted his "Saint Louis Blues"; a battery of composers including Hoagy Carmichael, Jerome Kern, Sigmund Romberg, and Irving Berlin played their own tunes at the piano; a teen-age Judy Garland sang "Over the Rainbow"; Deems Taylor narrated for the symphony; and the incomparable John Charles Thomas rang the rooftree with "Old Man River."

WESTWARD THE FUTURE

The fair closed financially in the red, but it had made its mark in other terms. Every great world's fair since the first one—the Crystal Palace in London in 1851—has been an index to its times, a reflection of the achievements of an era, the arts and sciences, the technology and cultural values. In the centennial summer of 1876 the Philadelphia Exposition exhibited the Corliss engine and other technological wonders that heralded the burgeoning of industry in the expansive post-Civil War era. The Paris Exposition of 1889 featured not only Little Egypt but the precursor of the skyscraper city, the Eiffel Tower.

The first world's fair in the United States, Chicago's Columbian International Exposition of 1893 (Daniel Burnham, chief architect), initiated the classic revival in architecture and gave great impetus to city planning. At Chicago that year and at the Paris International at the turn of the century, historian Henry Adams was both dazzled and puzzled by the new force in the world represented by the dynamo; both of the fairs provided chapters for *The Education of Henry Adams.*

St. Louis in 1904 ("Meet me in St. Louie, Louie, meet me at the fair . . .") celebrated the centenary of the Louisiana Purchase and succeeded in its expressed determination to outdo Chicago in classic splendor. "The world has never seen so marvelous a phantasm. . . ." wrote Henry Adams. In 1915 San Francisco celebrated its revival from the ashes of 1906 and the opening of the Panama Canal. Eighteen years later Chicago displayed the technological achievements of a "Century of Progress."

Far more than most of its predecessors, the Golden Gate International Exposition of 1939 was a look forward. Although the 1915 fair here had officially celebrated the promise of the new canal, architecturally and artistically it commemorated the past, most notably in Maybeck's neoclassical Palace of Fine Arts. In 1939 the theme was the Pacific, which necessarily meant the future, because America had never before looked thoughtfully westward from these shores. We had been too busy settling and developing our own West—and looking backward at Europe—to see very far beyond the Golden Gate.

The 1939 New York World's Fair also emphasized the future, but its "World of Tomorrow" (like its 1965 exposition later) was a world of mechanical gadgetry; San Francisco's was an anticipatory blending of the arts and cultures of the Pacific. It was implicitly a statement that the Era of the Atlantic was drawing to a close and the Era of the Pacific was about to begin. The prevailing architecture was an adaptation of Aztec-Mayan and Cambodian. Murals and sculpture portrayed the traditions of East and West in arts, crafts, and religions. One of the most impressive of the fair's murals was a gigantic bas-relief in the Court of Pacifica representing the meeting of cultures of the Orient and the Occident.

END OF INNOCENCE?

The fair's view westward into the future was undoubtedly too optimistic. It was a product of a decade that had begun in a time of bread lines and bankruptcy but had developed in the Roosevelt years into a national resurgence of hope and creative energy. It ignored the war clouds gathering around the far shores of both oceans. Before the fair closed for the winter in September of 1939, Hitler had invaded Poland, opening World War II. By the time it closed its doors forever a year later, the conquering Nazis had marched down the Champs Elysées; and the Luftwaffe was setting fire to London. Then followed the years of war and cold war, the tragedies of Korea in the 1950's and Vietnam in the '60's, and, at the beginning of the 1970's, widespread pessimism and increasing violence in American cities. In these years there has been no unifying symbol, no affirmative vision to counterbalance the threats and terrors of war and domestic violence, pollution, and overpopulation.

Was the vision of the 1939 fair the final display of American innocence and optimism, or was it an idea whose time had not yet come? Perhaps the question is unanswerable. Yet in the America of the 1970's, in a general miasma of gloom and doubt, there seems to be a hunger for new ideas, new approaches. It is particularly significant that among many members of the younger generation there is an intense interest in Asian philosophies and life styles. Perhaps, then, it is time to revive and expand the interrupted vision of the exposition. Perhaps it is time to contemplate not only the genuine dangers and disasters of our era but the equally genuine possibilities of a new renaissance inherent in the meeting of East and West.

It may be time again to mobilize the talents of artists in all fields to create visible symbols of possibilities beyond the Pacific. The vision this time might well be embodied in less expansive but permanent form—in an exhibition that could fire the imaginations of a new generation with the inestimable opportunities lying westward, in culture and commerce, in philosophy and the arts. Our age needs affirmations of faith in the human potential. No city is better suited to provide them than San Francisco, historically the symbol of opportunity in the West.

4

Isle of the Ancients

As THE BOAT leaves Richmond and approaches Brooks Island, the morning mists are rising from the surface of the bay, obscuring the horizon, and the island seems to be floating there between the water and the sky, like Mont-Saint-Michel off the coast of Normandy. There are no medieval spires rising from this island, but it contains the remnants of a far older culture, antedating the Gothic cathedrals, the monuments of the Roman Empire, the temples of ancient Greece.

Four thousand years ago, when Europe was populated mainly by primitive tribes and the Egyptians were building their pyramids in the Valley of the Nile, there was a colony of Indians on this island in San Francisco Bay, catching shellfish, fashioning tools, building crude structures probably comparable to those in Europe at the time. Doubtless their children ran along these beaches, shouting at their games; men speared fish from the rocks along the coves; women ground seeds into meal while they kept an eye on the youngsters. Doubtless, too, they watched the fogs moving in through the Golden Gate toward the Berkeley Hills and took shelter on the lee side of the island when winds riffled the bay into whitecaps.

You can see remains of the colony in the big shell mound on the lee side at the water's edge, where archeologists have cut away a cross section of a village site in attempts to reconstruct the life patterns of the inhabitants. In the Bay Area a century ago there were about four hundred of these Indian village sites—mounds containing shells, tools, bones, weapons, and other implements left by many generations. This is one of the few shell mounds that remain. Many have been leveled and paved over for subdivisions and parking lots.

Others have been bulldozed and their contents sold commercially to house owners who want rich soil on which to plant lawns.

At many of the remaining sites around the bay archeologists have been engaged in a frantic race with the bulldozers to try to sift through the mounds before they were destroyed, but in a few days they could not hope to make the kind of analysis that should be carried on with utmost care and precision over a period of months or years. In other cases they have arrived after the bulldozers had done their work. The destruction of these mounds, whether by subdividers, souvenir hunters, lawn-fill merchants, or government construction agencies, is the destruction of knowledge—in the same category as burning books.

FOUR HORIZONS

From the evidence of the Bay Area mounds that have been analyzed, archeologists probing the remains, painstakingly cataloguing each object with a record of its exact location and immediate context, have begun to piece together a complex picture of life in the Bay Area over a period of several thousand years. They have isolated the remains of three distinct cultures, with some signs of a fourth. The earliest men in the Bay Area, the Paleo-Indians, left few surviving traces here, but it is known from evidence elsewhere in California, such as Santa Rosa Island, that their campsites extend back as far as twenty-five thousand years, with a possibility that they may go back forty thousand years—well into the last Ice Age, when climate, geography, and wildlife were far different.

The Paleo-Indians hunted animals that have long since disappeared—bison, camels, sloths, mammoths. They may have been the earliest men on this continent, having crossed the Bering Sea when lower sea level exposed a land bridge from Asia. Oddly, they were more like Caucasians than the Mongol peoples who came later. Doubtless many of their campsites were near the ocean for fishing reasons and were inundated by rising sea level as the ice sheets melted and the oceans overflowed. The only Bay Area sign of a Paleo-Indian is a skull discovered in 1922 embedded in the steep banks of San Francisquito Creek at Stanford, known as "Stanford man." It may go back some ten thousand years.

The first culture of which more substantial signs have been found here is "Early Horizon" culture occupying the period from about 4000–1000 B.C. A "Middle Horizon" culture extended up to about A.D. 700 and "Late Horizon," continued to the coming of Europeans around 1800. The evidence from the mounds shows distinct cultural and technological improvements from one horizon to the next: from crude stone implements to polished and well-fashioned tools and ornaments; from spears to the bow and arrow; from a diet very high in shellfish to greater use of nuts, seeds, berries, and, particularly in the Late Horizon, acorn meal.

Early Horizon Indians had few tooth cavities, but their teeth were worn down by a coarse diet. Late Horizon people had a more refined diet that resulted in less tooth wear but extensive cavities. In the Middle Horizon are found some small figurines representing humans or gods that seem superior in workmanship and conception to any work of local tribes and are oddly similar to figurines found in cultures of the Pueblo Indians of the Southwest. Conceivably there was some trade between people over these vast distances. Many of the shoreline mounds were partly under water, indicating a considerable land subsidence or rise in sea level (owing to glacial melt) that took place since the sites were first inhabited.

BAY MUSSELS AND RUSSIAN BEADS

In the Brooks Island mound there are remains of four separate cultures. The earliest are those of Middle Horizon people who lived there from about 2000 B.C. to about the time of Christ. For many years excavation at the mound has been supervised by archeologist George Coles of Contra Costa College, who points out that the Middle Horizon remains occupy about the lower ten feet of the cross section that has been exposed.

"We judge from the shells," he says, "that their principal food was bay mussels, supplemented by other fish, game, and acorns. In the earlier part of the period the shells are mostly from mature mussels, but later they are mainly small, immature mussels which must have been less desirable as food. This could mean that the Indian population was growing and they were pushing on the food supply. Or it might mean that the bay was silting up and mature mussels were harder to find."

The second culture, Coles explains, was for some reason a short one, lasting only one hundred years or so, and is represented by new types of beadwork, changes in techniques of working obsidian, and different ways of burying the dead. Still different techniques are visible in the tools and implements of the third culture, which occupies about four feet of the mound's depth and extended from about A.D. 100 to 1000.

"Then there is a big gap in the record," Coles says. "Evidently there was nobody living here at all for about eight hundred years. We have no idea why they left or what happened. But evidence from the top six inches of the mound seems to indicate that the island was reoccupied by at least 1800. We have found beads of the kind we know were distributed by the Russians in trade, when they had their base up at Fort Ross early in the nineteenth century. The Russians may have traded directly with these Indians here on the bay, or the beads may have reached here after being traded among the tribes."

The Brooks Island mounds, like others around the bay, have been jeopardized over the years by vandals, souvenir hunters, and potential developers. There have been various plans for leveling the island and joining it by fill to the nearby mainland at Richmond for industrial or residential development. In the mid-1960's, stimulated by Coles and other archeologists and conservationists, William Penn Mott, then general manager of the East Bay Regional Park District (and later state park chief), launched a campaign to save the forty-five-acre island. The effort was successful, and in 1968 Brooks Island became part of the district, although it was not opened to the public at that time for lack of funds. It continued for some years as a private hunting preserve, leased to a group of sportsmen, including Trader Vic Bergeron and Bing Crosby, who hunted pheasants that had been released there.

THE WARS OF THE MICE

Biologists as well as archeologists have a special interest in the island as a natural museum, preserving the native grassland habitat which elsewhere in the Bay Area has been wiped out by the spread of introduced species such as wild oats and eucalyptus. There are some fifty species of native grasses, creating a mosaic of colors and patterns on the slopes. In sheltered places a few willows and buckeyes grow. Baccharis (coyote brush) blossoms in the fall throughout the island, and in the spring the slopes are ablaze with wild flowers.

Zoologist William Z. Lidicker, Jr., of the University of California, has found two species of salamanders on the island, both showing characteristics different in some respects from mainland salamanders —an indication that the island had been cut off from the mainland long enough for new characteristics to evolve.

Lidicker also tells the story of the Brooks Island mouse wars: There are no native mammals on the island, but at one time there was a large population of house mice, which had originated on a ranch that stood there around the turn of the century. In 1958 a University of California graduate student in biology experimentally planted three pairs of field mice on Bird Island, a small satellite of Brooks Island one hundred yards off the west shore. Within a few months the field mouse population of Bird Island had reached such a point that some of the hardier individuals, evidently spotting greener pastures on the larger island, migrated across the channel on the exposed mud at low tide. That was 1066 in the history of Brooks Island. The resident house mice were no match for the larger, more aggressive field mice. The invaders took over the island, and the house mice were driven to retreat on the long breakwater stretching to the west, where a few survivors remain. The field mouse population now reaches a seasonal peak of about thirty thousand, offering succulent viands to owls and hawks.

Shore birds and upland birds are both abundant. Curiously, the island is the only place in the Bay Area used as a breeding ground by mallards, and by Canada geese, which normally breed only much farther north.

Fortunately East Bay Regional Park officials plan only minimum development for the island, in order to retain its character as an outdoor museum. For generations to come, visitors will be able to roam Brooks Island, explore its coves and beaches, gaze at the sweeping panoramas of San Francisco and the far shores, watch the distant freighters move up the Richmond Channel, listen to the calls of the curlews, see the flashing white wings of flocks of avocets, and hear in imagination the voices of the ancient peoples who worked and played on these shores four millenniums ago.

5

The Crusade of Joseph Strauss

AT THE LOOKOUT POINT near the San Francisco end of the Golden
Gate Bridge stands a bronze statue of Chief Engineer Joseph B.
Strauss, the man who did not build the bridge. The full story of the
construction of this span has never been told and probably never
will be. Too many of the participants have died, taking their stories
with them.

This much can be said: The legend of Strauss, "the little giant
who conquered the Golden Gate," is compounded in about equal
parts of fact and myth. It does not detract from his very great
achievement to set the record straight as to what he did and did not
do.

The legend of his early life is well known. How much of it originated in his own mind or that of publicists may never be entirely
clear. It has an undeniable appeal—the small man who went out for
college football, was mauled by the behemoths on the team and while
convalescing in the hospital developed an obsession with size: He
would become an engineer and build the biggest bridge in the world.

For whatever reason, he did seem to operate under a compulsion
to do things that had never been done, to build bigger and newer
and better than anyone had ever built before. He frequently succeeded in doing so; owing in part to a fortuitous combination of
talents. As a boy in Cincinnati, he had pleased his artistic parents—
his father was a painter, his mother a musician—by showing an
early talent for writing romantic poetry. But he had also surprised
them with a bent for mathematics and mechanics. The two sides of
his character, the imaginative and the practical, became the source

of his genius. When the engineer in him warned that something could not be done, the poet challenged him to do it anyhow. And usually the engineer found a way. In the latter part of his career, however, the poet outreached the engineer, and therein lies the untold story of the Golden Gate Bridge.

His first practical inventions as a bridge builder were not quite on a scale with his undergraduate thesis—a bridge joining North America and Asia across the Bering Strait—but they were nevertheless revolutionary. While working for an engineering firm he designed a new type bascule, or lift, bridge which was upended on a fulcrum by use of a concrete counterweight. When his boss laughed it off as impractical, he stalked out the door, found an office, and went into business for himself. He submitted his bascule design to a railroad that was planning a new bridge, but the railroad officials were almost as skeptical as his former boss had been.

The youngster was so persuasive, however, that they tossed the ball right back to him. If he really believed in the contraption, he could go ahead on it—provided he would build the bridge himself and prove it would work. He accepted the challenge, begged and borrowed the funds, took on the job, and built the bridge. To the surprise of everybody but the builder, the new bascule worked and saved the railroad thousands of dollars in construction costs. It not only worked; it ultimately helped revolutionize the building of movable bridges. Eventually the Strauss bascule became a recognized design around the world.

THE PURSUIT OF THE SUPERLATIVE

Strauss continued to develop new ideas in movable bridges, but despite a growing reputation he still had to fight an uphill battle for every innovation.

"The value of an idea," he told an interviewer, "depends not only on the sweat you put into thinking it up, but also on the sweat you put into getting people to recognize and accept it."

Several of his innovative bridges spanned the Chicago River, including one which when upended was as high as an eighteen-story building. But Chicago was merely a training ground. Strauss traveled around the world to find spectacular new bridge sites and to convince foreign governments that he was the man for the job. He built a major bridge at Copenhagen Harbor and spanned the Neva in St. Petersburg at the entrance to the Winter Palace of the czars; the latter made history a few years later when revolutionary mobs stormed across it to take the palace. Other

Strauss bridges went up around the world—in Japan and China, Egypt and South America. Among his biggest jobs in the United States were the center span of the Arlington Memorial Bridge in Washington, D.C., and a big cantilever across the Columbia at Longview, Oregon, at the time the longest span of its kind in the country.

Between bridges, Strauss's fertile imagination worked overtime on a variety of inventions. Often his imagination outran his know-how, and he produced several failures—a device to put springs on automobile wheels in place of tires, and when that didn't work, a new type of tire, which didn't work either; an "air tram," an overhead railroad that anticipated the monorail but never got beyond the Sunday-supplement stage; and a "room cooler" that didn't cool the room but heated it instead. Every failure drove him on to new experiments, some of which were successful: a bascule door for aircraft hangars; a portable searchlight unit and a concrete freight car, both used during World War I; and an "Aeroscope" constructed for the San Francisco Exposition of 1915, a big enclosed observation platform that hoisted a roomful of tourists into the air on the end of a 150-foot boom. Always there was the restless drive, the nervous compulsion to outdo everything that he or anyone else had done. Often he could scarcely get one project under way before turning the details over to his staff and he was off to develop something bigger, better, newer. He had yet to find a job big enough for his runaway imagination. But in the back of his mind there was one immense possibility. It was probably planted there during his work for the 1915 exposition, although the idea evidently did not mature until 1917, when he stood on the hill at the narrows of the Gate above old Fort Point.

THE BRIDGE'S ENEMIES

For a century and a half, men had talked of bridging this strait. Back in 1872 Charles Crocker, one of the builders of the transcontinental railroad, had even made some vague plans for a suspension bridge to carry his railroad north from San Francisco. But bridge builders had looked at the Gate and had shaken their heads. Ordinarily a bridge across a mile of water would be a routine job. The Golden Gate was something else again. It was the only place where the Pacific, in its perennial assault on the continent, had breached the coastal mountain wall. Twice a day the waters of the ocean poured massively through this narrow gap on the flood tide. Twice a day the waters of fifty-mile-long

San Francisco Bay charged out the Gate on the ebb. On a maximum ebb tide, the volume of water flowing out the Gate was fourteen times the average flow of the Mississippi River.

To sink foundations for a bridge in such currents was a prospect to give pause to the most daring engineer. To do so in the formidable depths of the Golden Gate seemed a compounding of impossibilities. The currents had carved out a channel fifty fathoms deep, and at one point the bottom lay sixty-four fathoms below the surface—enough depth to swallow a thirty-story building. The Golden Gate was not only a funnel for the tides but for wind and weather as well—for blinding fogs and for howling gales that churned the water into a white roiling fury.

Generations of engineers had failed to find a way to bridge this wild stretch of water. But it was Strauss the poet and visionary who stood on the south shore of the Golden Gate that day in 1917, gazing at the nearby cliffs, the far shore, the whitecapped water below. Here was possibly the most dramatic meeting place of land and sea on earth, the ultimate challenge to the bridge builder. Here at last was a project to match Strauss's unbounded ambition.

San Francisco officials were surprised when he presented the city with a design for a Golden Gate bridge at an estimated cost of $27,000,000. Newspapers ran pictures of the design and enthusiastic articles. But as soon as the idea began to take hold, the enemies of any attempt to bridge the Gate drew up their battalions for combat. There was opposition from Army and Navy officials who feared that in case of war the bridge might be destroyed by enemy action and block the entrance to the bay. There was opposition from the owners of the ferryboats, which would be put out of operation by the bridge. There was opposition from shipowners who were afraid that the bridge would interfere with shipping, from north-coast lumber interests who didn't want swarms of motorists in their domain, from bankers who said the bridge could never be financed, from big taxpayers afraid they would be forced to pay for the bridge's failure, from engineers who said it could never be built anyhow.

Against this formidable array of opponents the diminutive Strauss went into action like David after a regiment of Goliaths, armed with messianic zeal and all the experience born of decades of convincing skeptics and overcoming enemies. He had a flair for personal publicity, and for months and years, in speeches to businessmen's clubs, in public appearances, in statements to the press,

1. Arthur Brown's concept of classical elegance is visible in this interior view of the City Hall, taken in 1915, just before completion.

2. In the recent aerial view below Brown's War Memorial Opera House and Veterans' Building are partially visible to the rear. The entire ensemble seems to affirm a civilized tradition as against the threat of the encircling freeway. (San Francisco *Chronicle*)

3. "Sunny Jim" Rolph in a familiar posture. On other occasions he posed waving a baton as band leader and on a locomotive in the overalls of a railroad engineer. (Wide World)

4. Arthur Brown, Jr., in the uniform a Membre de l'Institut de France, c of the few Americans to receive t honor. (San Francisco *Chronicle*)

5. Posed though it is, this picture captures something of the intense driving energy of Adolph Sutro. (Nevada State Historical Society)

6. Arthur Putnam sketching in pocket notebook. (Mechanics' Institu

7. Telegraph Hill rises above the lights of Fishermen's Wharf against a long swinging arc of the Bay Bridge. (San Francisco Convention and Visitors Bureau)

8. The northeastern corner of the city: Telegraph Hill near the center, the Golden Gate and Mount Tamalpais beyond. Since both of these pictures were taken, high-rise buildings have risen to mar the view. (Aero Photographers)

9. Willis Polk at his desk. (From *Daniel Burnham*, by Charles Moore, Houghton Mifflin, 1921)

10. Daniel Burnham at the Twin Pea cottage designed for him by Polk. (Fro *Daniel Burnham*, by Charles Moo Houghton Mifflin, 1921)

11. The view seen by Polk and Burnham from the Twin Peaks cottage seven decades later. (San Francisco *Chronicle*)

12. The mirrorlike curtain wall (if not the lacy ironwork) of Willis Polk's Hallidie Building was the forerunner of all glass-and-steel skyscrapers. (San Francisco *Chronicle*)

13. Fort Point, once the guardian of the Golden Gate, now is overshadowed by the steel arch of the bridge (U.S. Army, Courtesy Fort Point Museum Association, Presidio of San Francisco)

14. Bernard Maybeck
(Moulin Studios)

15. Maybeck's Pal
ace of Fine Arts
(San Francisco
Chronicle)

16. Clifford Paine, the man behind the man behind the Golden Gate Bridge. (San Francisco *Chronicle*)

17. Joseph Strauss displays an early version of the bridge. (San Francisco *Chronicle*)

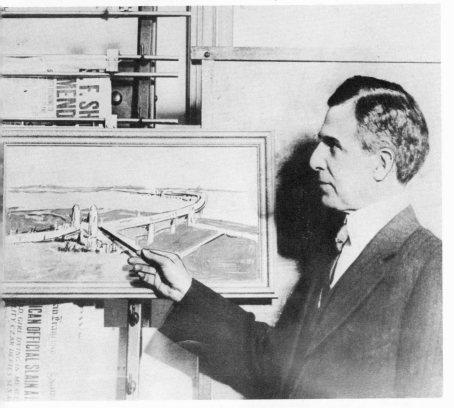

18, 19, 20. The Gate in various weathers: On a summer afternoon a low mass of fog moves slowly in over the bay like a glacier; on a winter night the city glitters through the harp-string cables of the bridge. (18. Redwood Empire Association. 19 and 20. San Francisco Convention and Visitors Bureau)

21, 22. History and prehistory: On Treasure Island in 1939–40, Ralph Stackpole's colossal figure *Pacifica* was the theme statue of the Golden Gate International Exposition. Except for some of the sculpture in the foreground, the fair has vanished as completely as the Indians of Brooks Island, whose four-thousand-year-old village site is being sifted by archeologists. (21. From *Treasure Island*, by Jack James and Earle Weller, Pisani Printing Company, 1942; 22. San Francisco *Chronicle*)

23. The Ferry tower, the Bay Bridge, and part of the East Bay. Visible over the top of the Berkeley Hills is the snowy summit of Mount Diablo, thirty miles away. (San Francisco *Chronicle*)

24. President Robert Gordon Sproul a
commencement speaker in Faculty Gla
1948. (University of California, Berkel

25. The John Muir house at Martin
Muir planted most of these trees a
from the cupola surveyed operations
the farm. (National Park Service)

26. Mount Tamalpais: the East Peak from the ridge above Mill Valley. (Redwood Empire Association)

27. John Muir and William Kent at the Muir Woods Inn, about 1910. (Photo courtesy Roger Kent)

28. Audubon Canyon Ranch. Egrets are visible feeding in Bolinas Lagoon and nesting in the redwoods up the canyon beyond the farmhouse. (Photo by Clerin W. Zumwalt)

29. Two young egrets in a nest high in a redwood put on a dance to obtain food from the parent. (Photo by Clerin W. Zumwalt)

30. The channel at the entrance to Bolinas Lagoon, where the battle of the oil spill took place. Stinson Beach and Bolinas Ridge are in the distance. Audubon Canyon Ranch is on the far shore to the left of the picture. (San Francisco *Chronicle*)

31. Muir Woods. (Redwood Empire Association)

he hammered home his theme: a bridge across the Gate would link San Francisco with the north, place the city in the main stream of Pacific Coast travel, and open a new era for the Bay Area and the northern Redwood Empire.

THE SHOWDOWN

San Francisco, which traditionally loves dreamers, was swept up in Strauss's vision. Around him rallied scores of community leaders who believed he could do what he promised. In 1923 they formed the "Bridging the Golden Gate Association" and pushed through the State Legislature a bill enabling San Francisco and five north-coast counties to form the Golden Gate Bridge and Highway District. But the opposition included some of the most potent political interests in California. For six years the pro-bridge forces were held to a standstill by a series of taxpayer's suits to block the project. The climax of the long campaign came in 1930, when the issue went to the voters.

In the bond election the bridge's enemies fought the bridge by radio and newspaper. They claimed that even if the bridge could be built it would cost well over $100,000,000, as compared with Strauss's estimated $27,000,000, and that the difference would have to be made up by property-owning taxpayers. House-to-house canvassers told voters: "A vote for the bridge is a vote to confiscate your property." And they claimed that an earthquake along the infamous San Andreas Fault, on the ocean bottom a few miles west of the Golden Gate, would bring the bridge down in a mass of wreckage. Thirteen prominent engineers, including the City Engineer of San Francisco, signed statements opposing the project, and a San Francisco banker called it an "economic crime."

Strauss was in the kind of a battle he loved. He countered the earthquake talk by pointing out that a quake strong enough to knock down the bridge would level most of San Francisco first. He heaped scorn on those who said the bridge couldn't be built. And he appealed to local pride. San Francisco would have in the Golden Gate Bridge not only the greatest span on earth but one of the mightiest structures of any kind ever built—"the eighth wonder of the world." Strauss's crusading zeal was indomitable and contagious. When the ballots were counted, the voters by a big majority had approved the bonds.

That night, while the bridge supporters painted the town, Strauss was already busy planning the next step. There was still one more major obstacle to hurdle. The bonds had been approved, but they still had to be sold. Bond houses had politely declined to buy; the bridge was too speculative. To raise the money at the bottom of the Depression was a job that seemed beyond possibility.

Strauss went to see another man who had a reputation for specializing in the impossible. San Francisco's A. P. Giannini had defied all the financial powers of Wall Street and all the accepted canons of banking to build the West's largest financial institution, the Bank of America. In the granite-jawed banker, Strauss found the imagination and daring he was looking for. "California needs that bridge," Giannini said. "We'll take the bonds."

Still the workmen couldn't go to work. Another two years were consumed by last-ditch legal maneuvers from die-hard enemies and by further financial problems, which Giannini ultimately solved. Finally, early in 1933, Strauss stood triumphantly on the south shore of the Golden Gate for the ground-breaking ceremony near the spot where he had first visualized the bridge sixteen years before. The day was declared an official holiday; schools were closed; the United States fleet steamed by; and the city staged an all-out pageant to mark the beginning of the world's biggest suspension span.

6

The Building of the Bridge:
Myth and Fact

IN HIS DECADE-LONG CAMPAIGN for a bridge across the Gate, Joseph Strauss defeated the opposition in a series of hard-fought battles, but when the long crusade was ended he faced a battery of even more formidable opponents—the elements. At this point the life of Strauss took a strange turn. For he confronted not only the elements but himself. And that fatal flaw of his genius—the conflict between the poet and the engineer—again came to the surface.

During the long years of struggle for the right to build the bridge, the poet had been dominant. The battle had been led by Strauss the visionary, the blazing-eyed crusader who had persuaded people by the sheer force of personal conviction that he could build the bridge. But now that period was at an end. No oratory, no persuasiveness, no amount of personal zealotry could tame the raging currents of the Golden Gate or raise a quarter billion pounds of steel into the air. No poetic vision could fasten the bridge's foundation securely to the tide-swept rock on the bottom of the strait.

Now that it was time to translate his dream into steel and concrete that would withstand the stresses of wind, weather, traffic, and tides for perhaps a thousand years, Strauss paused. Exactly what went on inside him at that crucial point will never be known. He brought his junior partner out from Chicago, placed him in charge of construction, and left the city.

Associates who assumed that he had gone away for a few days' rest were surprised when several weeks passed and Strauss still did not reappear. It was reported that he had come close to a nervous breakdown as a result of the years of strain during the fight for the bridge, had taken a ship to the East Coast and was recuperating someplace in the Adirondacks.

Strauss returned after work was three months under way, reportedly fully rested. What was not reported was the fact that his absence from San Francisco had made little difference as far as the bridge was concerned. Almost nobody—even the bridge's directors and his most avid supporters—knew Strauss very well. His solemn dignity and fierce zealotry held people at a distance. The truth was that while fighting the long political and legal battles for the bridge he had been out of touch with practical, hard-hat engineering. Increasingly he had left engineering matters to his staff in Chicago, headed by his junior partner.

THE DISSENT OF CLIFFORD PAINE

Young Clifford Paine, brilliant, hardheaded, down to earth, shy of the limelight, had talents which neatly complemented those of his boss. Strauss's single-minded dedication and his easily wounded ego made him a hard man to work for. Most associates were afraid to disagree with him. Paine, as outspoken as Strauss, had no such inhibitions. There was an unwritten understanding that he would always speak his mind to Strauss and pull no punches. And over the years the older man had come to depend more and more heavily on his assistant.

When the time came to go to work on the Golden Gate Bridge, it was entirely logical that Paine should come out from Chicago and take charge, under Strauss's nominal direction. Paine was well prepared for the job. Years before, Strauss had asked him to check over the plans for the bridge. Characteristically, Paine began by telling him where he was wrong.

Strauss's preliminary design for the bridge had envisioned two cantilever arms connected by a suspension span, an ungainly type of structure, totally unprecedented. Paine disapproved of the oddball design. Strauss held out for a time but finally yielded to Paine's common-sense reasoning—a plain suspension span would do the job best. Strauss's flamboyant plans for architectural gingerbread on the bridge—including entrances resembling Napoleon's Arch of Triumph—were also opposed by his assistant, who felt that the structure should be kept as simple and functional as possible.

The most risky part of the entire project—and the feature of Strauss's plan which had drawn the concentrated fire of his enemies —was the construction of the foundation pier for the south tower. The north tower—on the Marin side—could be built on the rocks at the water's edge; but its twin to the south would have to be planted underwater in the turbulent currents of the Gate. This, Strauss said later, possibly with pardonable exaggeration, "was undoubtedly the most difficult engineering feat men have ever attempted."

From the geodetic charts, Strauss knew there was an underwater ledge of rock extending out from Fort Point on the south shore for about a quarter-mile before the bottom dropped off into the three-hundred-foot depths of mid-Gate. It was on the end of this ledge at a depth of sixty-five feet that he had long ago planned to build the south tower. But so swift are the currents at that point that a diver trying to work there would be buffeted like a balloon in a high wind—except for short periods at the turn of the tide. So Strauss had planned to enclose the site with a permanent concrete breakwater or fender, providing quiet water in which the construction men could work. After the pier was finished, the fender would protect it from tides and passing ships.

THE WRECKING OF THE TRESTLE

Strauss's original plan had been to build in drydock a prefabricated steel framework for the fender. The frame would be contoured to fit the sloping rock surface of the ledge, floated to the site, and lowered to the bottom by filling it with concrete, in effect forming a cofferdam around the construction area. But now when the time came to begin the job, Paine checked over Strauss's plan and scowled. The big framework would be unwieldy to float into place; fitting its contours to the rough bottom would be an uncertain thing at best; the clumsy structure might be hung up on boulders or caught in the powerful currents before it reached the floor of the Gate.

Paine got out his pencil and slide rule and went to work. His solution was to build the frame in twenty-two small sections, sink one section at a time and pour the concrete in before lowering the next one, building stability as the work went on. Paine had solved "the most difficult engineering feat men have ever attempted"—on paper. But would his plan work at the bottom of the Golden Gate?

The effort to find out soon turned into a battle of men against the sea. In the initial stages it was a frustrating conflict against what seemed overwhelming odds. To get to the pier site, nearly a quarter-mile offshore, contractors under Paine's direction built a working trestle out from Fort Point on the San Francisco shore. Shortly after it was finished, an inbound freighter loomed out of a thick fog, plowed through the middle of it, sank one hundred feet of it, and uprooted most of the rest. As soon as the trestle was rebuilt, an attack came from another quarter—the ocean itself. One day a tall guide tower at the end of the trestle was lowering into the water some of Paine's steel forms for the fender when giant swells came rolling in from the ocean and set the trestle swaying. As workmen looked on helplessly, the guide tower began to rock ominously under the impact of each swell. Gradually it was loosened until a single wave toppled it with a crash and it went to the bottom, together with three of the steel forms.

Laboriously the tower and the forms were fished up out of the depths and put back to work. But crewmen no sooner resumed work than an even greater storm assaulted the coast. Mountainous swells humped in from the open sea, sent ocean liners pitching, pounded the headlands, rolled through the Gate, and engulfed the trestle. When they subsided, more than half of the structure had gone to the bottom.

Paine was in the East conferring with manufacturers on materials. Strauss calmed the bridge's alarmed directors. "We can still build the bridge and finish it on time," he assured them. At that point no one, including Strauss, knew exactly how. Paine returned from the East and planned with the contractors a new king-sized trestle. The deck was twenty-five feet above the water, and the piles were guyed with steel cables anchored to the bottom. It took three months to build, but in the end it was able to withstand the worst the ocean could do.

THE ASSAULT OF THE OCEAN

Even though the ocean was temporarily defeated, the bridge's enemies were not. Dr. Bailey Willis, a bearded professor of geology at Stanford, broke into headlines with a blast against Strauss for planning to build the south pier on what he called weak serpentine "puddingstone," subject to landslides and "unstable to a degree likely to endanger the structure." Strauss denied the charges, but the report had its effect. The bridge's opponents gloated; and in Washington officials read Willis' charges and decided against giving the project financial help.

Willis' attack was in progress when the ocean mounted still another offensive. Paine's steel frames for the fender had been gradually lowered to the bottom and concreted, in spite of rough seas and high winds, until all but the last few units were in place, resulting in a horseshoe-shaped concrete wall about thirty feet thick. Then a giant caisson, which had been prefabricated in a Bay Area shipyard, was floated into the enclosure through the open end. The plan was to finish off the fender, enclosing the caisson in quiet water so it could be sunk gradually to the bottom, forming the base for the pier. The ocean remained quiescent until the caisson was moored inside. Then, that night, before the fender could be closed off, the waves rose again, ripped the caisson loose from its moorings and began to toss it violently against the surrounding concrete.

Strauss was rousted out of bed for a midnight decision. Paine was again in the East, unavailable for consultation, and the chief engineer faced the crisis alone. Just that afternoon geologist Willis had loosed another barrage, warning that the caisson should not be sunk to the "puddingstone" bottom. Strauss knew that to discard the caisson now would give the public the impression that he was unsure of himself and had been dissuaded by Willis. But the ocean was in command. Strauss made the decision he had to make and ordered the caisson towed out. Since it could not be towed in again without risking a repetition of the same situation, it was subsequently sunk in deep water.

The abandonment of the caisson was all the evidence some people needed. Again the bridge's enemies scored heavily. And again the bridge builders had to change strategy to meet the challenge of the elements. If a prefabricated foundation caisson could not be floated into the enclosure, the foundation would have to be built on the spot, from scratch. So the final units of the fender were put into place and concreted, closing it off. Inside, concrete men laid down an underwater floor sixty-five feet thick. The water was pumped out, and there, inside the fender, in a dry area the size of a football field, construction men went to work. Paine's final revision in the design of the pier had been to unite pier and fender into one solid unit below the waterline, thus spreading out the load of the bridge over more than double the original rock area occupied by the pier alone.

The fender had hardly been completed when a ship loomed out of a fog heading directly toward it, sending workers sprinting for the trestle. The vessel veered in time and missed the concrete wall by a few feet. The incident emphasized the wisdom of building the fender as a permanent protection. Probably a glancing blow would have been warded off by the concrete. Since the fender was shaped like a narrow oval with pointed ends toward oncoming ships, the chances for a head-on impact were almost zero.

THE BIG NET

With the completion of the south pier, it looked as if the principal fight against the elements had been won. But the ocean was yet to take its greatest toll. On the far shore, the easier north pier had long been completed, and its tower was rising from the water's edge 750 feet into the air. All the while, Paine was supervising the engineering staff and the contractors, flying to Eastern cities to oversee the manufacture of parts, rejecting materials that did not conform to his near-perfectionist standards, and trying to keep the complex construction schedules in gear.

Strauss's health, frail ever since his near-breakdown at the beginning of construction, declined steadily. As the months and years went by, his restless mind turned to grander schemes, inventions, and ideas. He envisioned new bridges. He composed poems, one characteristically, about the giant redwoods:

> The greatest of earth's living forms,
> Tall conquerors that laugh at storms;
> Their challenge still unanswered rings
> Through fifty centuries of kings . . .

He wrote lyrics to songs and found composers to set them to music; one, a patriotic song called "Flags Aloft," was performed at a band concert in Golden Gate Park. He tried unsuccessfully to organize youth groups and even had uniforms designed for one such organization he planned to call "The American Sentinels." At meetings of the bridge's directors, when he was required to discuss problems of construction, he showed flashes of the old brilliance. But usually the loyal Paine was sitting quietly behind him for any necessary prompting. And toward the end, even the iron-willed composure Strauss had always maintained while in the spotlight showed signs of cracking. On one occasion, when someone questioned an engineering decision, Strauss jumped up in hot anger. "I resent and object to that!" he shouted. "I'm not on trial here!" And he walked out.

Strauss was further unnerved by the bridge's one major accident. Both he and Paine had known from firsthand experience the truth of the bridgebuilders' axiom: "The bridge demands a life." Traditionally, accidents have been responsible for one death per million dollars of bridge. Considering the extremely hazardous conditions under which the Golden Gate Bridge was built, the death rate might easily have been several times normal. But Paine believed he could beat the odds. With Strauss's approval he devised a new safety scheme—a tremendous net beneath the bridge from shore to shore.

Contractors and other engineers were incredulous. Such a thing had never been done before. A net to catch performers in a circus was one thing; a net more than a mile long was fantastic. It would cost $130,000. But the directors gave their approval, and the net was built, establishing a practice since followed on all big bridge jobs. Critics were silenced when over a period of months nineteen men tumbled from the structure and bounced harmlessly in the rope mesh. They formed the exclusive Halfway-to-Hell Club.

THE FALL OF THE SCAFFOLD

In the first four years of construction not a single life was lost— an unprecedented safety record. Then early in 1937 a derrick toppled in a high wind and killed one man. A few days later, within three months of the bridge's scheduled completion, eleven workers were standing on a sixty-foot wooden scaffold beneath the deck, pulling boards away from the bottom of the completed concrete roadway. Two more men were in the net directly below, picking up odd pieces of wood that had fallen in the mesh. A day or so before, an inspector had checked over the scaffold and informed the contractor's superintendent that the aluminum brackets holding the platforms needed extra strengthening for safety. The superintendent had complied by installing some supporting bolts. But the inspector was still worried and wanted to check it again. At nine-fifteen on the morning of February 17 he met with the representatives of the engineering staff and the contractor at the south end of the bridge. They all decided to look over the scaffold and were walking out toward the center of the span when they felt the bridge shake and heard from ahead a sudden series of loud reports as if someone were firing guns.

Workmen on top of the deck saw the scaffold tip down as one of the brackets broke, hang tilting from the remaining brackets for an instant, then plunge down into the net with its human cargo. The net had not been designed to hold the several thousand pounds of men and wood and steel that came hurtling down from above. It stretched, sagged under the load, then began to rip. The sound of the hemp mesh snapping under the tension was like a battery of machine-guns going off all at once. Several hundred yards of net tore loose and billowed out in the wind as it was carried down by the weight of the scaffold.

The crewmen on the deck heard the yells of their falling comrades. They watched in horror as the victims tried to reach for pieces of net or timber. The fall, prolonged by the gradual ripping of the net, was agonizingly slow. Men, timbers, and parts of the net hit the water simultaneously. The men disappeared beneath the brown racing ebb tide, then some bobbed again to the surface, still grasping frantically for anything within reach in the tangle of wreckage. Slowly the wind billowed the still-falling portion of the net and folded it back over the struggling men like a deadly shroud, carrying them down as it sank.

Ten men died. Two who had succeeded in catching the net and riding it down into the water were picked up by a fishing boat, alive but badly injured. And one was discovered still dangling desperately from a girder beneath the deck. Workmen hauled him up to safety.

The ocean had at last claimed its price for the taming of the Gate.

THE RADICAL ARCHITECT

Bay Area residents had watched with awe and pride as the bridge grew to its full size. The most spectacular part of the job was the spinning of the giant cables from which the deck was suspended. On either side of the channel two big shuttles moved back and forth from anchorage to mid-span, sometimes swaying in the seventy-mile winds howling through the Gate; each carried a total of 27,252 strands of pencil-thick wire—enough to circle the earth three times—binding them into a cable a yard in diameter and a mile and a half long. The main span of the suspended deck was 4200 feet long (longest in the world until the completion of the 4260-foot span of New York's Verrazano-Narrows Bridge in 1964). The tops of the stepped-back steel towers were a dizzy 750 feet above the water, nearly twice as high as San Francisco's tallest buildings. The steel-cell maze of the towers' interiors was so complicated that some workmen got lost overnight in one of them, and a twenty-six-page manual was published for inspectors as a guide to the vertical labyrinths.

The appearance and design of the bridge owed much not only to Strauss and Paine but to a third member of the team, an extraordinary young architect named Irving F. Morrow. Strauss may have chosen him—as he had chosen Paine—for certain characteristics compatible with Strauss's own qualities. Morrow, like Strauss, was a visionary and a poet. But he was like Paine in his indifference to publicity and his willingness to let Strauss occupy the spotlight alone.

The choice of Morrow had taken the architectural community by surprise. It had been assumed that the job would go to the city's leading architect—Arthur Brown, Jr. With his fondness for classical ornamentation, Brown would doubtless have designed a very different bridge. Morrow was often regarded as a radical—a modernist long before modern architecture was respectable. He designed what may have been the first modern house in San Francisco, for Mr. and Mrs. Henry Cowell, on a hillside in Forest Hill. But owing to his uncompromising belief that architecture should speak for its own age and not copy traditional styles, he had been able to find very few clients. He did not increase his popularity with other architectects by his caustic criticisms of San Franciso's Renaissance and Gothic skyscrapers of the 1920's. And he had been perhaps the only architect to praise Willis Polk's daring Hallidie Building.

By the time he was called in to work with Paine on the architectural details of the bridge, the basic structure had been dictated by engineering necessities—the height and proportions of the towers, the lengths of the center and side spans, the location of the cable anchorages, the curve of the cables, the height of the deck. For the towers above the deck, Paine had chosen to use "portal" bracing (with four "portals" above the roadway) giving a sense of spaciousness, rather than the more conventional X-type bracing used on the Bay Bridge. On the piers below the deck, he used X-type bracing for added strength.

RED FOR THE BRIDGE

Paine was inclined toward "functionalism," suspicious of any decoration, whether classical or modern. He wanted to leave all the structural parts of the bridge visible. Morrow, however, was able to convince him that the skeleton steelwork of the portals should be covered with steel plates. And Morrow decorated the plates themselves with a series of vertical facets, smaller on each successively higher brace, emphasizing the height of the towers. The facets were Morrow's theme in the bridge decoration, appearing also, much larger, on the concrete piers at the water level. Also to emphasize the height, Morrow convinced Paine that the portals above the deck should similarly diminish in size upward. Morrow's greatest problem was that he was dealing in magnitudes larger than any previous designers had ever had to cope with. With no precedent to guide him, he often had to guess at the visual effect.

Perhaps Morrow's most startling innovation was his decision that the bridge should be painted red. There were many howls of protest. The idea seemed preposterous. Who had ever heard of a red bridge? It would be a colossal eyesore, said the doleful prophets, and ruin the Golden Gate. They wanted to paint it black or gold or aluminum. Morrow held out for red (or, more technically, "international orange"), claiming that it would loom colorfully against the brown or green of the far hills, complement the reddish Franciscan rock of the Marin cliffs, and be the most visible color in the dense fogs that roll through the strait. Paine and Strauss backed him up, and the bridge was painted the dramatic color that has become part of its character.

Morrow's hand was also visible in two other principal features of the bridge, the lights and the railing. His graceful arching electroliers, or lamp standards, each consisted of a structural steel beam curved at the top and split at the end to hold the lights. On the bay's other bridges the view from the deck is annoyingly blocked by an eye-level railing, but Morrow devised a rail with open balusters, permitting users to look through it and see the spectacular panoramas in both directions.

"AT LAST THE MIGHTY TASK IS DONE . . ."

In May 1937, twenty years after Strauss first stood on the hill above Fort Point and dreamed of spanning this strait, the bridge was completed. It was testimony to Strauss's vision—and Paine's engineering skill—that in spite of the obstacles, delays, and rising prices of materials, the final construction cost was slightly under the budget of $27,000,000, Strauss's original estimate.

San Francisco and the Bay Area observed the opening with razzle-dazzle festivities eclipsing anything the city had seen since the days of '49. Strauss himself, though by now weak and palsied, was the hero of the day. Because of the construction difficulties and delays, he netted almost nothing financially from his twenty years work. But he had his final moment of victory over those who had said it couldn't be done. And Strauss the poet observed the occasion by writing his final poem:

> At last the mighty task is done;
> Resplendent in the western sun,
> The bridge looms mountain high;

Its titan piers grip ocean floor,
Its great steel arms link shore with shore,
Its towers pierce the sky.

On its broad decks in rightful pride,
The world in swift parade shall ride,
Throughout all time to be;
Beneath, fleet ships from every port,
Vast landlocked bay, historic fort,
And dwarfing all—the sea.
. . .

High overhead its lights shall gleam;
Far, far below, life's restless stream
Unceasingly shall flow;
For this was spun its lithe fine form,
To fear not war, nor time, nor storm,
For fate had meant it so.

For Joseph Strauss, the bridge was the end of the road. Shortly after signing the final "Engineer's Report," he died of a heart attack at the age of sixty-eight. Paine, probably the only man who ever really knew Strauss, was, unlike his chief, no artist in words, but in his precise and understated engineer's prose, he wrote in later years a final tribute: "My many years of association with Mr. Strauss impressed me with his many admirable attributes, foremost of which were ingenuity, vision, steadfastness, and resilience of spirit. All of these played an important part in his noteworthy achievements and without them the Golden Gate Bridge would not have been built for many years."

At the lookout point just below the bridge's toll plaza, sight-seers stare curiously at the bronze statue of the man who conceived the Golden Gate Bridge and fought the long crusade that it might be built. The figure is that of a very small person with the sensitive features of a poet or an artist. The towering bridge behind him is his triumph. But perhaps there should be a companion memorial to share the triumph, the figure of the hard-hat engineer who quietly and without acclaim finished the job envisioned by the poet.

PART THREE

———◆———

EAST OF THE BAY

1

The Burning of Berkeley

THE VIOLENCE that has afflicted the city of Berkeley in recent years—student-police clashes involving tear gas, shootings, and mass arrests—has shaken the community to bedrock. Yet these contemporary troubles cannot compare in destructiveness and terror with an earlier disaster—the great fire that swept through the city within the memory of many living residents.

Most people assume that such a calamity as the great fire could not occur nowadays. But that is precisely what most residents assumed in the middle of September 1923.

The first omen came late on a Sunday night. By the time Berkeley residents went to bed, they noticed that the summer fog, which had enshrouded the Berkeley Hills every night for a week, was gone, and an odd warmth pervaded the air. At nine o'clock the temperature strangely began to rise, and it soared steadily from sixty-two to seventy, then seventy-five. By midnight the thermometer in the weather station on the University of California campus stood at eighty-two.

From the northeast came a hot wind, rustling in the eucalyptus groves along the crest of the hills. Sleepers stirred restlesssly in the sudden heat, threw off their blankets, got up to secure windows and doors which had begun to bang in the wind. Then they went back to bed, assuming that all was well.

For some four thousand residents of the hillside district just north of the university campus, the assumption was tragically wrong. Each person slept in quiet ignorance of the fact that this was the last night he would lie in his bed, in this house.

All during that Sunday night the wind came in fits and gusts, and by dawn Monday morning—the fateful seventeenth of September—it was blowing steadily at gale force over the crest of the hills and down to the bay. Early risers noted that the skies were clear and dry. They could feel static electricity in the air. Their hair crackled as they drew the comb through it; wool sweaters and cats' fur generated sparks. The unseasonal wind chased flapping remnants of Sunday papers through the still vacant streets of Berkeley and Oakland and San Francisco. Out on the bay passengers on the early ferries watched the wind whip up whitecaps on the water and send flying banners of spray up from the bows of the boats.

FIRE WEATHER

The abnormal weather around the bay was no mere local phenomenon but the result of a major disturbance in the balance of forces over an area of several million square miles. The pattern was one which occurs, with variations, two or three times a year. Westerly winds from the Gulf of Alaska roared onto the continent through the valleys of the Yukon and the Fraser and poured over western Canada. Then, deflected by the rotation of the earth, they veered to the right and circled around in a great clockwise arc to the high plains of inner Washington, Idaho, and Oregon. They poured south across the California border, whistled past the sky-scraping peaks of Lassen and Shasta, and howled down through Sierra passes from the Feather River to Donner to Tioga.

The moving air had long since lost the moisture of the sea where it was born, and had taken on the dryness and warmth of the continent. Descending to the Sacramento Valley, it grew even warmer and drier. It crossed the hot valley and hit the Bay Area like a blast out of a furnace. Residents could feel the desiccating air in the dryness of their lips and the parched sensation of their throats and lungs.

The four thousand people in their homes just north of the campus rose and dressed as usual that Monday morning, blinking sleepily and thinking vague early-morning thoughts. If they had received premonitions of what was going to happen that day, they might have looked carefully at the familiar sights they would never see again—the color of the bedroom walls, the view out the window into the yard, the chairs and tables and treasured volumes in the bookcase. But no one suspected that the highly complex structure of civilized living, which urban people take for granted, was fatally weak at one point and about to give way.

Or perhaps some did suspect, subconsciously. One of the four thousand, a newspaper editor arriving at work through the wind-blown streets of Berkeley, remarked to a colleague: "This would sure be a bad day for a fire." City officials gave out warnings against the lighting of bonfires in the wind. Firemen, aware that this was "fire weather," were on the alert, and early in the morning were answering minor alarms. But for most Berkeley residents it was just another of the hot windy days that sometimes occur at that time of year.

THE WILDCAT BLAZE

At nine-thirty that morning the deputy state fire warden received a report of a blaze in Wildcat Canyon, just over the ridge east of Berkeley, an area that is now Tilden Park. He drove to the canyon, found no sign of fire, and reported it as a false alarm. A few minutes past noon Mrs. Marion Randall Parsons, a prominent club-woman and a resident of the hill area above the campus, saw smoke to the northeast and phoned the fire department. But as always in this kind of a wind, alarms were coming in rapidly, and the firemen could not attend to all of them immediately.

At that moment the fire warden was leading a team of men battling a brush fire which had broken out in Dimond Canyon near Oakland. At twelve-forty he received word from a patrolman of the East Bay Water Company that there was a fire in Wildcat Canyon which had been burning for about forty-five minutes. Hoping that it was not another false alarm, the warden broke away as soon as he could and returned to Wildcat Canyon with twelve men. There, just north of the area where the golf course is now located, he confronted a dismaying scene. A blaze had started in the dry grass near a Pacific Gas and Electric high-tension line and had been fanned by the wind with such force that it had already covered several acres and was spreading up the hill toward the crest above Berkeley. The warden and his men set to work with hoses and shovels, but they were forced to retreat. There had been no rain for six months, and the sun-bleached grass, further dried out by the wind, burned almost as if it had been doused with gasoline.

At one-twelve the crew of a railroad car working in the dock area of Oakland looked up toward the Berkeley Hills, spotted a cloud of smoke rising from behind the ridge above Berkeley, and saw flames begin to appear along the crest north of Grizzly Peak. Unluckily, residents below the blaze were still unaware of it—for geological reasons. Along the western front of the Berkeley Hills runs an ancient rift in the earth—the Hayward fault. In the area just north of the University campus, between Strawberry and Codornices canyons, the fracture took the form of a series of "step faults," steep slopes with relatively level terraces between them. For residents of most of the houses on the terraces, the crest of the hill was blocked from view by the intervening step faults.

FLYING SHINGLES

Propelled by the strong draft that whipped down Codornices Canyon, the flames raced through the grass, and by one-thirty the uninhabited hillside at the head of the canyon was ablaze. Newspaper reporters in downtown Berkeley saw the smoke, which by this time was forming a menacing cloud over the city; they telephoned the fire department, the police, the Pacific Gas and Electric office, and most other conceivable sources, but oddly enough no one had any report of a fire in the area. Mrs. Parsons' call to the fire department had evidently been overlooked in the confusion, and the state warden fighting the blaze in Wildcat Canyon apparently did not suspect that it had burned its way over the hill into Berkeley. It was not until two-five that the fire department received an urgent call about a grass fire from the resident of an isolated house high on the hill.

Fire companies were still busy with a number of small blazes, however, and by the time the trucks had chugged up the narrow, winding streets to the scene, the conflagration had descended to the edge of the hillside residential area and about two-twenty ignited several houses on Keith Street, Shasta Road, and Tamalpais Road. The firemen immediately went to work, too busy to notice that the grass fire was spreading into a large eucalyptus grove along the crest above them. The fire raced through the trees and suddenly burst out into the residential area on La Loma Street several hundred yards away from the fire fighters.

Within a few minutes, before additional fire fighters could be summoned, the blaze was advancing into the fringe residential areas on a quarter-mile front. Most of the homes on the hillside north of the campus were relatively new—predominantly large, two-and-a-half-story frame dwellings. Unluckily, most of them had shingle walls; nearly all had shingle roofs. Many shingles were cracked and curled on the surface, offering perfect lodging places for sparks. Like the grass and trees, they had been dried out further by the hot winds, and they ignited like paper. As soon as the shingles had been loosened by the fire, the wind ripped them from the roofs and carried them through the air, still flaming. Within forty minutes after the first house was on fire, burning shingles were sailing over the rooftops throughout an area a half-mile square. As the firemen fought the blaze at one house, its flying shingles would touch off another house several doors down the street.

THE CAMPANILE'S TOCSIN

In California Hall on the university campus, Dean of Men Joel W. Hildebrand was sitting at his desk, talking with a student, glanced out the window and spotted the cloud of smoke to the north. He thought instantly of his wife and children at home north of the campus and rushed for the door. At the same moment a phone rang on the desk of Comptroller Robert Gordon Sproul. The superintendent of buildings and grounds was calling with word that the fire had reached menacing proportions. Sproul told him to offer the university's facilities and personnel to city authorities to help fight the fire. Then he headed up the hill toward the Campanile for a firsthand look at the burning area.

Hildebrand, a mountain climber and athlete, raced the half mile uphill toward his house with scarcely a pause for breath. As he headed up Euclid, he first realized the magnitude of the disaster. Down the hill came the first wave of refugee families, lugging a few possessions out of the fire zone. A truck full of furniture was careening down the street, its driver unaware that his load was ablaze. When Hildebrand arrived at his home at Le Roy and Buena Vista he could see the fire approaching across the rooftops, still a block or two away. He and his family ripped blankets from the beds and dumped them in the bathtub in order to wet them and lay them on the roof. But the bathtub spigot yielded only a trickle of water.

As the fire crept closer, Mrs. Hildebrand left with the children for the safety of the campus, pushing a baby buggy ahead of her, while her husband remained behind. A moment later the house on the opposite corner caught fire. In front of the house firemen coupled a hose to a hydrant but no water came. Plainly Hildebrand's own house would shortly be ablaze. Quickly he jammed some clothes into two suitcases and followed his family to the campus.

The Berkeley fire chief, watching his men fall back before the advance of the flames, put in an emergency call for help from Oakland, but at that moment thirteen Oakland fire companies were fighting fires of their own and could not be spared. He tried to phone San Francisco for help, but the phone lines were jammed. University students had been mobilized for the emergency by a more ancient means of communication—the bell of alarm. The elderly elevator operator at the Campanile had gone to the top of the tower and frantically pushed a big wooden bell handle, sending the tocsin out over the campus and the city. Classes were dismissed, and students and faculty ran to the base of the tower. There university authorities told the men to report to the fire area and the women to organize relief centers for the refugees, who were already gathering on the campus. Co-ed Jean Gregory gasped to fellow-student Robert Hill that her invalid grandmother was at home in the burning area on Euclid. Hill raced half a mile to the home, carried the frightened old lady out on his back to the family car, and drove through the burning streets. The top of the car caught fire and a tire exploded from the heat. On reaching safety Hill collapsed from exhaustion.

THE RETREAT OF THE REFUGEES

When the alarm was sounded, John Edy, Berkeley's city manager, had been in the office of the East Bay Water Company complaining that the water mains had not been enlarged to give adequate service to the newly developed areas on the hillside terraces north of the campus. Unfortunately, the complaint was too late. All of the fire companies tapping hydrants in the stricken area found only a weak flow of water. The water supply tapped by Engine No. 2 gave out completely as Engine No. 3 began to draw on a hydrant a block away. Engine No. 2 then moved another block—to the corner of Euclid and Cedar, and found that hydrant dry. The draft on the water supply—both from fire trucks and residents using garden hoses to wet down roofs in the path of the flames—was too great for the small water mains. The firemen found themselves helpless in the face of the holocaust.

Throughout the area north of the campus, most residents gave up battling the rooftop flames and concentrated on hauling furniture and valuables from the lower floors of blazing buildings to the street. In the confusion they grabbed whatever was at hand, and one dazed housewife wandered down the street clutching a telephone book. From the smoke-darkened sky fell a hot hail of ashes and blazing fragments of wood. Ambulances raced through the area. Intersections were jammed with cars escaping the flames. There were several collisions; more than one speeding automobile failed to negotiate curves on the winding hillside streets and over-turned. The passengers crawled out and continued their flight on foot, ignoring injuries in their anxiety to outrun the fire.

University students directed traffic; some walked through the streets using football megaphones to direct refugees to relief centers; others helped residents carry belongings out of burning houses. Several rescuers, headed by Otis de Rimer, were themselves trapped inside a blazing house and had to batter their way with axes through the basement walls to safety. Elderly Alice Chittenden refused to leave her home and had to be carried out by her son-in-law. Mrs. Martha Spaulding, stumbling down the hill with her six-year-old son, had to stop repeatedly when her clothes caught fire from flying fragments. Tennis star Helen Wills found her way to the university infirmary, temporarily blinded in one eye by a cinder.

Sproul, learning that the flames were menacing the home of President Emeritus Benjamin Ide Wheeler, quickly rounded up a platoon of students and faculty members and led them to the Wheeler house. The elderly educator had been evacuated earlier, perched on the tail gate of a truck with a few belongings. Sproul and his recruits lugged books and furniture out of the blazing building. California's championship football team, at practice on the field when the alarm sounded, was led to the fire front by Coach Andy Smith. Still in their uniforms, the athletes hauled furniture from the endangered homes.

THE DESTRUCTION OF THE MANUSCRIPTS

In spite of the valiant efforts of an army of students and other fire fighters, many eminent members of the faculty suffered heavy property losses. Historian Herbert Bolton lost irreplaceable historical materials collected in world tours over a period of decades. Law professor Max Radin was unable to salvage his legal documents. Samuel Haines of the physics department lost in the burning basement of his house a set of delicate instruments he had invented to test the electrodynamic wave theory of physical force.

Architect Bernard Maybeck and his wife were at Lake Tahoe on vacation, and their daughter Kerna, a co-ed, was able to save only one box of documents and a suit of clothes for her father. All of Maybeck's architectural photographs and records from his years in Europe were destroyed, and some twenty houses he had designed were consumed in the flames. Sociology professor E. J. Taggart arrived at his home in time to find it ablaze from roof to basement; inside had been the almost-finished manuscript of his treatise of world populations, the work of a lifetime. But later at the refugee station he was philosophical. "I got out alive, didn't I?" he asked jauntily, munching a sandwich. Geology professor Andrew Lawson had built his house of concrete to withstand possible earthquakes. Valuable articles carried into the street burned while the house was spared.

By late afternoon the swiftly moving flames had spread to houses across Hearst Avenue from the campus and were threatening the business district on Shattuck. Fire companies from Oakland and San Francisco had finally arrived—the latter by ferry—to help battle the blaze. Nearly every city within fifty miles also sent fire fighters, but without sufficient water they could only fight a series of losing campaigns, falling back block by block. The Berkeley fire chief had declined to use dynamite to level buildings in the path of the blaze, believing that it would be ineffective in the face of the wind. Some amateur fire fighters, trying hurriedly to dynamite a burning apartment house on Euclid at Ridge, succeeded only in blowing holes in the walls and throwing them ten feet out of line, while the fire continued unabated.

THE TURN OF THE AERIAL TIDE

By this time the fire companies had been forced to fall back to the downtown shopping district, sometimes compelled to retreat so hurriedly that they had to abandon hoses and equipment en route. The Odd Fellows building at Shattuck and Addison caught fire at four-thirty, and residents were stamping out flames on the roofs of other buildings in the block. The blaze had gathered such momentum that it appeared nothing could prevent it from consuming downtown Berkeley and continuing through Oakland.

Then came the decisive moment. Fire fighters and refugees alike felt instinctively that a major change had occurred, paused, looked at each other wonderingly. Someone pointed up at the cloud of smoke. It was no longer billowing southwest over Berkeley but seemed to be heading back toward the hills. Gradually everyone realized what had happened. The wind had changed. The battle front in the upper air had turned. The northeast gale had blown itself out, and now a gentle breeze, damp with the smell of the sea, was coming up from the bay. Though it brought the salt tang of the ocean, it was sweet and cool in the hot lungs of the weary fire fighters. The turning point had been reached. The efforts of man had been of little avail. The holocaust was too big to be stopped except by the element that had started it—the wind.

From that blessed moment when the wind changed, the fire fighters were able to establish a holding action and contain the flames within the area already ablaze. The small fires along Shattuck were gradually extinguished.

Though the conflagration was no longer spreading, it continued in the area north of the campus. Fire fighters speculated nervously as to whether the wind would rise again. Throughout Monday night refugees wandered through the burning streets, looking for relatives, hoping that this was some nightmare from which they would awaken to find families safe and homes intact. Like most urban dwellers, who live in a man-made world normally insulated from the harsh impact of the elements, they had never dreamed that such things as this could happen to themselves. They blinked at the smoking rubble through a haze of confusion.

LIFE IN THE RUINS

Rumors spread about the numbers of people killed. There were eyewitness accounts of people falling through blazing roofs and disappearing in collapsing buildings. Across seventy-two blocks of what had been a modern residential area there was scarcely a wall left standing. Fires in the rubble threw an eerie light on the charred stumps of trees and the brick chimneys standing like tombstones in a graveyard.

Jets of gas from broken conduits flared high into the night. Small streams of water like pitiful fountains spouted from severed pipes in the ashes. Where a fire hose was played on the ruins, clouds of steam rose in grotesque shapes and turned pink in the light of the dying flames. An ominous red glow flared up on the hilltop, then died, the last gasp of the original blaze.

Soldiers patrolled the streets to prevent looting. Spectators thronged the hills above the burned area to stare at the ruins. Sidewalks and curbs were strewn with furniture and other goods, much of it charred or still burning. Red Cross shelters were set up, and sleeping accommodations were hastily arranged in university buildings—Stephens Union for women and Harmon Gym for men.

By Tuesday and on following days the magnitude of the damage could be assessed. A total of 584 buildings, mostly single-family houses, had been completely destroyed. Some four thousand people were homeless. Total damage was estimated at $10,000,000. It was generally expected that the death count would be high. But final calculations were astonishing. Though the hospitals had been jammed with hundreds of people treated for burns and minor injuries, no one had been seriously hurt.

One by one, people reported missing turned up alive and well, including several students believed dead. Among them were Stanley Mattoon, who had last been seen falling down the stairs in a building but escaped with nothing worse than a sprained ankle, and Ed Norton, who had fallen through the blazing roof of his home but received only some scratches and bruises. There was a report that charred human remains had been found in the wreckage of a house on Euclid, but they turned out to be the remnants of a beef roast. A blackened human skull was unearthed in the ashes of another house but was sheared off so neatly that it was assumed to be the keepsake of some biology student with a grisly sense of humor.

NEVER AGAIN?

Although the cause of the fire's origin in Wildcat Canyon—now Tilden Park—was never conclusively ascertained, there seemed little doubt that carelessness in some form was responsible, whether the fire was ignited by poorly maintained high-tension lines or a discarded cigarette or match. The Berkeley fire department, because of a faulty warning system, was not aware of the grass fire in the hills and did not go into action until two hours after it began. Even so, had the residential area been adequately provided with water mains and hydrants, the fire might have been stopped much earlier. If the law had required fire-retardant roofs, as had often been recommended by fire experts, the houses would not have gone up like tinder. If the fire department had been adequately equipped, it would have been more effective. The residents of Berkeley, assuming, as city dwellers inevitably do, that someone, somewhere, was taking the proper precautions against possible disaster, lived with a false sense of security.

Precautions were taken to prevent a recurrence of the disaster. A fire lookout was established on Grizzly Peak to give early warning of any future blazes in the dangerous hill area. Roads were built giving access to the hilltop areas, including the extension of Grizzly Peak Boulevard south to Tunnel Road. The discredited East Bay Water Company was replaced by the East Bay Municipal Utilities District, which installed new reservoirs and water mains.

It would be foolish to assume, however, that a repetition of the 1923 fire is impossible. Despite modern fire-fighting methods, recent brush fires have destroyed many homes in suburban hills, including an area behind Oakland. The Grizzly Peak fire lookout was abandoned in the 1950's as no longer necessary, yet hundreds of homes with highly flammable shingle and shake roofs have been built in the old fire area and the hills above. The very lack of fires in the intervening years has increased the chances of a big one; in the natural areas of Tilden and the adjacent hills, dead brush and dry leaves have accumulated to such a great depth as to provide tinderlike fuel for a holocaust. A program of controlled burning there would seem to be highly desirable.

Whenever in early fall after a dry year the hot winds roar down through the canyons, set doors and windows to banging and trees to bending before the blast, there are still old-time residents of Berkeley who look uneasily toward the hills, half expecting to see that dreaded cloud of smoke, and at night turn nervously in their beds, wondering whether all is well. Their concern may well be justified. Such nightmares as the great Berkeley fire should not be forgotten.

2

Demosthenes of the University

THE UNIVERSITY OF CALIFORNIA in recent years has come to bear dismayingly little resemblance to the hallowed groves of Academe. The once-parklike five-hundred-acre campus at the foot of the Berkley Hills has been wracked by both social and architectural violence. The demonstrators, however, have done far less permanent damage than the builders and pavers, who have covered with structures and asphalt the broad lawns and bucolic glades where you could once stroll in sylvan serenity and contemplate the cosmos.

Yet there are still a few places on the campus where it is possible, at least in off-hours, to find some measure of detachment and perspective, to consult the muses or your own conscience, to feel the palpable presence of a mighty tradition. One is the area around University House, where rambling gardens surround the Victorian mansion inhabited by most of the university's presidents in this century. Another is the foot of the Campanile, where you can sit in a classic grove of sycamores or gaze westward to the Golden Gate. Faculty Glade, despite some encroachments, remains a green enclave of lawns and oaks and redwoods by the curve of Strawberry Creek.

The most profound experience of the Berkeley campus may come from standing in the Greek Theater on a quiet afternoon looking up the green hillside to the high groves above, peering out through the eucalyptus trees past the Campanile to the sunlight on the bay. If you were to listen carefully at such a time you might hear in imagination some of the voices that have echoed from these stones over the generations—Sarah Bernhardt playing *Phèdre* on this stage shortly after the earthquake of 1906, with the smoldering ruins of San Francisco visible in the distance; Theodore Roosevelt vigorously exhorting the multitudes as he jabbed his fist toward the sky; the portly William Howard Taft on a hot day congratulating the university on the "bake-oven" qualities of its amphitheater. You may hear, too, the chanting of thousands of voices in the firelight at successive re-enactments of that primitive rite known as the Axe Rally. But for tens of thousands of alumni who were students during the 1930's, '40's and '50's, the dominant sound heard here in recollection will always be the stentorian tones of the university president in those decades, Robert Gordon Sproul.

THE SOUND OF HOMER

In those years, the university itself was symbolized in the person of the big man with the prodigious voice and commanding presence, whose eloquent speeches defining the high purpose of the university reverberated from this amphitheater and from the spinal cords of generations of students on all of the campuses. In an age when oratory seems a lost art, Sproul has perhaps been the last of the orators in the classic tradition. Like the addresses of his illustrious predecessor, Benjamin Ide Wheeler, his speeches were resonant with classical allusions; he gathered insights from science, the arts, and humanities and projected them onto the contemporary scene in a voice of ringing affirmation, firing the imaginations of his listeners with the infinite possibilities of man's illimitable mind.

Sproul's unsurpassed popularity among the students was partly the result of his fabulous memory for names, his unerring ability to find a quip to match every occasion, his gregarious habits (he often dropped in on Telegraph Avenue malt shops to chat with students), and his lusty sense of humor, which owed a great deal to his youth in San Francisco's Mission District and sometimes scandalized his ivy-minded colleagues.

Sproul's Homeric laugh was an experience in contagious sound. It lighted up faces for a distance of at least two hundred yards across the campus and could set a stadiumful of spectators chuckling by sympathetic vibration. He denied the story that it once shattered a wineglass across a banquet table.

THE HAND AT THE PLOW

His ability to deal with student disorders was immeasurably enhanced by his sense of humor—and perhaps by recollections of his own student days when he was an editor of an anti-establishment student paper called *Brass Tacks*. There were student demonstrations in Sproul's time, too, some of them directed at him, but quite different from the more recent variety. One evening in 1939, several thousand shouting students massed in front of his home, University House, waving picket signs and demanding that he appear. In response to the summons, he came out on the porch, listened to the shouts, peered at the signs, and grinned broadly. The signs read: "WE WANT SPROUL" . . . "GREETINGS, SPROUL, WE RAISE A HOWL" . . . "BOBBY IS OUR HOBBY."

The undergraduates were raising their howl at the prospect of losing their president, who had been offered the presidency of a major bank at several times his university salary. He raised his hand to quiet the demonstration and began: "I have told those who wanted me to leave you . . ." The rest of the sentence was lost in a wave of cheering and band playing that resembled the uproar after a Big Game victory.

Eight years later a similar episode took place when Sproul was offered the presidency of Columbia University and after deliberation finally declared: "I will not take my hand from the plow to which it has been set these seventeen years." The position at Columbia was later accepted by Dwight Eisenhower, and Sproul continued to plow his chosen furrow for another eleven years.

For more than half the university's century of existence, Sproul was associated with the institution as student, cashier, comptroller, president, and president emeritus. From the beginning, he was the kind of person about whom legends naturally develop. One of the stories, which happens to be true, concerns the time in his student days when he was running the two-mile event in a track meet with Stanford and won the race in the rain carrying an umbrella he had accepted from a spectator. His astounding vocal prowess was apparent even in those days. On one occasion after a Big Game victory, he and some friends were whooping it up on the front deck of a ferry bound for San Francisco when a crewman tapped him on the shoulder: "Hey, bud, you'll have to pipe down. We can't hear the foghorns."

DEPRESSION CRUSADE

A year after his graduation in 1913, he was appointed to the university staff and eventually had an office adjoining that of President Benjamin Ide Wheeler, who one morning demanded to know what the commotion was in the next room.

"Mr. Sproul is talking to Sacramento," an aide informed him. The imperious Wheeler was not impressed. "Well, tell him to use the phone!"

His overwhelming vitality and enthusiasm made him a well-nigh irresistible force as a persuader on behalf of the university, beginning with his career as the university's lobbyist in Sacramento. As president during the darkest days of the Depression, he took to the radio and the road for a hard-fought campaign against attempts by the governor and the legislature to pare the university budget to the marrow. Over the years he was probably the world's champion money-raiser for education, and any faculty member who developed a promising research project requiring financial aid knew that Sproul would lend a sympathetic ear and quite probably convince some philanthropist or foundation to supply the funds.

During Sproul's administration, as his successor, Clark Kerr, has pointed out, the University of California "became one of the most eminent universities in the nation." As enrollment doubled, its total income rose from $13,000,000 to $209,000,000. Faculty salaries went from near the bottom among major universities to near the top. The American Council on Education rated Berkeley second only to Harvard in the number of distinguished departments, and the quality of its library was surpassed only by Harvard and the Library of Congress, each of which had had a long head start.

While these accomplishments cannot be attributed solely to Sproul's presidency, his vital role in bringing them about was one of the many factors that caused the late historian Dixon Wecter to deliver his much-quoted encomium: "Doubtless God could have made a better university president than Robert Gordon Sproul, but doubtless God never did."

RGS AND THE FSM

After his retirement as president in 1958, Sproul turned from education to conservation—an old interest. He was one of the organizers of the Save-the-Redwoods League and remained treasurer of the organization for half a century. He helped establish the East Bay Regional Park District in 1931, and was its long-time president. From 1959 to 1965 he served on the National Park Advisory Board, appointed by the Secretary of the Interior.

During his years as president emeritus, he scrupulously avoided involvement in the administrative affairs of the university, but it was characteristic that he contributed the sole note of humor in the otherwise grim confrontation between the administration and the Free Speech Movement in 1965. There was a rumor that student demonstrators had invaded his office in Sproul Hall during his absence and scattered the files. A reporter phoned him for confirmation.

"No," he replied with a laugh that set the newsman's eardrums ringing. "Nobody messed up my office. It always looks that way!"

For decades to come, alumni and faculty members with origins in the Sproul era will find it difficult to enter the Greek Theater —with its towering eucalyptus trees, its view of the Campanile, the bay, and the Golden Gate—without seeing in mind's eye the tall figure at the rostrum, booming out over the ancient amphitheater the old familiar salutation that was at once a greeting, an auspicious prelude, a sound of rolling drums, and a manifestation of sheer vital exuberance: "FELLOW CALIFORNIANS . . ."

3

Sanctuary in Oakland

THE WILD DUCKS are visible above Oakland first as a barely perceptible line in the sky, like a thin wisp of smoke. Then as they approach, you can see them come in ragged file around the big silver slab of the twenty-eight-story Kaiser Building, slide down the air currents over the river of traffic on the Nimitz freeway, and alight on the bright water of Lake Merritt, stinging the surface with a rapid series of splashes as they ski in on spread feet.

Arriving in spring or fall, the wild ducks bring to this anomalous urban scene eloquent signs of the turning earth and the changing seasons, symbols of the far north from which they come—the waters of the Yukon and the Mackenzie and the cold lakes of the Canadian prairies.

Inevitably they head for the southeast reach of the lake and the shelter offered by the lake's five small islands. There are pintails and widgeons that come in September and October by the score, canvasbacks that arrive in November by the hundreds, along with other migrants—terns and herons and gulls and grebes, occasionally some loons and egrets—all converging on the lake after flights that in some cases amount to thousands of miles. Here they join the resident species—the colorful mallards, the swift-winged cormorants that come in from the bay during the day, the colony of Canada geese, and the flock of huge white pelicans.

The birds come to Lake Merritt in preference to the wilder shores of the bay, ignoring the surrounding skyscrapers of downtown Oakland and the roar of freeway traffic, perhaps because they know that they will not be greeted with birdshot from the guns of hunters. They have been protected here for more than a century. The Lake Merritt Wild Duck Refuge was the first legal wildlife sanctuary in the nation, and a few years ago was proclaimed a National Historic Landmark by the National Park Service.

THE MIXED MOTIVES OF MAYOR MERRITT

For these blessings the birds have reason to be grateful to Dr. Samuel B. Merritt, who in 1852 bought the land around Peralta Slough, a tidal inlet of the Oakland estuary, which in turn is an arm of San Francisco Bay. The dynamic physician later became mayor of Oakland and in 1869 had a dam constructed across the narrow entrance to the slough, converting it into a salt-water lake. Hunters had long converged on the slough to pop away at the birds that flocked there, and anyone else wanting to stroll the shoreline or picnic near the water was in jeopardy of being punctured by birdshot. Mayor Merritt instigated a bill in the state legislature establishing Lake Peralta as America's first wildlife refuge, and the bill became law on March 18, 1870.

The mayor's motives, like all motives, were doubtless mixed. The banishment of the hunters measurably raised the value of his own lands around the lake, some of which in 1891 became Oakland's Lakeside Park, containing one of the last stands of the live oaks that gave the city its name. At the same time Lake Peralta became Lake Merritt. Whatever his purposes, Dr. Merritt's maneuver worked out very well not only for the birds but for the nearly half million people who come to the lake annually to see the bird show.

Major-domo of this aerial-aquatic carnival is Oakland's park naturalist, Paul Covel, who combines certain qualities of John Burroughs, Aldo Leopold, and the Pied Piper of Hamelin. He is perennially surrounded by flocks of birds and children and takes immense delight in both. The kids call him "Paul" and fire continuous barrages of questions. Inner-city youngsters who know little more of nature or wildlife than the rats in the alleys gaze in wonder at Covel's wild birds, his caged birds, his mammals, and bees and snakes and wildlife exhibits in the Rotary Natural Science Center.

TO RESCUE THE WING CRIPPLES

For forty years Covel has walked the shores of this lake, explaining the birds to visitors, and the State Park and Recreation Commission has awarded him an unprecedented citation for his long-time "leadership role in the cause of ecology and environmental quality." He first appeared at the lake in 1931, a young Bostonian employed part time at the Oakland museum. He joined forces with Brighton C. Cain, a Scout naturalist who was Oakland's unofficial man-at-the-lake in his off hours. "Bugs" Cain (the nickname originated in his Stanford training as an entomologist) banded birds and talked to park visitors on weekends with no pay and little thanks from the city.

After World War II, Oakland's moribund park system was brought to life by a new superintendent—the redoubtable William Penn Mott, Jr., later state park director. Mott persuaded the city to hire Covel as full-time naturalist while Cain continued to help at the park in his spare time. Some of the other results of Mott's persuasive powers and money-raising talents are visible elsewhere around the lake—Children's Fairyland, the Rotary Natural Science Center, the Buckminister Fuller geodesic aviary that houses some of Covel's birds, and four of the lake's five man-made islands, containing fresh-water ponds to provide nesting grounds and sanctuaries for the burgeoning bird population.

To supplement the flocks of Lake Merritt, Covel travels to wildlife refuges in the Sacramento Valley and rescues "wing cripples" —birds whose wings have been injured by hunters' birdshot. Although many farmers consider the migrant birds enemies that raid their crops, Covel remembers with gratitude one Sacramento Valley rancher who presented him with nine wing-crippled Canada geese he had saved. They became part of the lake's resident colony of these impressive birds. The young remain three or four years, until they hear the call of the wild and fly to join their migrating cousins from the north.

Other birds that have found permanent sanctuary here are five big white whistling swans and the even larger eight white pelicans from Pyramid Lake, with wingspreads reaching nine feet. They rank with the California condors and certain albatrosses as the biggest flying birds on earth.

THE PERILOUS PROCESSION OF THE MALLARDS

Among the most populous birds on the lake are the resident mallards, numbering thousands. They nest on the islands and offer visitors an unforgettable lesson in the grimmer aspects of nature. When the eggs hatch out and the half-dozen young mallards are ready for their first swim, the mother leads them as they paddle on a perilous crossing to the mainland, one hundred yards away. The peril comes from the sky, where squadrons of fierce gulls swoop down to prey on the ducklings. Although the mother may be able to protect most of them as they are herded across the water, when they land and scatter, the gulls move in for the kill.

But Covel and his assistants, like the United States Cavalry, are ready for the rescue. They scoop up the ducklings as fast as they can, leaving the mother the one or two she is able to protect, and dump the rest into a big glass-enclosed "hatchery." There the ungainly young birds are fed and sheltered for three weeks, then released when they are too big for the gulls.

Some forty-five thousand people a year go through the museum and hear Covel's lectures. Ten times that number visit the refuge, annually buying tons of birdseed for distribution. Retired folks come every day, holding rendezvous with their favorite birds—ducks or sparrows or geese, or perhaps Covel's Ichabod the Crane. Early on most mornings an Oakland merchant known as the Goose Man brings crates full of lettuce discarded by local markets and feeds it to the geese. He often returns after work with more lettuce and helps guard the birds from would-be vandals. Occasionally, with permission from Covel, he takes an ailing goose to the veterinarian or hauls it home temporarily to nurse it back to health.

Covel refuses to guess at the numbers of birds that have taken advantage of his hospitality, but estimates a population of about five thousand on a top day. Birds he has banded, particularly ducks, have shown up in Alaska and Northern Canada, and in 1954 one of his bands was returned from a pintail found on the Chukotski Peninsula in Siberia.

In a time when Americans are increasingly turning to nature for relief from a fouled-up, plastic environment, men like Covel are the guides and prophets, and urban oases like Lake Merritt are sanctuaries not only for birds but for humans as well.

4

The Berkeley Hills:
Backdrop to the Bay

FORMING THE EASTERN SIDE of the basin around San Francisco Bay
is the fifty-mile section of the Coast Range known as the Berkeley
Hills—a colossal backdrop to the stage of the bay and its shores,
changing in aspect hour by hour and season by season.

At the end of a clear day in midsummer the light from the
setting sun strikes fire to the houses on the slopes opposite the
Golden Gate. From the bay or the city, you can see the windows
glitter along the far wall like a thousand blazing jewels. Then, as
the sun sinks, the lights along the lower tiers begin to go out. Almost
imperceptibly the twilight rises like a tide until the last flames
along the rim are finally extinguished, and the spectacle is ended.

On a winter morning the same hills may present a totally different
aspect as the early sun, shining from the rear, brilliantly backlights
a cloud deck over the range, and the steep slopes below are a wall
of black in the shadow. As the sun climbs and illuminates the
sloping plain between the hills and the bay, you may see the
Campanile and other spires silhouetted negatively in white against
the dark backdrop.

Conversely, if you live in the hills and have a view to the west,
you are part of a permanent audience in the vast amphitheater
overlooking the bay. You watch an ongoing drama of ships and
bridges, winds and clouds and storms. The show is continuous except when the curtain of fog is drawn and the thick masses of
vapor billow through the high streets on the hillside terraces.

THE REGIONAL PARKS

Whether as backdrop or amphitheater, this range along the rim of the basin is as essential to the total spectacle as the bay itself. It extends down the eastern side of the basin behind all the cities of the far shore, from Carquinez Strait south to Richmond, Berkeley, Oakland, San Leandro, Hayward, and Fremont. But it is far more than a wall. The Berkeley Hills (sometimes called the Contra Costa Hills) are about twelve miles wide, highest at the western edge and dropping off eastward to the San Ramon Valley and the Ygnacio Valley, where Walnut Creek is located. They embrace such smaller valleys and towns as Orinda, Moraga, and Lafayette.

Drive through the steep residential districts facing the bay or across the hills on Highway 24 through the Caldecott Tunnel to Walnut Creek and you might conclude that the range is thoroughly urbanized. However there is far more than meets the eye from the main roads. There are hundreds of thousands of acres of open rolling hills, canyons, valleys, and woodlands, where the principal inhabitants are black-tailed deer; where golden eagles soar over the ridges; where gray foxes and bobcats are common; where an occasional mountain lion moves silently through the chaparral.

Fortunately, a large portion of this near-wilderness region will be preserved from the bulldozers and accessible to the public as part of the remarkable East Bay Regional Park District, embracing some twenty-two thousand acres and twenty parks. Within the park are hundreds of miles of hiking and riding trails and special areas for dozens of kinds of recreation activities. In Tilden Regional Park, for example—two thousand acres of hills and valleys behind Berkeley—you can go swimming and boating in Lake Anza, study nature at the Jewel Lake Nature Area, play golf, ride horseback, engage in archery and tennis, picnic, botanize at the state's largest garden of native plants, or stroll over miles of trails. Farther east is three-thousand-acre Briones Regional Park, entirely dedicated to the hiker or horseback rider who would explore the hills and valleys and groves in the heart of the Berkeley Hills; cars must be left at the entrances.

THE LAST OF THE REDWOODS

Behind Oakland is two-thousand-acre Redwood Regional Park, containing some of the last of the redwoods that filled these canyons and valleys before they were logged over in the decade following the Gold Rush. The present trees are highly impressive, although second growth. The original trees were reputed to be as large as any now standing in the northern redwood forests. It is significant that the redwoods were concentrated in this section of the range opposite the Golden Gate, the gap in the coastal ridges which allowed rain and fog to penetrate to the bay's eastern shore.

Once the giant trees covered nearly twenty-five square miles of the Berkeley Hills, from the slopes facing the bay back through the canyons almost to the Moraga Valley. Those on the western slopes overlooking Oakland and Berkeley were known as the "San Antonio redwoods," after the Peralta family's Rancho San Antonio. The "middle redwoods" were those in and near the present Redwood Regional Park, in the north-south valley drained by Redwood Creek. The trees farther east, in the canyon of upper San Leandro Creek, were the "Moraga redwoods."

Early navigators used certain tall trees along the crest of the Berkeley Hills as landmarks. Captain F. W. Beechey in 1826 wrote that a ship entering the bay should line up the northern tip of Yerba Buena Island with ". . . two trees . . . south of Palos Colorados, a wood of pines situated on top of the hill, over San Antonio, too conspicuous to be overlooked." By doing so the navigators would avoid a submerged rock off Telegraph Hill later known as Blossom Rock, which did serious damage to Beechey's own ship, HMS *Blossom*. Although "Palos Colorados" means "redwoods," and historians seems certain that Beechey's "pines" were redwoods, there may be some doubt as to whether the landmark trees were Douglas firs. Redwoods seldom grow on windy crests and prefer sheltered canyons.

The East Bay Regional Park system was established in 1934, beginning with watershed lands declared surplus by the East Bay Municipal Utilities District—initially Tilden, Temescal, and Roundtop (now Sibley). These lands would have been ideal for subdivisions but were preserved by long, hard-fought struggles led by such conservation crusaders as Robert Gordon Sproul; William Penn Mott, the ebullient general manager recruited by Sproul; and more recently by Richard Trudeau, who succeeded Mott when the latter became state park director.

THE RISING OF THE RANGE

Geologically the Berkeley Hills, like most of the rest of the Coast Ranges, are relatively young. This edge of the continent has been a particularly unstable section of the earth's crust, covered by the waters of the ocean through long eons, emerging as islands, archipelagoes, and ranges through other eons, only to fall back into the sea. During most of the Pliocene period, for example, which began about twelve million years ago, the relation of the Berkeley Hills area to San Francisco Bay was almost the reverse of what it is now. Where the bay is now located was a long north-south ridge, and the Berkeley Hills area was a valley. Earlier the valley had been partly occupied by another bay, which was connected with the ocean to the south, but the bay was replaced by sediments washed down from the ridge. Volcanoes rose throughout the area like bubbles in mud pots, spewing lava and ash over hundreds of square miles.

Toward the end of the Pliocene, about 2,500,000 years ago, the surface of the earth began to heave and buckle under pressures from deep in the earth. The crust bent and broke into rising and falling blocks. The long ridge dropped and became a valley which was later invaded by the ocean to form San Francisco Bay. The old valley to the east began to rise, forming the beginnings of the Berkeley Hills. At first, the hills were low and undulating, but at intervals through the past two million years they were lifted higher, particularly along the western edge facing the valley of San Francisco Bay. Perhaps the most pronounced uplift came during the past few hundred thousand years—and may still be going on.

SIGNS OF THE UPLIFT

Explore the Berkeley Hills now and you can read this whole dramatic story written in the visible rocks. In roadcuts along the top of the range you can see the hardened sediments that washed down from the ancient ridge and accumulated here when this was a valley. They are called the Orinda formation and consist mainly of light brown beds of conglomerate and sandstone. One good place to see them is in the roadcuts on Highway 24 just east of the Caldecott Tunnel. Although the beds were laid down horizontally in the old valley, here they were steeply upended when the Berkeley Hills rose.

You can also see the lava (the Moraga formation) that flowed over some of this area during the age of the volcanoes. Since the lava was particularly hard and resistant to erosion, it now forms some of the highest summits of the range—1700-foot Grizzly Peak, for example. Drive along Grizzly Peak Boulevard to the road cuts just below the peak and you can see the very dark basaltic lava beds. These once level beds now dip steeply to the east.

Little Grizzly Peak, a few hundred yards to the northwest, consists of some younger lava, mainly rhyolite. The rhyolite flowed in various directions from Little Grizzly, and you can see it in whitish outcrops in the nearby groves of Monterey pine. Lava outcrops are also visible in Indian Rock Park in Berkeley, where Sierra Club rock climbers practice on the volcanic crags.

In many places along Grizzly Peak Boulevard and its continuation southward as Skyline Boulevard behind Oakland, there are broad, gently rolling summit areas, contrasting sharply with the steeper slopes in the canyons and along the west base of the range. These relatively level upper areas are an old erosion surface—remnants of the low rolling hills that succeeded the ancient valley. As these smooth hills were lifted, streams running down the steepening slopes cut deep V-shaped clefts, such as Strawberry Canyon, above the University of California, and the parallel canyon occupied by Highway 24 to the tunnel. In future geologic times the old smooth uplands will diminish as the streams cut their way back into them.

Geologists have found other evidence of the rising of the range. On the slopes above San Pablo Bay, north of Richmond, there are old oyster beds, obviously laid down when the hills were lower and the bay covered this area. Under Oakland and Alameda are sands (Merritt sands) laid down on ancient beaches which were lifted above sea level when the hills rose. Immediately above these sands are the remains of old sea cliffs carved at the same time. The cities of the eastern shore are all built on alluvium laid down by the streams flowing down from the rising hills.

EARTHQUAKE COUNTRY

The lifting of the range produced numerous cracks in the crust —faults along which the earth still occasionally moves, both in slow, creeping action and in major convulsions. Along the foot of the steep western face of the range is the Hayward Fault. Along the eastern slope, facing the San Ramon Valley, is the Suñol-Calaveras Fault. Between the two are several parallel lesser faults including such active cracks as the Wildcat and Chabot faults.

Best known and most visible is the Hayward, a branch of the San Andreas, which it joins southward near Hollister. It is marked, over much of its distance, by a long valley just inside the Piedmont Hills, occupied by Lake Temescal, Warren Boulevard, portions of the MacArthur Freeway, Foothill Boulevard, and Mission Boulevard. Northward the fault extends beneath the University of California stadium, and beyond the campus, as we have noted previously, it takes the form of step faults—a series of terraces convenient for building houses. It continues along upper Arlington Avenue through El Cerrito, across the Mira Vista Golf Course. Streams flowing westward out of the Berkeley Hills jog northward as they cross the fault, then continue westward toward the bay, indicating that the bay side of the fault is moving northward relative to the hill side.

Some geologists believe that the Berkeley Hills were lifted along the Hayward Fault. Others are convinced that the fault's position above the foot of the range rules out this possibility; they believe the range was formed not by faulting but by bending or warping. Perhaps both processes were involved. On one point the geologists are agreed—the Hayward is still active. In 1836 it gave a great jolt, causing damage as far away as Monterey, one hundred miles south. In 1868 it lurched again, and rifts opened up along a twenty-mile stretch of the fault. By this time the town of Hayward had been built up. Every building was thrown off its foundations and some structures collapsed. Five people were killed in San Francisco, and chimneys topped from Santa Cruz to Santa Rosa.

THE FAULT FLAME

The 1868 jolt was comparable to the San Francisco quake of 1906 and probably would have caused an equivalent catastrophe if the East Bay had been extensively built up at the time. In the past one hundred years, however, the region has been almost solidly urbanized, and thousands of people live directly in the fault zone. Even reservoirs and water tanks have been built on the fault. Presumably most of the residents are unaware of the danger. Even in the absence of an earthquake, several homes have been destroyed by rainy-weather landsliding along the fault zone in Oakland.

The Chabot Fault is over the first ridge east of the Hayward, running through Lake Chabot. Farther north, behind Berkeley, the Wildcat Fault runs through Wildcat Canyon, now largely occupied by Tilden Park. Near Tilden's Jewel Lake nature area is a surprising manifestation of the fault. The crack is clearly visible for about fifty yards, where Laurel Creek flows through it. "Rock flour" is visible along the crack—a fine white powder mixed with mud where the rocks have been ground together by friction along the rift. Decaying marsh plants have collected in the crevice of the fault. Mixed with water from seepage, they give off methane gas. Park naturalists, demonstrating the fault, strike a match to the jet and produce a blaze, to the gasps of visitors.

The flame at the Wildcat Fault is merely the most spectacular piece of evidence that the Berkeley Hills are geologically very active. Over the long stretches of geologic time, all hills and mountain ranges rise and fall like waves on the surface of the ocean. This range is like a rising wave with its steep front slope facing the bay, and the houses on that slope resemble surf riders heading west. Residents can expect to be jolted sporadically, but since the wave has been rising for a couple of million years, they have little reason to fear that it would "break" over less than a 100,000-year period. Meantime the folded hills and valleys, the woods and canyons, the ridges and peaks offer superb opportunities for residence and recreation, for venturesome explorations and dazzling panoramas.

Look westward from these summits to the bay, the far mountains, the Golden Gate, and contemplate the prophetic words of Bishop Berkeley, for whom the city and the range are named:

> *Westward the course of empire takes its way;*
> *The first four acts already past,*
> *A fifth shall close the drama with the day;*
> *Time's noblest offspring is the last. . . .*

5

Muir of Martinez

IN APRIL, the lilacs bloom in the dooryard at the old house on the knoll in the Alhambra Valley near Martinez, fourteen miles northwest of Mount Diablo. The butterflies are flashes of yellow and orange in the spring sunshine, and the air is full of aromas from the incense cedars, the blossoming acacias, and the pink tamarisk in the deep grass at the bottom of the hill. From the top of a tall cedar of Lebanon, a mockingbird often pours out a lusty song.

There is no visible indication that the events that once took place inside this big house had a significant impact on the history of the United States and have touched intimately the life of every American who has ever visited a national park. For a quarter of a century this was the home of John Muir. He planted these trees, tended his orchards and vineyards here, and in this house planned many a campaign against the prodigal wastage of the nation's forests, against the destruction of the soil by overgrazing, against the commercial despoliation of the watersheds and the continent's superb natural parklands. The conservation movement and the beginnings of the national forest system and the national park system flowed out of his writings with an old quill pen in his cluttered study-den on the second floor of this house. One spring day in 1895 he wrote in his journal:

Fine balmy day. Mount Diablo one mass of purple in the morning. Nature is always lovely, invincible, glad, whatever is done and suffered by her creatures. All scars she heals, whether in rocks or water or sky or hearts.

DOWN IN THE VALLEY

Until he was over forty, John Muir had been a footloose wanderer in the mountains. "As long as I live," he had written in 1871, "I'll hear waterfalls and birds and winds sing. I'll interpret the rocks, learn the language of flood, storm, and the avalanche. I'll acquaint myself with the glaciers and wild gardens, and get as near the heart of the world as I can."

Around many a mountain campfire he scribbled in his notebooks the most eloquent prose that has ever been written about the American land. On a visit to the Bay Area in the late 1870's Muir's eye was caught by the comely daughter of a pioneer horticulturist in the Alhambra Valley, Dr. John Strentzel. Over a period of years, between his mountain trips, Muir visited the Strentztel family at the ranch, where he customarily arrived tattered and hungry.

"They pitied my weary looks," he wrote, "and made me eat and sleep, stuffing me with turkey, chicken, beef, fruits, and jellies in the most extravagant manner imaginable, and begged me to stay a month."

The mountaineer doubtless suffered many an inner struggle between conflicting forces—the attractions of gray-eyed young Louie Strentzel and his love for the freedom of the wilderness. On a showery fourteenth of April in 1880 the two were married at the ranch, and the mountain wanderer began a new life as a farmer in the Alhambra Valley.

Dr. Strentzel and his wife presented the old ranch house to the Muirs, and they built for themselves the big house on the knoll. When Dr. Strentzel died in 1890, the Muirs moved into the big house with two small daughters, Wanda and Helen.

Clear and cool. Beautiful silvery haze on Mount Diablo this morning, on it and over it—outlines melting, wonderfully luminous.

THE GOSPEL OF THE WILDERNESS

Muir poured into his career as a farmer the same energy and imagination that had characterized his studies of the mountains. His knack for nature was not confined to the wilderness. His premium Bartlett pears and Tokay grapes, marketed with tenacious Scottish shrewdness, always commanded top prices on the market, and at the end of ten years he had more than fifty thousand dollars in the bank—a good-sized fortune in those days.

When relaxing from his writing or farm duties, he loved to take his two daughters walking over the green rolling hills of the Alhambra Valley. He named two hills near the house Mount Wanda and Mount Helen.

Another lovely day, mostly solid sunshine. Took a fine fragrant walk up the West Hills with Wanda and Helen, who I am glad to see love walking, flowers, trees, and every bird and beast and creeping thing. . . . The oaks are in full leaf. A fine fragrant walk, the babies delighted.

It was while he lived on the Alhambra Valley ranch that he planned the beginnings of the conservation movement. During his Sierra Nevada explorations he had watched with alarm as the range was increasingly ravaged by overgrazing, leaving the meadows and slopes barren and eroded. In the midsections of the range, the giant Sequoias were threatened with extinction by the loggers.

By temperament Muir was a shy individualist who preferred mountains to cities and trees to people. But he put his inhibitions aside and went into the public arena to preach the gospel of wilderness like a latter-day John the Baptist. His brilliant articles in national magazines aroused the conscience of the nation, and his herculean efforts to persuade legislators as well as the public led to the creation of Yosemite and Sequoia national parks in 1890.

THE BIRTH OF THE SIERRA CLUB

Around the inspiring figure of the crusading mountaineer there developed a circle of men who could see, as he did, that the establishment of the two big parks was not the end of the battle; it would have to be the beginning of a much longer effort to create other national parks and preserve the remains of the American wilderness against the inevitable attacks by commercial interests. On Saturday, May 28, 1892, Muir and several others, including faculty members from both the University of California and Stanford, met in the office of Attorney Warren Olney in San Francisco; and the Sierra Club was created as a corporation, with Muir as president, "to explore, enjoy and protect the Nation's scenic resources. . . ." That night he returned to Martinez in triumph.

"He came home jubilant . . ." a guest reported, "and regaled them all with an account of it at the supper table . . . I had never seen him so animated and happy before . . . I venture to say it was the happiest day of his life . . . Hitherto, his back to the wall,

he had carried on his fight to save the wilderness. In the Sierra Club
he saw the crystallization of the dreams and labor of a lifetime . . .
He was hilarious with joy."

A list of the charter members of the club was almost a Who's
Who of the Bay Area in 1892: President David Starr Jordan of
Stanford; old William T. Coleman, who had been leader of the
Vigilance Committee of 1856; Andrew S. Hallidie, inventor of the
cable car; Charles F. Crocker of the Southern Pacific; Professor
George Davidson, pioneer scientist, for whom Mount Davidson in
San Francisco was named; William Hammond Hall, founder of
Golden Gate Park and first state engineer; artist William Keith;
Mayor Adolph Sutro; and many other famed names including Le-
Conte, McAllister and Hopkins. Shortly after the founding, William
E. Colby joined the club, became Muir's chief lieutenant, and was
the club's executive secretary for forty-four years.

The fledgling organization had an early baptism by fire and
successfully repulsed major attacks on the parks by commercial
interests. In 1913, however, it lost the climactic battle of a ten-year
nationwide struggle to prevent Hetch Hetchy Valley in Yosemite
National Park from being flooded by a reservoir, and the defeat
doubtless contributed to Muir's death by pneumonia the following
year.

HEIMGANG

In those last years, after the death of his wife and marriages
of his daughters, Muir lived alone in the big house, writing for
long hours while there was still time. The vital instinct was strong
to the end. In the final summer of his life he went to work modern-
izing the old house, bought new rugs and furniture, built bookcases,
and wired it for electricity—perhaps in the hope that the family
of one of his daughters would move in. He died of pneumonia
while working on the proofs of his last book on Christmas Eve of
1914.

*The rugged old Norsemen spoke of death as Heimgang—home-
going. So the snow flowers go home when they melt and flow to
the sea, and the rock ferns, after unrolling their fronds to the light
and beautifying the rocks, roll them up close again in the autumn
and blend with the soil.*

In 1952, to save the old house from destruction by vandalism
and decay, Mr. and Mrs. Henry Sax, admirers of John Muir,
bought it and moved in, hopefully as a holding action until some

public agency could take over. They restored the house, installed the original types of furniture, rounded up an impressive collection of Muir material, and invited the public in for group tours. In 1966, their hopes were fulfilled when Congress created the John Muir National Historic Site, consisting of the house and nine surrounding acres, administered by the National Park Service.

The view from the big house on the knoll has changed greatly since Muir's day. Most of the Alhambra Valley is occupied by subdivisions, and a freeway has been built just south of the house, cutting off parts of Mounts Wanda and Helen. But the tops of the two hills are still green in the spring; there are still portions of his orchards on the valley floor; and the far hills to the west remain much as he knew them.

Despite time's changes the intense, zestful spirit of the man who once lived here still is felt strongly in the old house, in this valley and over the green hills he named for his daughters.

Walked over the hills with Wanda and Helen. How the wind did surge and hiss and rustle and shout in the rocks and trees and grass! How the tall grain waved, the billows sweeping onward in endless succession with racing enthusiasm. . . .

6

The Mountain of the Devil

THIS MOUNTAIN is young. Only yesterday, in geologic time, the central core was thrust upward from deep in the earth with titanic force, breached massive layers of bedded rock several miles thick and rose four thousand feet into the sky.

This mountain bears an aspect of splendor. See it when the morning sun, rising from behind the far Sierra, strikes the peak with a rim of fire while the visible world below lies in deep shadow. See it after a winter storm when its summit is resplendent with snow or wreathed in long banners of cloud.

Watch it as you drive toward it across the flat San Joaquin Valley. It looms on the horizon for one hundred miles, offering a landmark-guide for present-day travelers as it did for the wagon trains of the pioneers. Observe it at twilight from the towns and villages at its base when the afterglow lingers on its upper slopes and it seems to hover over the hills and valleys below like a benediction.

From any vantage point at any season, this is undeniably one of the major mountains of California, one of the notable peaks of North America. Its 3849-foot altitude is not impressive when compared to the elevation of far higher peaks, but such heights are relative. Diablo begins almost at sea level and rises as high above its immediate base as many famed mountains of far greater total elevation. Diablo's uniqueness lies in its character as a peak standing alone, a massive, broad-shouldered individualist among mountains, dominating the surrounding landscape.

It is more than a thousand feet higher than Mount Tamalpais across the bay and twice the height of the nearby Berkeley Hills.

Because of its key position at the edge of California's five-hundred-mile-long Central Valley, it commands a panorama which is said to be unsurpassed in extent by any in America or Europe and second only to that visible from Mount Kilimanjaro in Africa.

THE FOSSIL GRAVEYARD

Although the mountain itself came into being very recently in geologic time, long after the other main features of the Bay Area landscape were formed, its ancestry is ancient. A few miles east of the Berkeley Hills, beneath accumulated sediments six miles deep, lay a mass of rock originally formed in the Jurassic period, a million and a half centuries ago, when the dinosaurs ruled the earth and the first ungainly birds of evolution took to the skies.

Pressured by tensions deeper in the earth's crust, the rock mass began to rise. It forced its way up through strata which had been deposited during the Cretaceous period for sixty million years, the time when the Rocky Mountains were formed; through layer after layer of Tertiary sediments representing another sixty million years, the time when the Alps and the Himalayas were born and the higher mammals developed; and finally through the topmost sediments laid down at the beginning of the Quaternary period, when the human race came into being. Some time in the past million years, that mighty rock upthrust breached the surface, forcing the overlying beds up into a vertical position and even throwing some of them over backward.

Climb the mountain now and you can see the results of this violent upheaval. One good view is near the south entrance to Mount Diablo State Park, overlooking the spectacular Devil's Slide, where the jagged, fractured ends of the Cretaceous and Tertiary beds thousands of feet deep are exposed to the sky. Continue up the mountain past the remains of millions of years of strata and eventually you reach the reddish rock mass that formed the core of the upheaval and now constitutes the upper slopes of the mountain. This rock may seem familiar in color and texture; it is part of the same Franciscan formation that also lies exposed at the Golden Gate, where a gorge had been cut deep into the ancient beds.

Owing to the great mass of broken strata of various geologic epochs exposed by the upthrust, the Diablo region is rich in minerals from these earlier eras and in the remains of prehistoric animals whose "burial grounds" were disrupted by the upheaval. On the Black Hawk Ridge in the Devil's Slide area is one of the richest fossil beds in California. It is almost impossible to dig there without finding remains of a mastodon, a four tusked, elephant-like pachyderm that lumbered around this region in herds some twelve million years ago. Here, too, are found the bones of primitive three-toed horses, saber-tooth tigers, and oversized prehistoric camels. Not far away, from another epoch, are fossil remains of oysters, scallops, and clams that were embedded here when this region was ocean bottom.

GHOST TOWNS

Around the north side of the mountain, in Eocene rock, are other evidences of the Diablo upheaval. Fifty million years ago this was a damp subtropical area; plants and trees decayed in the moist, swampy ground; their remains, buried beneath millions of tons of rock, became coal which was subsequently brought to the surface by the rise of the mountain. Between 1855 and 1900, fifteen million dollars' worth of coal was mined here, and there are still some ghostly remains of two of the six vanished coal towns, Nortonville and Somersville. Other commercially valued mineral deposits were also partly unearthed by the upthrust—limestone at Cowell, quicksilver near Clayton, silica (used in glass making) on the east side of the mountain.

Ironically, the red core of Franciscan rock, which was strong enough to force its way up through six miles of the earth's crust, met its match when it burst through to the surface. It encountered greater resistance in the thin air than it had met in all the strata of overlying rock in millions of years of its ascent from the depths of the earth. The weathering processes of wind, frost, heat, and rain eroded its exposed surface, and an unknown amount of the core rock—possibly five hundred feet or more—has thus been worn away. Much of this fragmented rock has come tumbling down the mountain in landslides. There are slides more than a mile long (partly overgrown) on the southwest side of the main peak and on the north side of the north peak, a half-mile distant from the principal summit. Landslides themselves are very vulnerable to erosion, and the fact that they have not yet been worn away is evidence that the mountain is young.

Other evidence of the mountain's youth is found near the eastern base of the peak where Marsh Creek flows northwest through a broad valley for several miles. The creek might be expected to continue to the north and empty into Suisun Bay—as it is believed to have done in the geologic past. But instead, it encounters a flank of the mountain and suddenly makes a sharp turn, veering off to the

east through a steep (and therefore young) canyon to empty eventually into the San Joaquin River. Evidently its former course to the
north was blocked by the more recent elevation of the mountain.
The rise of Diablo may be still going on, although too slowly for
accurate measurement.

THE SPECTER OF DIABLO

The nineteenth-century origin of the mountain's name has been
the subject of considerable speculation. According to an unauthenti-
cated story, some Spanish soldiers camped on the mountain or
near it were awakened by their sentry, who had been badly scared
by a ghostly figure and yelled, *"El diablo!"* The soldiers left the
mountain in considerable haste and thereafter referred to the area
as "El Monte del Diablo."

The story was recalled a few decades ago by some campers who
spent the night on the summit and awoke at sunrise to see several
gigantic apparitions in the sky. When they were fully awake, it occurred to them that they were looking at their own shadows projected on a fog bank by the rising sun—the Specter of the Brocken,
also visible on rare occasions at San Francisco's Grand View Peak.
It is quite possible that the *"diablo"* seen by the Spaniards was the
same phenomenon.

In the state park headquarters on the mountain hangs a large
oil painting portraying another version of the story of the mountain's name. It illustrates a Bret Harte short story which told of a
certain Padre José Antonio Haro of Mission San Pablo (both fic-
tional) who climbed the peak with a muleteer and two Indian con-
verts in the early days of Spanish occupation. As he looked out over
the great panorama and mused on the glorious future of New Spain,
the padre was confronted by a cadaverous caballero who predicted
the departure of the Spaniards and the invasion of the Yankees
(both depicted in the painting)—an eventuality which could be
prevented only if the padre would renounce his faith. The priest,
spotting the caballero's cloven hoof, refused to yield to temptation.
The enraged caballero then fell upon the padre, who lost consciousness. When he awoke, his frightened companions informed him that
he had been attacked by a grizzly.

ROCK CITY

The Indian name for the mountain was "Kah Woo Koom," which
has been translated both as "Laughing Mountain" and "Everywhere
Seen." The latter translation is probably more accurate, and the

California Legislature of 1865, observing its appropriateness, considered making "Kah Woo Koom" the official name. However, after due deliberation the legislators decided to stay with "Diablo," perhaps believing that in a state where most places are named for the saints, it was only fair to give some recognition to the opposition.

According to what is probably the most authentic of the several stories of the origin of the mountain's name, the whole thing was a mistake. Some Spanish soldiers, engaged in a battle with the Indians near the site of the present town of Concord, were scared into a hasty retreat by the appearance of an Indian medicine man, fantastically painted and decked out in wild plumage. Believing that the devil himself had joined forces with the natives, they named the willow grove where the battle had taken place "El Monte del Diablo." In common usage at the time, "monte" meant "woods" or "grove," but the American explorers in the 1840's assumed that the word meant "mountain" and erroneously transferred the name to the peak.

The practical-minded Americans immediately put the mountain to use. So strikingly did it dominate the landscape that it was designated in 1851 as the base point for surveys of northern California and Nevada. The Mount Diablo Base Line, which runs east through Yosemite National Park, appears on all topographic maps of California and Nevada.

In 1931, the upper slopes of the mountain became a 2168-acre state park. Some two hundred thousand visitors a year drive up the tortuous mountain roads to see the fractured and twisted rocks at Devil's Slide, the aeolian caves carved by the winds at "Rock City," the weird shapes of such formations as Elephant Rock and Turtle Rock—all carved in Cenozoic sandstone raised by the upheaval of the mountain.

The more adventurous visitors sleep out in the park's campgrounds or hike on its thirty miles of trails over high grassy slopes and through groves of oak, laurel, and the gray-needled Digger pine. They meander through sycamore-lined canyons along streams or drink at some of the mountain's one hundred springs—one of which rises within three hundred feet of the summit and flows so abundantly that it provides much of the park's water supply. The existence of a large spring so close to the summit has been the subject of considerable speculation, including the intriguing theory that the water could flow out near the peak in such volume only if its ultimate underground source were at a far higher point—which could only mean the Sierra Nevada. Most geologists are inclined to believe an easier explanation—that the rock of the summit is sufficiently water-retentive to supply the spring in the normal fashion.

THE FAR SIERRA

The greatest attraction is the summit itself. The road ends there at an observation house built by the WPA in the 1930's from fossil-bearing stone from the Cretaceous beds near the Devil's Slide. Nearby are an obsolete aircraft beacon and several radio relay transmitters, one of them a microwave relay station carrying both telephone conversations and network television programs to the Bay Area.

Falling away on every side are the contorted folds and faults and fractured strata overthrown by the upheaval of the mountain. To the west, beyond the rolling San Ramon Valley and the low wall of the Berkeley Hills, is San Francisco Bay, with the bridges and cities and ships of the bay sharply outlined on a clear day. Around to the north are the waters of Carquinez, Suisun Bay, and the vast jigsaw-puzzle mass of islands and marshes of the delta, the junction of California's two great rivers, the San Joaquin and the Sacramento. The two rivers can be traced to the north and south until they disappear in the vast alluvial plan of the Central Valley, which is so flat and long that its far ends disappear beyond the curvature of the earth.

Rising beyond the valley, more than one hundred miles to the east, is the climax of the entire panorama—the great wall of the Sierra Nevada. For generations, visitors lucky enough to ascend the mountain in very clear weather have been enthralled by the sight. The famed minister and orator Thomas Starr King climbed the mountain in May of 1862 with a party of the State Geologic Survey and found that the view of the Sierra taxed even his ample supply of superlatives.

"Look at the magnificent barrier," he wrote. "What majesty! What splendor! There you see the wonderful wall of the Sierra, its foothills that roll in huge surges, all reduced by distance to regular slopes of unbroken bulwarks. For 250 miles the mighty breastwork is in view, and along the whole line crowned with blazing snow! . . . Nowhere in Europe can such a vast mountain line be seen as Diablo showed us on that clear day."

Even the experienced geologists in the party, accustomed to mountain panoramas, were so awed by the sight that they found themselves unable to pay attention to their instruments and scientific duties.

"What a grand sight!" wrote William H. Brewer, leader of the party. "The peaks of the mighty chain glittering in the purest white under the bright sun, their icy crests seeming a fitting helmet for their black and furrowed sides! There stood . . . hundreds of peaks . . . vying with the Alps themselves in height and sublimity—all marshaled before us in that grand panorama!"

VIEW INTO TIME

Brewer finally was able to regain his presence of mind sufficiently to check the map and make some calculations. The most distant points visible—two hundred miles away in opposite directions—were Mount Lassen in the north and a peak to the southeast which Brewer later named for his boss, the state geologist, Josiah Dwight Whitney.

"I found," wrote Brewer, "that the extent of land and sea embraced within the extreme limits of vision amounted to 80,000 square miles, and that 40,000 square miles, or more, were spread out in tolerably plain view. . . ."

Brewer's eighty-thousand-square-mile panorama embraced half of California—an area greater than the size of all New England. Among the peaks that can be seen is Yosemite's Half Dome, visible because the axis of Yosemite Valley is very close to the line of sight from Diablo. Unfortunately, air pollution is such that the view seen by King and Brewer is rarely visible nowadays.

There have long been arguments as to whether it is possible from the summit to see Mount Shasta, 14,162 feet high and 240 miles due north. Some observers claim that, under extraordinary weather conditions, they have sighted Shasta's snowy crown on the northern horizon, but mathematicians calculate that the curvature of the earth makes a direct line of sight to the mountain impossible. They do not rule out the possibility, however, that the mountain could conceivably be seen by a refraction of light in the atmosphere, a phenomenon which on extremely rare occasions enables observers to see objects beyond the horizon. Whatever the explanation, the optical phenomenon is in keeping with the character and history of the diabolic mountain with its long tradition of visions, illusions, and hallucinations.

In any case the view from the summit is not merely geographical but geological, affording a vision of the geologic past represented by the thirty-five thousand feet of strata upended by the rise of the mountain. As the observer gazes at the jumbled rock from many epochs of the earth's history, it is almost possible to hear the earth-shaking tread of the tyrannosaurus and the thunder of herds of mammoths. Once again reptile-like birds flap unsteadily through misty Jurassic skies, the saber-tooth tiger roars in attack, and man's four-footed ancestor, the first mammal, cowers fearfully from the giants who rule the earth. This mountain offers not only a matchless view into space but a glimpse back into unending spirals of time, as dizzying to contemplate as the panorama spread below.

PART FOUR

———◆———

WEST OF THE BAY

1

Tamal Land

As VESUVIUS RISES above the Bay of Naples, so Mount Tamalpais dominates the Bay of San Francisco, towering above the low summer fogs or standing sharp and clear from base to summit on the crystalline days of winter. From San Francisco itself the mountain is the climax of all views northward beyond the Golden Gate. Few other major cities have such a superb symbol of wildness constantly in view. You may emerge from a downtown building on a hectic afternoon and the sight of it there, rising half a mile into the sky, puts you for a moment on a trail beside a creek flowing through dense woods and grassy meadows. You can almost smell the pungent aromas of laurels, live oaks, Douglas firs, and redwoods.

The Indians called the mountain the Sleeping Maiden. The Sun God, according to legend, one day came to earth, fell in love with the winsome daughter of a chief, caught her up in his arms and bore her away toward his abode in the sky. But he stumbled over Mount Diablo, and the maiden fell to her death. The impression made in the earth by the impact of his fall was the valley which was invaded by the ocean and became San Francisco Bay. The maiden still lies there asleep by the bay, her profile visible in the long ridge of Tamalpais. And they say when the summer fogs flow in from the ocean around the mountain, the Sun God is wrapping his beloved in a soft white blanket.

TABLE HILL

Explorer Pedro Fages in 1772 called the mountain "La Sierra de Nuestro Padre San Francisco." Later Spaniards gave it the present name, evidently for the Tamal Indians who lived at the foot of the mountain. The unimaginative English explorer Henry Beechey in 1826 called it simply "Table Hill," owing to its flat-topped appearance from the bay. Actually Beechey's view was a delusion; the tablelike summit is not flat at all but forms a long narrow ridge from east to west. The Americans used Beechey's ill-fitting name, plus such variations as Table Mountain and Table Butte. Fortunately the maps of historian Hubert Howe Bancroft in 1866 restored "Tamalpais," and the name has remained, corrupted occasionally by some Marin County residents who insist on referring to it familiarly as "Tam." Ironically, they are usually the same people who explode in wrath whenever they hear the equally profane term, "Frisco."

For generations the mountain has been a mecca for hikers. Jack London and his friends used to tramp the trails up the mountain from the grove that later became Muir Woods. When naturalist John Muir himself was wintering in San Francisco in the 1870's, writing up his Sierra notes, he used to head for Tamalpais to escape the pressures and confinements of city life. In the days of the bay ferries, scores of San Franciscans arose on Sundays in time to catch the early boat to Sausalito, where they entrained to Mill Valley, trooped up the steep steps behind the old mill, followed the Pipeline Trail to Mountain Home and on up the East Peak or out to Bootjack Camp, Rock Spring, and Laurel Dell.

THE MOUNTAIN BY THE CLEFT

The mountain's greatest attraction is its surprising variety of natural landscapes, which result from special geographical conditions present nowhere else on earth—its precise location between the ocean and the bay, just north of the Golden Gate, the only sea-level cleft through California's Coast Ranges to the inland valleys.

In the winter Tamalpais intercepts the storm clouds sweeping across the bay, and the resulting annual rainfall around the mountain is more than double that in San Francisco. In late spring and early summer when the streams begin to run low, the seasonal fogs, flowing in from the ocean in late afternoon, keep the lower slopes damp and green through the long rainless season. Here, in sheltered, well-watered canyons and valleys, grow the redwoods of Muir Woods and Steep Ravine and the shaded northern slopes, with their accompanying plant communities—ferns, sorrel, huckleberry, laurel.

The upper ridges of the mountain, however, rise through the fog zone into the inversion, a layer of warm air high above the cool damp ocean breeze. Here are open fields of wild flowers and chaparral-covered slopes where there is more sunshine, summer and winter, than anywhere else around the bay.

Between the two extremes the environment is modified by ridges and valleys and changing levels of fog into infinite variations of meadows, manzanita slopes, and woods of live oak, Douglas fir, and the aromatic laurel. The woods and fields are abundant with black-tailed deer and the shy gray fox. Hawks and buzzards hover overhead; meadowlarks sing in the fields; jays and crows raise their raucous cries in the wooded areas; and deep in the forests you can hear, far off, the haunting call of the hermit thrush.

There are certain perils in these wild areas, hard by sprawling suburbia, but they are perils primarily created by man. As the towns below the eastern slopes of the mountain—Mill Valley, Larkspur, Ross, Kentfield, San Anselmo—expand up the hillsides and into the canyons, developers who care less for ecology than for profits clear brush and cause erosion and floods, or they gouge away hillsides and set off landslides, or they build on steep slopes that give way when saturated by winter storms. To protect these developments, fire departments suppress the small natural fires that would regularly clear away debris. Consequently dead leaves, brush, and fallen trees accumulate into piles of potential fuel, ready to be ignited by any spark when the hot dry winds blow. On occasion, the result has been disaster.

2

The Crookedest Railroad and the Mill Valley Fire

JAKE JOHNSON, engineer on the Mount Tamalpais Railroad, had noticed a haze over the lower part of the mountain as his little steam engine huffed up the tortuous grade from Mill Valley to the summit on the morning of Tuesday, July 2, 1929. But such a haze was common around the mountain, and Johnson was not actually conscious of it except later when he thought back and wondered if it might have been a forewarning of the disaster.

His sixty-five vacationing passengers were in a holiday mood and were preoccupied with the spectacular panoramas opening up below—the bay, the cities on its shores, and the surrounding mountains, all etched sharply in the clear, fogless air. Since Sunday the Bay Area had been flooded with warm, dry continental air moving down from the high plains of the Great Basin, beyond the Sierra. The normal cool sea winds with their fogs had been driven back or came only occasionally between hot blasts from the interior.

For Clinton Thoney, who had succeeded his father as Mill Valley fire chief the day before, the dry air meant trouble. This was "fire weather." He still had fresh memories of the fire that had devastated Berkeley six years earlier at such a time as this. Whenever the wind comes to the Bay Area from the northeast for several days, humidity drops to near zero, and dried-out grasses and leaves fairly crackle in the desiccating air.

Since the 1890's, the narrow-gauge Mount Tamalpais and Muir Woods Railroad had been one of the region's most famed tourist attractions. Particularly thrilling to vacationers were the ride along the dizzy switchbacks at the Double Bow Knot and the gravity cars that rolled like a gentle roller coaster down from the summit. Although some Mill Valley residents had originally opposed construction of the railroad, the line did not significantly detract from the town's highly prized isolation. The isolated quality of the hill districts is attributable to a vagary of nature.

The valley happens to be one of California's most favored locations for redwoods, which grow so densely—along with introduced eucalyptus, pine, and natural undergrowth—that many houses seem to have been built in clearings in a primeval forest. Obviously this lush vegetation and the narrow winding roads entail some risks, but because the redwood forest is normally damp and green, the danger of fire seemed remote. Yet the fire scars on the older trees should have been a warning. On that second of July in 1929, after several days of northeast winds, the situation was made to order for tragedy.

THE LOST LOCOMOTIVE

At two-thirty that afternoon, hawk-eyed, seventy-year-old Hugo Legler, the veteran fire lookout at the summit of Tamalpais, spotted a billow of smoke rising out of upper Blithedale Canyon and phoned Fire Chief Thoney. The siren rang out across the valley, summoning volunteer fire fighters, who hopped aboard a train and headed for the site. The blaze had begun along the railroad right-of-way near the Garden of Allah, the palatial hillside mansion of Ralston White, president of the Tamalpais Land and Water Company. Unfortunately there was little that firemen could do; their hoses did not fit the garden-size hydrants on the White estate. Soon gusty northeast winds were whipping the flames toward Mill Valley.

The upper part of the valley from which the town takes its name is enclosed between two great flanks of Tamalpais—Blithedale Ridge on the east and Throckmorton Ridge on the west. Between them is another spur of the mountain known as the Middle Ridge, lower and more heavily wooded than the other two. It was down the Middle Ridge that the wind-fanned fire roared through the thick woods on that unforgettable Tuesday afternoon. Frightened residents of the Middle Ridge saw first the pall of smoke blowing overhead, then the flames; they hastily collected some belongings and fled. Fire engines screamed into Mill Valley from San Anselmo, Ross, San Rafael, and Fairfax, but there was little they could do to stem the wind-driven wall of flame.

At the summit of Tamalpais, engineer Jake Johnson, afraid that his passengers might be trapped by the fire, had decided to make a run for it. He bundled his charges into the train, fired up the locomotive, and began to rattle down the rails. Down the mountain, below the Double Bow Knot, a train crew and fire fighters with another engine on a side track were trying to hold back the flames. Careening down the curves through clouds of smoke came Johnson with his trainload of scared vacationers.

Johnson was nearly blinded by the smoke, but he could have piloted the locomotive home in his sleep; he had been engineer since the day the tiny railroad ran its first load up the mountain in 1896. Skillfully he barreled the train through the burning zone past the fire fighters into the cool canyons below, unloading his shaken passengers at the Mill Valley depot.

Up on the mountain the valiant engine crew and fire fighters retreated when the fire leaped the track. But they discovered that one volunteer was missing, and they headed the locomotive back into the flames to find him. They located the fire fighter and hauled him aboard, but as they did so some charred cross ties gave way and the engine rolled off the track. They abandoned the locomotive and sprinted down the tracks only to encounter Superintendent Bill Thomas running toward them and waving his arms. "You can't leave her there!" he yelled. "You'll get fired for deserting your engine!"

There is no record of their reply. It is known only that they escaped both the fire and the wrath of Thomas by jumping into a gravity car and rolling down the Muir Woods Branch.

THE SHIFTING OF THE WIND

At six-thirty that evening San Francisco fire companies arrived in Mill Valley via the Sausalito Ferry only to find that their hose couplings didn't fit the Mill Valley fire plugs. As the holocaust roared down on the business district, the hundreds of fire fighters prepared for a last stand to save the town.

Then, in the nick of time, came the turning point. The same critical change in the weather that had saved downtown Berkeley in 1923 also rescued Mill Valley. The hot wind that had been whipping down from the Middle Ridge carrying flaming brands for miles, setting roofs afire far to the south, suddenly shifted. A cool breeze came from the ocean, bringing relief to the scorched fire fighters. It turned back the flames into the burned area. The fire continued to spread across the mountain all night and through Wednesday, occasionally shifting direction with the wind.

On the burned Middle Ridge more than one hundred chimneys stood over the eight-hundred-acre blackened area marking the location of destroyed homes—a loss totalling more than one million dollars. As in the Berkeley fire, there had been no fatalities. Railroad Superintendent Bill Thomas was the first reported missing but was later discovered unhurt, mourning his lost locomotive—in the tavern atop the mountain.

The cause of the fire was never officially determined, although many people suspected that it may have started when one of the passengers on the railroad tossed a match or cigarette off the train. The railroad resumed its runs up the mountain soon afterward, but its days had been numbered ever since a competing automobile road had been built to the summit. It made its last trip a year later with old Jake Johnson at the throttle, tootling the whistle in a final salute.

The track bed is now a fire road, and along the way there are still some station platforms and water tanks—sole remains of the "the crookedest railroad in the world." Along the narrow winding streets of the Middle Ridge the lush vegetation has long since grown back, but evidence of the fire is still visible. Many of the young redwoods are the same size—about forty years old—and here and there can be seen a larger tree whose bark is still blackened.

Tamalpais is now laced with fire roads and other fire-fighting facilities to prevent a recurrence of the disaster. But on the slopes of the mountain above Mill Valley, the dead brush and leaves have been accumulating for four decades, and hundreds of wooden houses have been built on the ridges and in the canyons that were unoccupied in 1929. Mill Valley residents cannot afford to be complacent, particularly on those few days each year when the hot dry winds blow from the northeast.

3

The Redwoods of William Kent

IN DEEP REDWOOD CANYON, at the foot of Tamalpais and west of Mill Valley, lies Muir Woods—the best-known grove of redwoods in the world. No one knows precisely how it came to be there. Possibly many millenniums ago a strong, dry wind, blowing at gale force from the northeast across the valley now occupied by San Francisco Bay, may have carried over the ridge great quantities of dust, leaves, and flying debris. And possibly among that debris were some seeds that filtered through the leaves of the trees growing along the bottom of the canyon—oaks, maples, madrones, alders—and came to rest in some fresh soil where a small animal had plowed up the earth in making a burrow.

Under the protecting cover of the older trees, one or more of the new seeds took root. Winter rains nourished the green shoots, and summer fogs, dripping down from the leaves of the older trees, kept the soil damp during the rainless summers. In a few years the fast-growing trees towered above the older vegetation. Small native horses and rhinoceroses grazed beneath the new trees, and later when several generations of the redwoods had created a grove in the canyon, saber-tooth tigers may have roamed through the quiet forest aisles.

Much later, within the past few thousand years, Indians ventured into the woods to hunt small animals and to fish for the salmon that in winter migrated up Redwood Creek. The name of the first white man to enter Muir Woods is unknown, but it is not surprising that the event was unrecorded. The big trees of these woods were no larger than many that were growing elsewhere in the region. The Forty-Niners and their successors soon learned that the tall trees growing in abundance in the these hills made highly durable lumber, and a good part of San Francisco was first built of redwood from Marin. Today, around the old mill in Mill Valley, for example, it is possible to see stumps of trees as large as those in Muir Woods. Fortunately the high ridge separating Redwood Canyon from the settled areas around the shores of the bay made these trees inaccessible for lumber. However, around the turn of the century, when most of the rest of the Bay Area had been logged over, lumbermen began to think about ways of getting over the ridge.

"SAVE THE TREES YOURSELF"

Hikers had discovered the giant groves in the 1880's and '90's. One anonymous nature lover was so concerned that the trees might be logged that he tried to persuade a number of people to buy the grove and save it from the lumbermen. One of the men he approached in 1890 was William Kent, a large Marin property owner, but Kent had never seen the trees and was not interested.

In 1892 some members of San Francisco's Bohemian Club decided the grove would be a fine place for the club's annual summer encampment. One of the members put up fifteen thousand dollars to buy the grove for the club, and others went to work building a giant plaster figure of the Daibutsu Buddha, then a club symbol. The encampment took place as scheduled, but the club membership afterward vetoed the purchase of the grove. The place, it seemed, was too close to the ocean, and the summer fogs moving up the canyon at night made the camp cold enough, in the approximate words of one member, "to freeze the ears off a brass monkey." The Bohemians moved to the Russian River, but the plaster Buddha remained for many years in what is now called the Bohemian Grove of Muir Woods.

A decade after the Bohemian encampment, the Tamalpais Land and Water Company, which owned Redwood Canyon and other large tracts in the Tamalpais region, decided to sell out. Lovell White, the president of the company, suggested again to William Kent that he buy the woods to save them from the loggers. Kent, an irascible businessman, was still uninterested. "Save the trees yourself," he snorted, "I can't afford to buy any more white elephants."

Nevertheless, Kent decided to visit the woods, along with his friend and business associate Samuel B. Cushing, who had built the Tamalpais railroad. The giant trees made a deep impression on Kent, and afterward he could not quite get out of his mind the disturbing thought that they would be logged. He asked White the price of the land. It was forty-five thousand dollars for a little over six hundred acres, a reasonable price even for that era. But Kent was already in debt, and business conditions were bad. When he contemplated borrowing the money, his wife asked him how it would ever be paid off. Apparently he made up his mind that instant. He barked out: "If we lost all the money we have and saved those trees, it would be worth while, wouldn't it?"

Mrs. Kent's response was not recorded, but the discussion for all practical purposes was over. Kent borrowed the money and bought the property in 1905. To make the grove accessible to visitors, Cushing decided to run a spur of his railroad down to the edge of the woods, and Kent planned to construct a hotel at that point. (The Muir Woods Inn was built there in later years, on the site now occupied by Camp Alice Eastwood, and the old railroad grade is now a hiking trail from Mountain Home to the camp and on to the bottom of the canyon.)

TO DROWN THE WOODS

It looked as if the trees had been saved. Actually the struggle had hardly begun. The first attack came from an unexpected quarter. The North Coast Water Company decided that Redwood Canyon would make a fine reservoir. A dam halfway up the canyon would impound the waters of Redwood Creek, which could then be pumped over into Mill Valley. It would also enable the company to log the trees on the reservoir site at a tidy profit—which may have been its principal motive all along.

The water officials had developed a shrewd stratagem for wresting the land from Kent. They found a provision of California water law that would enable them to ask the court to condemn the property for reservoir purposes. Domestic water supplies were legally the highest use of any undeveloped land, and there appeared to be no way to prevent the water company's seizure. But Kent was a fighter, and the water company's attempted land grab got his dander up. He charged into battle with all the vigor of the man he most admired, President Theodore Roosevelt. The water company had found a law to fit its purpose. Kent would find a law to suit his.

He discovered his weapon in the form of a bill Congress had recently passed enabling the Federal Government to accept donations of land of outstanding historic or other interest, particularly Civil War battlefields, to be established by presidential action as national monuments. Kent might have had a hard time proving that a Civil

War battle had been fought in Redwood Canyon, but he felt that the area was certainly of "other interest." If he could present the grove to the Government, it would be safe, he believed, once and for all.

First, however, he had to persuade federal authorities that the trees were of outstanding value to the nation. To get public support, he organized a publicity program that would do credit to Madison Avenue. It was the first nationwide save-the-redwoods campaign. He had pictures taken of the trees and sent them to newspapers and magazines. He induced university professors to write the life history of the trees. And he enlisted the help of the nation's leading naturalist and conservationist, John Muir, who brought all his literary talent to bear on behalf of the project, as he had done earlier on behalf of Yosemite and Sequoia national parks.

The campaign was long and hard-fought. Kent's most formidable opponent was the Secretary of the Interior, James R. Garfield, who was opposed to the Government's accepting property with a condemnation suit attached to it. "This was particularly maddening . . ." Kent wrote later, "but Roosevelt took the bit in his teeth and the woods were accepted."

MUIR'S MONUMENT

Kent asked President Roosevelt to name the monument for John Muir, who had first popularized the big trees of California and the need for preserving them. But the President wrote back: ". . . I have a very great admiration for John Muir, but after all, my dear sir, this is your gift . . . I would like greatly to name the monument the Kent Monument if you will permit it."

For once Kent refused to go along with Roosevelt. He wrote: "So many millions of better people have died forgotten that to stencil one's name on a benefaction seems to carry with it an implication of mundane immortality as being something purchasable. I have five good, husky boys that I am trying to bring up to a knowledge of democracy . . . If these boys cannot keep the name of Kent alive, I am willing that it should be forgotten."

The President was impressed. "By George!" he wrote back. "You are right. . . . Good for you, and for the five boys who are to keep the name of Kent alive! I have four who I hope will do the same thing by the name of Roosevelt."

Muir Woods National Monument was established by Roosevelt in 1908, and Muir himself was deeply touched by Kent's gesture. "This is the best tree-lover's monument that could be found in all the forests of the world," he wrote to Kent. "You have done me a great honor and I am proud of it. . . . Schools here and there have planted Muir trees in their playgrounds and long ago Asa Gray named several plants for me. . . . A Sierra peak, also, and one of the Alaska glaciers bears my name. But these aboriginal woods, barring human action, will outlast them all, even the mountain and the glacier.

"Compared with Sequoia forests lifting their domes and spires to the sky, mountains great and small, thousands of them, have been weathered, ground down, washed away and cast into the sea, while two of the many species of Sequoia have come safely through all the geological changes since Cretaceous times, surviving even the crushing ice-sheets of the glacial period. Saving these woods from the axe and saw, from the money changers and water changers is in many ways the most notable service to God and man I have heard of since my forest wanderings began."

"DAMN THE PUBLIC SCHOOLS!"

The creation of Muir Woods National Monument did not end Kent's problems with the grove. For many years the Government lacked sufficient funds to maintain the monument. Kent paid a custodian out of his own pocket and also paid for maintenance of the road leading down into the woods from the ridge. He was not a man to be satisfied with stopgap measures. Disgusted with the lack of action from the Government, he decided to go to Washington and take action himself. He got himself elected to Congress on the Progressive ticket in 1911 and proceeded to spearhead the fight for the bill creating the National Park Service. Although the maintenance of national parks and monuments improved as a result, Kent was soon to learn that the fight for conservation is never ended.

On a visit to Muir Woods in 1921, he found that the forest was filled with automobiles, spilling out people who overran the hillsides, trampled the ferns and flowers, carved their initials on the trees and even endangered the redwoods by trampling the soil around their roots. He fired off a volley of protest to Washington; as a result, cars were prohibited in the woods and confined to a parking area on property Kent donated for the purpose. A new supervisor was assigned to enforce stricter rules on park use.

Invigorated by the Muir Woods battle, Kent leaped into the fight to preserve other redwood groves. On one occasion when the Governor of California complained that there was not enough money to purchase a particular grove because of the demands on the state budget from such other sources as the public schools, Kent pounded the governor's desk and shouted: "Damn the public schools! Close 'em up for a year and save those trees!" The startled governor somehow managed to find funds for both trees and schools.

After Kent's death in 1928, members of the Tamalpais Conservation Club brought a three-and-one-half-ton boulder down on the railroad to Muir Woods and over a period of many Sundays rolled it by hand several hundred feet to the base of a giant Douglas fir, which they dedicated to the park's donor. The Kent Tree stands a short distance off the main Muir Woods trail on the Fern Creek path.

THE PERENNIAL STRUGGLE

In the years since Kent's fight to save the trees, Muir Woods has become the most popular of all the redwood groves. It has been visited by millions of people—at the current rate about a half-million a year—including presidents, queens, and prime ministers. In no small measure the impetus to the nationwide effort to preserve the redwoods—which grow only in a narrow strip along the coast of California and southern Oregon—stemmed from Kent's original efforts on behalf of Muir Woods.

As in Kent's time, there are still continual setbacks in the effort to save the remaining groves of the giant trees before they are logged over. Conservationists were unable in 1959 to prevent the destruction by loggers of the redwood grove in the canyon adjacent to Muir Woods. The big grove on Butano Creek, south of San Francisco, had been similarly destroyed a few years earlier. In the Rockefeller Grove on Bull Creek in Humboldt Redwoods State Park, five hundred of the giant trees were uprooted when loggers denuded the land upstream, causing flood damage in the park. Long after the creation of the Redwood National Park on the northern coast in 1968, lumber companies continued to denude the slopes above the park, endangering the park's groves in the canyon bottoms. The fight against such destruction is led by the Sierra Club, the Save-the-Redwoods League, and numerous smaller groups, valiant battlers in the tradition of William Kent.

Kent's brand of crusty vigor is badly needed in the fight today. He was a man of action to the end. In the last months of his life, bedridden by a stroke, he had himself propped up on the porch of his big house in Kentfield beneath Mount Tamalpais and lustily blasted away with his shotgun at the crows making depredations in his orchard.

4

The Birth of the Peak

TO INQUISITIVE GEOLOGISTS the long ridge of Tamalpais rises above the bay like an enigmatic sphinx, posing a series of complex riddles. It is a major peak of the Coast Range, but the principal ridges of the range elsewhere run parallel to the coast itself, while Tamalpais stands at right angles to the coast and to the direction of the range. It rises 2600 feet above the bay, inexplicably three times as high as the peaks and ridges on either side.

It has never been mapped geologically, perhaps because visiting geologists have been too dazzled by the panorama from the summit to look at the mountain under their feet. However, the job has finally been undertaken by a resident geologist, Salem Rice of the State Division of Mines and Geology. Rice, who lives in Mill Valley, has explored the area for ten years, puzzled at the contradictory pieces of evidence in rock fragments on all parts of the mountain.

Most of the Bay Area's bedrock (like that of the rest the Coast Ranges) is composed of the Franciscan formation, principally sandstone, with quantities of shale and chert, all formed from sediments laid down on an ancient sea bottom and then thrust upward when the Coast Ranges rose above the ocean. Yet in exploring the mountain, Rice has come across minerals and rocks never before reported in the Franciscan—tourmaline on the East Peak, hornblende schist near Rock Spring, volcanic rhyolite near Lone Tree Spring. Even more puzzling is the fact that on many parts of the mountain Franciscan rocks are not found in the usual order but are broken, scrambled, and scattered in a mystifying conglomeration, like a sack of mixed nuts. Hard by some of the most chaotic masses, however, are large blocks of normal sandstone. It is this kind of jumble that makes life difficult for geologists.

PLATE TECTONICS

For years Rice was unable to work out any coherent picture of the mountain's origin or structure. Recently, however, the mountain has begun to come into focus in the light of a new theory that is revolutionizing geology as Einstein revolutionized physics. The theory indicates that the crust of the earth is composed of plates or blocks that "float" on the earth's mantle and underlie whole continents and oceans. These plates are slowly separating along some zones (where new crust is being created from molten rock below) and crushing together in other zones. The theory accounts for the previously unexplained "drift" of continents—their changing position on the globe over the geologic epochs.

At times the Pacific plate has been thrust hard against the edge of the North American plate, sliding under it and prying it upward. The rising Coast Ranges are evidently the result of this upthrust of the continent's edge. Along surfaces where the two blocks meet there has been massive fracturing, crushing, and grinding, producing a jumble or "melange" of many kinds of rocks. This has happened particularly among weaker formations; stronger rocks may retain their form.

Studying this theory of "plate tectonics," Rice felt that he had found a key to the mystery of Tamalpais. To see the evidence, go to the west flank of the mountain, between Muir Beach and Stinson Beach. Here along the sea cliffs you traverse a confused conglomeration of rocks—sandstone, chert, serpentine, and greenstone, scrambled so chaotically that the land is highly unstable, and immense masses of rock have tumbled into the ocean below. Here, if the theory is correct, you are on the jagged edge of the continental plate where it rises up over the edge of the Pacific plate and the rocks along the surfaces in contact are ground to rubble.

THE BIG SLIDE

Continue north, however, and within a mile of Stinson Beach you stand on a solid sandstone block which extends many miles northward as Bolinas Ridge. This block, with its greater strength, held its shape in spite of the pressures. The boundary between the two zones is Steep Ravine, where erosion of the crushed rock has created a canyon precisely right for redwoods. Oddly, another zone of the crushed Franciscan melange is found one thousand feet higher on the northwest side of the mountain at Rock Spring, above the sandstone block but partly wrapped around it.

Here, too, the melange is unstable and slides easily. On Cataract Creek a few hundred yards below Rock Spring is a landslide that gives evidence of the instability, and farther down the canyon are the remains of other landslides that also blocked the creek, creating lakes and ponds that silted to meadows. Although all of the meadows are being slowly eroded away, in time new landslides in this melange of rock can be expected to create new ponds and meadows.

By far the biggest landslide on the mountain is so overgrown and well disguised that it went unnoticed by Rice until he had been mapping rocks within it for several days. It occupies more than a square mile between the West Peak, at 2600 feet elevation, and Alpine Lake, nearly 2000 feet below. Perhaps several hundred years ago, long before the lake was formed by a man-made dam on Lagunitas Creek in 1918, the stream may have gradually undermined the foot of a loose mass of melange material constituting the entire west side of the West Peak. Then, possibly at a time when the ground was saturated after heavy rains, an earthquake may have shaken the mass loose and started it rumbling downward into the canyon.

The resulting scarp at the head of the slide is visible along the Bernstein Trail and above Potrero Meadows. The meadows themselves (once part of the West Peak) as well as several ponds and marshes below, are evidence that the slide is relatively recent. They were formed in pockets on the surface of the slide and will be eroded away fairly rapidly. Many of the big Douglas firs in the slide area lean out of line, indicating that the ground continues to move slowly.

THE MISSING FAULTS

Still unexplained is the remarkable height of the mountain's main ridge, rising 1700 feet above the 900-foot level of adjacent ridges both north and south. The ridge's origin, Rice believes, might lie in the kind of pressures that produced the melange materials—grinding of the continental and oceanic plates. But the impact of the plates has changed with time. The melange masses were created between 70,000,000 and 140,000,000 years ago, when the plates were meeting head-on. Subsequently, the motion altered until they began to move laterally, creating the San Andreas Fault.

The long ridge of Tamalpais may be the result of some extraordinary motion of the plates along the San Andreas, which here lies on the ocean floor just west of the mountain. Possibly a portion of the continental block was wrenched loose, pivoted to an east-west position, and thrust upward under pressure from the moving oceanic block. If so, there should be faults on both sides of the ridge where it was fractured and torn loose from the surrounding terrain, but no such faults have yet been found. Rice hopes to locate them during his continuing study of the area.

If the new theory is correct, Tamalpais is a product of the meeting of the ocean and the continent in far more profound ways than have been suspected. Now geologically, as well as aesthetically and altitudinally, Tamalpais can be seen as the climax of this incomparable landscape at the continent's edge, this place where the Pacific breaches the thousand-mile mountain barrier along the western rim of America.

5

A Mount for All Seasons

FROM MUIR WOODS, from Mill Valley, from almost any place around the base of Tamalpais, a trail network leads to all parts of the mountain, offering exploration and adventure, refreshment and renewal to all who can walk. In order to know this mountain of diverse moods, it is necessary to hike its trails in every season and every weather.

One August morning, for example, when San Francisco was dark beneath a heavy overcast, I drove to the mountain by way of Mill Valley and on the road above the town found myself in a thick fog. Switching on the windshield wipers, I continued slowly on the Panoramic Highway past Mountain Home, Bootjack, and Pantoll, then turned off for the road toward the summit, still fogbound. Suddenly I emerged from the mists and looked down on the roof of the layer of vapor, dazzling white in the sun. Below were big waves of fog, with shadows in the hollows. Slow volatile geysers rose from the crests of the waves to heights of one hundred feet or more and evaporated in the warm air above.

I parked near Rock Spring, where the sun was bright and warm. From the grove of big tanbark oaks next to the parking area came a crackling sound, as if some animal were walking among the dry leaves under the trees. I walked into the grove to investigate and was surprised to find that the trees were dripping copiously; the drops resounded as they hit the stiff brown tanbark leaves. For a moment I was puzzled as to why the trees were wet in the sun. Then it occurred to me that the fog had been in here all night, drenching the trees, and had burned off a few minutes before I arrived.

The theory was confirmed as I walked down the trail below the spring and noticed that the tawny grass in the meadow was still wet. The woods were aromatic with the smell of damp leaves in warm weather—the strong odor of the laurels, the special fragrance of live oaks and toyon and meadow grass, the Christmas-tree smell of the Douglas firs.

BRIEF CHRISTMAS

Rounding a bend, I came on a sight that brought me to a quick stop. There alongside the trail were several young Douglas firs still wet from the fog. From where I stood the sun was directly behind them, and every needle was bejeweled with drops of water that glistened in the morning light. Each drop reflected a different band of the spectrum, turning the sunlight into piercing reds and yellows, burning blues and purples. No Christmas tree was ever so brilliantly decked out as those Douglas firs with the fog jewelry on their needles.

The process of decoration had been a complicated one. Every drop of water had been lifted from the ocean by the moving masses of air, had been part of the great flowing fog bank, had been elevated two thousand feet above the ocean and hung with ten thousand others in resplendent array on these branches. All this elaborate preparation had taken place for a glittering display that would last only a few minutes, the interval between the lifting of the fog and the evaporation of the water particles. I had happened to come along at exactly the right time.

While I watched, the spectacle began to disappear as the sun dried out each needle. The moisture passed invisibly into the air, seeming to give it a polished brilliance that sharpened the lines of trees and rocks and ridges in the sun.

The coming of the sunlight after the fog had produced an array of sounds almost as brilliant as the light on the leaves. Excited finches and sparrows twittered in the chaparral. Big jays cawed and chattered and whistled as they swooped among the live oaks. Woodpeckers beat out industrious rhythms on tree trunks. Yellow jackets buzzed and hummed in the chaparral, and from somewhere along a high wooded ridge came the scream of a red-tailed hawk. Underneath all the other sound there was a barely audible roar that might have been the imperceptible stirring of the leaves in the big Douglas firs on the ridge or perhaps even the far-off pounding of the surf along the oceanward foot of the mountain.

At a point where the trail led through a stretch of deep woods, the sunlight filtering through the canopy made patterns on the forest floor, illuminating the rich red browns of the dead leaves, and from the damp mossy bole of a big conifer a shaft of golden light was raising a ghost of a vapor that drifted through the woods like an errant wisp of the vanished fog.

STORM MUSIC

The same trail at another time or season is quite a different experience. The summertime hiker, the sunshine mountaineer, the fair-weather outdoorsman can participate in only a fraction of the beneficences this peak has to offer. He knows the mountain only in a time of quiescence, when the natural forces that created this magnificient parkland are at rest. To see the mountain in its full splendor, go there in fog or wind or rain; see the sun set and rise again; explore the high trails by the light of the stars and the woods in the full of the moon. Above all, to see the forces of creation at work, go at the climax of a winter storm, when the rain turns rivulets to torrents, the wind sets the groves and forests to waving and shaking, and the aroused energies of the mountain seem to radiate from the rocks themselves.

I took the trail down from Rock Spring during a rain one afternoon in November, listening to the music of the storm—the wind in the high branches overhead and the full range of tones of the moving waters. Over the mountain ten thousand springs were flowing copiously from the early storms; every gully was filled with a stream. Creeks that in August had been a mere trickle were now impassable torrents; in the larger canyons, cascades and cataracts and waterfalls shook the air with their thunder.

Light showers were falling as I strolled down the canyon between stands of big shiny-leaved madroños, through aromatic groves of laurels, past contorted live oaks arching over the trail. Outcrops of wet rock gleamed more brilliantly than they do in the brightest August sunshine. Every drop of water on the rock surface acted as a prism, both brightening the natural color and reflecting the light roundabout. Rocks that had a dull surface when dry now sparkled as if polished by a lapidary. Dun colors turned to orange and yellow; dull reds became rich ocher; outcrops of pale green serpentine were transformed into masses of shining emerald.

THE EVOLUTION OF A MEADOW

In the storm I became intimately aware of the force of the rushing waters in sculpturing the mountain, in wearing away the rocks, in creating and deepening canyons, in depositing soil in the meadows and valleys. Consequently I noticed something that had not been evident to me before. About two hundred yards down the trail from Rock Spring, the canyon broadened to a grassy meadow. The stream, which above had been roaring over boulders in a white torrent, disappeared from view. I walked closer and found that the water had carved a miniature gorge with nearly vertical sides and was flowing six to eight feet below the level of the meadow. Here was an intriguing problem in geology. The walls of the gorge were not rock but rich alluvial soil that obviously had been deposited over a long period of time by slow-moving or still waters. I realized then that I was standing on the bed of an old lake or marsh.

At the lower end of the meadow the canyon bottom narrowed to about the width of the stream. Here, evidently, at some unknown time in the past, a landslide from the steep slopes above had blocked the stream, backing up the waters to form a lake. On the lake bed had been deposited the sediments I now saw being eroded away in the gorge. Probably in time the lake had been entirely filled with sediment and became a marsh or meadow. A flood breaching the landslide-dam would have caused the stream to flow swiftly again, rapidly cutting the gorge through the soft soil of the meadow.

At the foot of the old landslide a big Douglas fir, a century old or more, leaned precariously out over the stream, which was undermining the bank on which it stood. The curve of the trunk made me think that the tree had begun to lean about halfway in its lifetime, probably at the same time that the dam was breached and the stream began to deepen its bed. Another clue was that part of the gorge was thickly planted with relatively young Douglas firs, making a handsome wall of vegetation through the middle of the meadow. The firs were all about twenty-five feet high, indicating that they were of the same age. Evidently they had begun to grow here at the time when the stream had excavated the gorge down to the level of the new outlet and the cutting process was stabilized—perhaps thirty years ago. The gorge could not have been much older than that or its steep walls would have been eroded away long since. Such angularities do not last long in nature, and doubtless within a few more decades will disappear —along with most of the meadow.

Although I had hiked this same trail scores of times in fair weather, it had not occurred to me to look into the evolution of this meadow until I saw the full force of the flowing water during

the storm and was acutely conscious of the forces that are continually creating and re-creating the landscape.

A COLLISION OF WEATHERS

A totally different kind of experience with the mountain came
one day in January, after a series of storms had been followed
by a period of calm weather and tule fogs—the winter fogs that
form in the cold inland valleys and move slowly westward toward
the warmer ocean. From a high point in San Francisco I noticed
a strange situation: instead of flowing outward through the Golden
Gate as it would normally do at this time of year, the fog was
flowing in from the ocean, as it would do in the summer. Wondering what could be the cause of this meteorological accident, I got
in the car and headed for a grandstand view on Tamalpais. As
the car climbed to the ridge above Mill Valley, through a gap in
the hills I looked out to the bay and caught a quick glimpse that
gave me a preview of the spectacle I was about to witness. Through
Raccoon Strait, between Angel Island and Tiburon, a fog flood was
pouring west. Climbing higher, I could see similar tongues flowing
westward through the low saddles of the Tiburon Peninsula. There
could be no doubt that this was a normal tule fog, forming inland
and moving west. Yet at the same time the sea fog continued to
blow in from the ocean through the Golden Gate. The two fog
masses were on a collision course.

At Mountain Home, at the nine-hundred-foot elevation on Tamalpais, where the road leaves Throckmorton Ridge and turns west,
I parked the car and continued up the ridge on foot, following
the steep Throckmorton Trail. Here above the fog zone the sun
beamed down warmly, but as I climbed to the upper part of
the ridge, I felt a breeze from the west—the advance guard of
the fog moving in from the Pacific. The fog did not hang low
on the water, as it would in the summertime but was actually
a deck of broken stratus clouds several hundred feet above the
surface, as far west over the ocean as I could see.

This is the kind of fog-cloud that often heralds an approaching
storm front. Actually I learned later that there was at the time
a storm center moving from the ocean across northern California
and southern Oregon. I was standing at the extreme edge of the
storm area, around which the air masses were moving, as they
always do, in a counterclockwise direction, bringing the wind and
fog and clouds to this area from the west. It was this foggy
southern edge of the storm that was moving in over the coastal

hills and about to collide with the westward-moving tule fogs around the bay. I hurried on up the ridge to witness what promised to be a major clash of the elements.

MOUNTAIN ARTILLERY

Higher up, I looked out on an extraordinary sight. The bay itself was almost completely covered with a thin white film of tule fog, as if wind-blown snow had drifted across the surface of a frozen lake. The humpbacked deck of the Richmond-San Rafael Bridge seemed to rest on the white expanse, and its foghorn moaned a bass dirge. Near the bridge, two ships appeared to be half-sunken, the vapors level with their upper decks.

Suddenly I was startled by what appeared to be a silent explosion in a canyon directly below me. A big puff of white vapor forty feet high appeared from nowhere, rose, and drifted away. Then, at the head of an adjacent canyon, another smokelike puff appeared, boiled upward into a familiar mushroom shape, then disappeared. Responding to an old wartime reflex, I had an instinct to hit the dirt. In appearance the phenomenon was uncomfortably reminiscent of an artillery barrage.

Then, as similar "explosions" took place just at the heads of the canyons below, I realized what had happened. Masses of cool ocean air, moving in ahead of the fog and clouds, had reached the canyons above Muir Woods and Mill Valley, followed the canyons upward as if in a chute, cooled as they rose, and just below me had reached the point at which their moisture condensed into visible puffs of vapor.

I climbed on up beyond the area of "bombardment" to the summit of the East Peak of Tamalpais. Here a cold wind from the storm front was howling in from the west-northwest. I crouched on the lee side of the lookout station and gazed down across the bay. Along the near shore, the filmy fog covering the water had accumulated into drifts that buried the towns of San Rafael and Corte Madera, and was flowing like driven smoke up through the foothill canyons. San Quentin on its point was half hidden in the vapors, and the channels of Corte Madera Slough gleamed up through the mists like sinuous tracings of light.

"BEHOLD, I SEE NEW SHAPES ARISE . . ."

I had arrived at the summit just in time. The sea breeze, moving ahead of the fog and clouds it was carrying, had advanced over Mill Valley and across Richardson Bay and now met the edge of the advancing masses of tule fog along the Tiburon Peninsula. The forces from land and sea had come into contact, and the battle was suddenly joined on a front miles long. From the start there was little doubt as to which force was the stronger. The wind from the ocean had acquired too much momentum to be stopped by the low thin layer of tule fog from inland. The advance front of the tule fog was suddenly blunted and rolled over backwards like an ocean wave that hits a rocky cliff and rebounds. Everywhere along the battle front, in Raccoon Strait, in the passes through Tiburon Ridge, over the canyons between Mill Valley and Corte Madera, and then out over the surface of the bay itself, the misty tide was turned as the tule fog began to retreat before the battering attack of the sea wind. The advance salients of tule fog seemed to rear back before the onslaught like the dismayed cavalry of Napoleon before the British fire at Waterloo.

The encounter between the two forces created an array of fantastic fog shapes such as I had never seen in many years of fog-watching. All along the battle line, the nebulous forms appeared and disappeared faster than I could keep track of them. Vapory castles quickly formed and vanished. Fog masses thrown back by the advancing west wind were broken up into swiftly moving spirals and parabolas. Steeples and pillars and vaulted arches came into being for a few moments, only to be destroyed by the wind.

The artillery barrage I had seen earlier on the mountain was repeated in the valleys below on a mammoth scale. A mushroom cloud loomed over San Quentin. Over the bay's edge at Corte Madera a mass of white vapor slowly rose like a column of water, spread, and spilled over at the top in a gigantic fog fountain. Then it rose even higher and changed shape until it seemed to be a towering monoloth—a vaporous Washington Monument catching the last rays of the sun before falling back into the shaded valleys below.

Out over the bay the rout was soon complete. The filmy surface fog was swept quickly backward and piled into ridges that drifted and rolled and retreated eastward, revealing the bright surface of the water. Within twenty minutes the battle was over. Thousands of people in the valleys below had been oblivious to the spectacle going on above their heads. Looking up, they could only see that it was either foggy or clearing.

By the time the sun was about to set, the bay was cleared of all but a few pockets of tule fog along the far shores, and the sea fog was moving in force across the Marin ridges. As I left the peak,

numb from the cold northwest wind, I could see the giant shadow of
Tamalpais stretching across the bay to Carquinez and Vallejo,
twenty miles away. There was still a glow of twilight on the upper
slopes as I walked back down the ridge, but in the dark valleys
below, the lights of the towns and villages were shining mistily
through the advancing vapors from the ocean.

THE TYRANNY OF THE INNER TIME CLOCK

To innumerable people toiling in San Francisco offices, the sight
of that mountain across the Golden Gate on a clear day is always
a strong temptation, but in spring the attraction becomes well nigh
irresistible. One bright morning in May the pile of unfinished work
on my desk was reaching the point where I could not face it without
a sense of panic. The mountain was shining in the spring sun, and I
made the inevitable decision—or rather some primal instinct of self-
preservation made it for me. I got in the car, headed across the
bridge, took the road skirting the south side of Tamalpais, parked at
Pantoll, and set out at a quick pace along the Matt Davis trail
around the peak's western flank.

It was one of those bright May days when the mountain seems
to vibrate with life. Birds sang lustily; the grasses were refulgent
green; wild flowers, after the abundant winter rains, were spread
across the grassy slopes more profusely than in any previous season
in memory. Still I was unable to exorcise the compulsions of urban
living. I followed the trail from the open slopes into the woods,
rounded a couple of bends, and came upon a creek cascading down
a ferny ravine—a perfect spot to sit on a log and watch the light
on the water. But the inner time clock was not yet unwound and
kept senselessly insisting that I keep moving.

Fortunately the spell of the falling water began to overcome the
corrupt influences of civilization, and I sat on the log, observing
the flowing forms of the creek as it plunged down a small precipice
and glissaded over a smooth boulder into a clear pool where the
surface reflected dappled sunlight upward onto the leaning bole of
a big maple.

The creek flowed through a natural hillside rock garden displaying
a dozen shades of green—the brownish greens of a coat of mosses
draped over a big boulder like velvet, the duller green of the
chain fern, the pale green of the big-leafed thimbleberry, the darker
greens of the laurels above, and the brilliant spring green of the new
leaves on the maple, forming a back-lighted canopy over the entire
garden. The sounds were hypnotic—the high-pitched purling of the

cascade, the deeper note of a fall dropping into a pool, the cawing of a jay, the exuberant chatter of a sparrow, the rustling of the leaves of maple and laurel in an occasional breeze.

THE FLOW FROM THE GATE

When I finally got up and walked down the trail, I was able to saunter rather than trot—with only fading twinges of guilt over the wasted time. Walking through an opening in the woods, I suddenly came upon a big sloping meadow alight with color—the bright orange of the monkey flowers, the yellow of daisies, the scarlet of the trumpet flower, and the incredible blue of masses of lupine. The field of lupine seemed to change color as I watched it. Examining the plants closely, I could see the cause of this optical illusion. Each stalk of the flower carries petals of several shades, ranging from white at the top, through pale blue to a vibrant purple at the base. By exposing various parts of hundreds of stalks, a breeze causes the colors to change, and the white tops in the field of blue make the entire mass seem to scintillate like wind-rippled water.

I found a good spot on a grassy slope to doze in the sun, and when I opened my eyes after a few minutes I saw directly in front of me something I had failed to notice before: a perfectly formed web about eight inches in diameter, spun between three blades of grass with such engineering skill that the three stalks moved as a unit when riffled by a breeze. The web was spread like a fisherman's net to intercept whatever game might happen through that way. An iridescent-winged insect struggled haplessly in the entanglement. In the center of the web the spider waited patiently. The spider seemed to be the villain of this production, yet he was only making his living in the legitimate way nature had provided and was no more villainous, surely, than a fisherman netting his catch. As I stood up, I startled a foot-long lizard; his back was an intricate pattern of zigzagging black and yellow designs.

I wandered through groves fragrant with the spicy scent of laurels, then continued across open grassy knolls where the ocean came into view and the sweet odors of the trailside lupine were mixed with the salt smells of the sea. After a long descent through a Douglas fir grove like a big dim chamber with pillars four feet in diameter, the trail emerged onto a high rocky point with a superb panorama of the shoreline. The waves, in lines of white surf two miles long, were curving around Duxbury reef to the beach at Stinson where the currents have built a sand barrier across the entrance to Bolinas Lagoon. Offshore, contrasting sharply with the vast aquamarine expanse of the ocean beyond, was a long salient of brownish water that I recognized as the ebb from the Golden Gate, a current laden with silt and sand from the streams flowing into the bay and from the Sacramento and San Joaquin, the combined waters of a dozen rivers originating near California's summit peaks from Mount Shasta to Mount Whitney.

THE PATH OF THE HAWK

Here on this rocky promontory a thousand feet above the sea, facing the incandescent ocean, I could almost feel the geologic heaving of the earth's crust that created this spectacle. At the foot of this mountain, slicing southward into the ocean from Bolinas Lagoon and the Olema Valley, was the San Andreas Fault. Along this colossal rift the earth's crust has moved horizontally over the eons. Here in 1906 the land on either side of the fault slid about ten feet in opposite directions in less than a second. Before long, doubtless, it will move again.

I turned back along the trail toward civilization, with its lesser dimensions of time and space. By now it seemed to me that this day on Tamalpais had been not a retreat from duty but an advance—a salutary confrontation with the real world outside the human hive.

Crossing a high ridge with a view to the south, I spotted a red-tailed hawk riding the air currents and followed him in the binoculars as he swooped against a whirling montage of sea and mountains and sky—the wave-assaulted Marin coastline to Point Bonita, the breakers pounding the cliffs at Point Lobos, the white rows of houses where San Francisco slopes slowly up from the ocean, the eucalyptus forest on Mount Davidson and, on the far horizon, the distant peak of Loma Prieta down the Peninsula. Then the hawk seemed to top the north tower of the Golden Gate Bridge and sailed upward against a backdrop of Nob Hill skyscrapers and the observatory on Mount Hamilton, seventy miles away. I lost sight of him as he disappeared against the two massive summits of Diablo.

6

City of the Birds

IN THE DARK early-morning hours of Monday, January 18, 1971, two tankers collided in the fogbound Golden Gate. Within the next few hours several hundred thousand gallons of fuel oil spilled out across the waters of the channel and into San Francisco Bay on a flood tide. Then the tide reversed, and a major portion of the black mass was carried out of the strait into the ocean. Within twenty-four hours a northerly current moved it ten miles along the precipitous coast of Marin County toward the entrance to Bolinas Lagoon.

There, for the next thirty-six hours, was waged the major battle against the great San Francisco oil spill. The lagoon, with miles of tidal flats, is a superb wildlife habitat, centering on Audubon Canyon Ranch, which the National Park Service has designated a National Natural Landmark. For the sanctuary, the oil was a potential death warrant.

THE BATTLE OF THE BOOMS

On Tuesday morning, Audubon naturalist Clerin Zumwalt arrived at sunrise and found the ocean off the entrance coated with oil. Black waves lapped the sandspit enclosing the lagoon. He quickly got to a phone, asked help from Standard Oil of California (owner of the tankers), then went to the lagoon entrance, where he found scores of people already at work.

"Everybody seemed to sense the danger right away," Zumwalt recalled later. "The water was ebbing from the lagoon at that point so no oil was coming in, but the next flood tide was due that afternoon, and everybody knew we had to get something across that channel to try to skim the oil off. Nobody was in charge, but everybody found ropes and gunny sacks and somebody even brought a tennis net. By the time I got there they had already rigged up two makeshift booms across the channel. They had to swim out in that icy water to do it."

Zumwalt doubted that the booms themselves would hold back much oil, so he began to search the countryside for straw. He finally located a load at Point Reyes Station, a dozen miles away, and had it hauled to the channel and dumped into the water between booms to soak up the oil.

About that time a battered old cattle truck painted in psychedelic colors drove up to the lagoon entrance and out of it jumped a band of long-haired residents of a nearby commune. They hauled six telephone poles off the truck and lashed them to a cable, which was hauled across the channel by a small boat. At the same time, from the opposite shore, one-hundred yards away, hard-hat workers from Standard Oil were setting up their own boom—a ready-made, bright yellow polyethylene skimmer of the kind used at refineries.

When the tide began to come in that afternoon, the workers and volunteers watched and hoped. The polyethylene boom, unsuited to rough water, soon broke. But the makeshift booms held, and the straw between them soaked up immense quantities of oil. A good storm could have taken out all the booms and swept the oil inside the lagoon, but fortunately the weather and the surf remained relatively calm. That night an even higher tide poured through the channel, but the booms held again.

Overnight and through the next day hundreds of students from Marin County schools, other volunteers, the hard-hats from the refinery, and the long-hairs from the commune worked together to save the wildlife. Standard provided food for all. And the students at two Marin schools, unable to donate labor, took up a collection for Audubon Canyon Ranch. By Wednesday, although small amounts of oil had entered the channel, the main mass of black stuff had moved out to sea and the crisis was over. The lagoon, with its unique bird habitat, was saved from the oil, the most sudden and dramatic of a long series of threats to its existence.

OUT OF THE MISTS

My wife and I first saw Canyon Ranch on a spring morning early in 1962. We had driven north from San Francisco on State Highway 1, which drops down off the shoulder of Tamalpais to Stinson Beach and skirts Bolinas Lagoon a few feet above the water. The lagoon, drained by a minus tide that morning, was a mass of channels winding among archipelagoes of glistening sand flats. Diaphanous mists rose from the water like slow billows of steam, drifted across the flats in sinuous wisps and tendrils, and occasionally rose to meet a layer of fog above, creating vapory pillars between heaven and earth. Along the shoreline, pale sunlight filtered down through the edges of the vapors, producing vague, indefinable moving patterns like the first light appearing among the mists of creation.

As we watched the lagoon, out of a drifting bank of vapor appeared the shape of a bird so large that we at first thought it was an illusion wrought by the deceptive light and primeval mists. It was standing motionless when we first caught sight of it, its reedlike legs rising from a shallow channel, its long, graceful neck slightly arched, its head alert as if in anticipation.

Then, with incredible grace and dignity, the bird moved, spread long white wings, and with swift powerful strokes rose through the low mists into the clear air above. It was clearly an egret, pure white, adorned with plumes of the mating season. As it emerged from the edge of the fog bank into the light, it seemed to catch up in its bright plumage all the radiance of the morning sun.

We kept it in sight for several minutes as it soared against the high sunlit backdrop of Bolinas Ridge. Behind the great white bird were smooth grassy hillsides where cattle pastured a thousand feet above the ocean, steep canyons where streams plunged down cascades through groves of redwoods, and high ridges tufted by pointed Douglas firs rising into the cool morning sky. After a short flight, the egret turned into one of the canyons and disappeared.

THE VIEW THROUGH THE FOREST WINDOW

We drove along the road by the lagoon and turned off at the same canyon, where a sign read: "Audubon Canyon Ranch." An immaculate old white farmhouse stood among fruit trees, and pink and red roses grew over the front porch. We parked at the house and took a marked trail along the steep hill on the left side of the canyon. In a few minutes we were beyond the reach of the fog, and sunlight filtered down through the branches of the laurels and live oaks to the spring grass and wild flowers along the trail. A half mile up the canyon we came upon an opening in the live oaks to the right. Peering through the forest window, we looked down on an unforgettable sight.

There in the upper branches of a redwood grove was a congregation of more than one hundred huge birds. About half were the big white birds formerly known as American egrets, now called common egrets. The others were great blue herons, slightly larger than the egrets, a full four feet in height, with slate-colored feathers and patterns of black on their wings and head. Each bird of both species stood or sat solemnly on its own nest, protecting eggs or guarding two or three young birds. Every redwood was in effect a high-rise apartment house, with separate living quarters on each level.

As long as anyone can remember, the birds have come to this canyon at this season from the bays and marshes of seacoast Marin, from the tidal flats of Tomales, from the marshes and meadows near Olema, from the *esteros* off Drakes Bay, from the wild shores of San Francisco Bay and the delta. Here the egrets display with solemn pride their spectacular spring plumage, and both species perform the ceremonial dances and rituals of mating. Then, after the proper nuptials, they pair off and begin to raise a family.

THE CEREMONY IN THE TREETOPS

As we watched the silent spectacle, there was a flash of white through the treetops down the canyon. With an unmatched display of grace and rhythm, forming a perfect Euclidean pattern of planes and curves of wings and arch of neck, a big egret swooped and circled and settled into its nest. In its bill was a long stick, which it presented with a ceremonial bow and flutter to its mate, who had been standing vigil. The latter, with an equally appropriate gesture of courtesy, took the stick and began to weave it into the nest. Then, after a brief conference, the bird that had been standing guard spread its wings, rose above the redwoods, and flew down the canyon.

A great blue heron circled into its nest, and suddenly the silence of the grove was broken with a great squawking and bawling. Three young birds had observed that their lunch had arrived and demanded it instantly. They began to bite the bill of the parent and wrestle vigorously. After some token resistance, the big bird relented and opened its bill to provide food that it had considerably predigested. One of the youngsters was not appeased, however, and demanded a second course by more biting and wrestling. The parent tolerantly fended off the youngster for a few moments, then, apparently having had enough, sailed away to an adjoining treetop and perched there in peace. An egret in a nearby nest reached down with its bill, carefully turned over two pale blue-green eggs, and settled back on them.

Gazing at the spectacle, we lost all track of time, and it must have been a couple of hours before we reluctantly walked back down the trail. Since that first visit we have made many more, and the numbers of visitors to the hillside eyrie has increased to a steady procession on spring Saturdays and Sundays, apparently without disturbing the birds in the slightest.

THE APPROACH OF THE LOGGERS

The story of what has happened to the egrets in the United States over the past century is well known—their near extinction during the decades when their plumes were used for women's hats, their comeback after they were accorded legal protection in 1905, the current threat to their existence as their habitat gives way to yacht harbors, subdivisions, and shopping centers. By 1960 in Marin County, particularly along the San Francisco Bay shoreline, a dozen rookeries of the egrets and great blues had been abandoned as the subdivisions and marinas took over. But at Canyon Ranch, then a dairy farm, the rookery remained—the last major refuge of the big birds in central California.

In 1961, Dr. Martin Griffin, a Marin County physician and president of the Marin Audubon Society, was alarmed to learn that the ranch's new owner was planning to log the redwoods and subdivide. Together with Marin Audubon board member William S. Picher, a retired bookdealer, he called on the owner in San Francisco to find out if anything could be done to save the rookery. The owner cheerfully said he would be happy to sell them the 507-acre ranch—if they would care to pay the price: $337,000.

Griffin and Picher may have been privately dismayed, but they resolved to grasp the nettle firmly. At a meeting of the Marin Audubon Board they proposed that the society begin a campaign to raise the money. The society at that point consisted of precisely 125 people. The largest sum of money they had ever raised was two hundred dollars to help send a state park ranger to an Audubon summer camp. Even to think about raising a third of a million hardly seemed rational. So they made an irrational decision: They would not allow that superb wild refuge to be destroyed without making some attempt, however quixotic, to preserve it.

THE CRUSADE FOR THE BIRDS

The most urgent need was to hold off the loggers and stall for time until they could develop some long-range plans. The owner agreed to wait for ninety days if he were paid one thousand dollars as an option on the property. Griffin and Picher spent most of the next forty-eight hours on the phone and persuaded ten people, mainly Marin Audubon members, to contribute one hundred dollars each. Having bought three months' time, they next set about to raise another three thousand dollars for a further six-month option.

They described the plight of the ranch to anyone who would listen. With the help of a growing corps of volunteers and the thousand-member Golden Gate Audubon Society, which joined Marin Audubon as a co-sponsor, they parlayed the donations into a series of options that staved off the bulldozers time after time, and built up an equity in the property. New tactics were improvised to meet each deadline. Organizations and individuals were asked to buy one acre each for eight hundred dollars. The Marin Conservation League bought an acre, as did the Marin Rod and Gun Club and each of several Bay Area Garden Clubs. Altogether more than one hundred people and organizations purchased an acre or more each.

Pictures and news stories, typed in volunteers' living rooms, went out to every newspaper in California. Pledges for large and small amounts began to come in from across the country as Californians spread the word to friends and relatives elsewhere. The campaign snowballed, and the full price of $337,000 was paid off—in what surely must be a record in conservation fund-raising—by 1965.

When money kept coming in, Auduboners were able to buy adjoining property. They subsequently added several hundred acres of tideland feeding areas and 234 acres in the next canyon, now known as "Volunteer Canyon" in honor of the workers who stood at Bolinas channel during the big oil spill of 1971 and saved the lagoon. Another triumph came during 1971 when Audubon Canyon Ranch was able to purchase the next canyon to the north, expanding the ranch area to more than one thousand acres.

THE KENT ISLAND COUP

The success of Audubon Canyon Ranch has shaped the destiny of the entire spectacular coastline between the Golden Gate and Point Reyes National Seashore. This semicircle of two-thousand-foot ridges, redwood canyons, cliffs, sandy beaches, and tidal lagoon is probably unmatched for scenic beauty in any other metropolitan region, a fact that has not escaped the notice of the developers. Conservationists worked mightily for years to create parks there, and their greatest successes came in the 1960's with the establishment of the national seashore at the north end and the extension of Mount Tamalpais State Park on the south. The proposed Golden Gate National Recreation Area would tie down the south end. But the great gap has been in the canyon and lagoon area in the middle, between the two villages of Stinson Beach and Bolinas.

Innumerable developers have covetously eyed the lagoon itself. Properly dredged, it would make a good marina, the nearest small boat harbor outside the Golden Gate. The Bolinas Harbor District was formed under state law for that purpose and proceeded to draw up a plan for a sixteen-hundred-boat marina and a major resort, motel, and shopping center complex. The ambitious scheme would have resulted in transforming the entire semicircle of coast into a bustling commercial center. So the horrified Auduboners began to make counterplans. The key to the harbor district's proposal was 110-acre Kent Island in the lagoon, where the motel and boating center would be located. The district planned to condemn the island and take it over. But before the condemnation could take place, the Auduboners joined forces with the Nature Conservancy, raised enough money to make a down payment on the island, received title to it, and promptly deeded it to Marin County. The county supervisors quickly accepted the gift and dedicated the island as a wildlife park before the harbor district directors knew what was happening. Unable to condemn county property, the directors could only fume.

Largely as a result of this coup, the harbor district was dissolved by the voters at the next election, and the immediate threat to the lagoon was lifted. As further protection, Audubon Canyon Ranch deeded a mile of lagoon tidelands to the county as part of a waterfront park. These actions were catalysts inducing the county to make further purchases to acquire the entire lagoon shoreline from Bolinas to the ranch.

THE FREEWAY MENACE

There remain other threats to the ranch and the lagoon area, however. State Division of Highways plans call for converting tortuous State Highway 1 to a freeway. The result would be six lanes of traffic roaring between the ranch and the birds' feeding area in the lagoon—almost certain death to the heronry and the end of hopes to maintain this natural enclave of hills and lagoon free of urbanization. Repeated attempts by the state to proceed with this plan have thus far been staved off by vehement protest from the public and Marin County officials, citing the damage to the rookery. One proposed alternative is a "parkway" along the top of Bolinas Ridge. Although this route would by-pass the ranch and the lagoon, it would bisect Tamalpais State Park, a prospect no conservationist can contemplate with equanimity. In the new era of ecology, there can be no excuse for any major expansion of the road system in this fragile scenic area.

While these campaigns were taking place, the ranch itself was being converted from an abandoned dairy into an environmental education center. The old milking barn was converted into a well-designed museum of the geology, history, and ecology of the Bolinas basin. Some five thousand youngsters in classes from throughout the San Francisco Bay Area visit the ranch annually for regular classes in nature education. Volunteer Canyon, over the ridge from the rookery, is being developed as a residence camp in ecology. The Conservation Foundation of Washington, D.C., and the California Department of Fish and Game have made special studies recommending preservation of the entire basin in a near-natural state.

THE TOLL OF THE POISONS

The greatest potential threat to the rookery and the wildlife of the entire basin is the impact of pesticides. The egrets and possibly the great blue herons are evidently vulnerable to the same poisons that are causing reproductive failures among other fish-eating birds, such as the pelicans. Concentration of DDT and other pesticides through the food chain results in egg shells too thin to bear the weight of the parents.

At the rookery, in recent years, about half of the total number of egret eggs have failed to hatch for this reason. The herons have not been as seriously affected. Laboratory analysis of dead egrets has revealed dangerous quantities of both mercury and DDT and lethal quantities of dieldrin, a chlorinated hydrocarbon increasingly used for agricultural purposes to replace DDT. The birds evidently picked up the poisons not around the ranch but in the San Francisco Bay Delta area, where many of them spend the months from July to January, and where the waters are highly polluted with agri-cultural, domestic, and industrial wastes.

The best hope for reducing environmental poisons would seem to lie in informing the public about the values at stake. Audubon Canyon Ranch, attracting twenty thousand visitors a year, is a prime example of how to reach the public with this message. They come principally on weekends at the height of the nesting season,

March 1 to July 5, There is no admission charge, although most of them make voluntary contributions. Probably most of the visitors have had no previous concern with wildlife; they come to the ranch out of curiosity as they would attend any tourist attraction. There, in the museum and bookshop, in informational pamphlets, in naturalist talks, and in the awesome view of the rookery itself, they are exposed to the values of the natural world in an atmosphere of respect and understanding. On some spring weekends more than a thousand people make the short pilgrimage up the canyon. At the overlook, even small children stand quietly, wide-eyed at the avian spectacle. Not the least part of the experience at Audubon Canyon Ranch is a heightened sense of wonder.

On Tuesday, January 19, 1971, the day the volunteers stood at Bolinas channel and fought to repel the deadly black tide, twenty pairs of great blue herons appeared over the high ridge, circled the canyon, and sailed, spread-winged, into the redwoods—the first of the advance guard to arrive at the ancestral meeting place and begin the immemorial ceremonies attending a new cycle of life.

7

Road on the Continent's Edge

THIS IS NOT a road for the fainthearted. It swerves along cliffs high above the rocky surf, skirts deep canyons where streams plunge to the ocean, crosses the rumpled and fractured landscape of the continent's greatest earthquake fault.

It is not a road for anyone in a hurry. The compulsive speeder will fret and fume at its meandering route, its hairpin turns, its dilatory way of circling a ridge instead of slicing through it.

This is a road for the lover of adventure and spectacle. When Jack London came this way in 1911 behind a team of four spirited horses, he wrote of the "poppy-blown cliffs, with the sea thundering in the sheer depths hundreds of feet below and the Golden Gate opening up ahead, disclosing smoky San Francisco on her many hills. . . . It was on this part of the drive that I decided at last I was learning real mountain driving. To confess the truth, for delicious titillation of one's nerve, I have since driven over no mountain road that was worse, or better, rather, than that piece."

This is a road for people temperamentally able to drive slowly, to stop at turnoffs and unhurriedly enjoy panoramas of mountains and sea, to contemplate the fabled past, to absorb slowly the lessons of this solemn landscape and the majesty of its natural wonders.

THE SEAWARD OASIS

For fifty miles through Marin County from near the Golden Gate to the Sonoma line, California State Highway 1 traverses a land scarcely more built up than in Jack London's day. Marin's urban sprawl has confined itself mainly to the hills and valleys

along US 101 and has thus far ignored as inaccessible the shoreline
country beyond this outermost ridge of the Coast Range.

The road is deceptively misnamed; this is no highway, and
you'd better start out with a good breakfast and a full tank of gas,
because the villages are few and small. About five miles north of
the Golden Gate Bridge, on US 101, Highway 1 branches off to
the right, passes under 101 at the Richardson Bay Bridge skirts
the north side of Tamalpais Valley, and climbs into a dense forest
of eucalyptus planted on these hills around the turn of the century
when the Australian tree was planted throughout California in a
futile effort to promote it as a profitable source of timber. On
other slopes are deep hillside grasses, wild flowers in the spring,
and luxuriant groves of live oaks, laurels, buckeyes, and madroños.
At the summit of the ridge, just after the Tamalpais and Muir
Woods road branches off to the right, the landscape along Highway 1 undergoes a profound change. Now, suddenly, you are on the
steep coastal slope of Marin, a land possessed by the sea and its
winds. Trees are almost nonexistent; the chaparral is low and
clings to the ground; the mood of the landscape shifts from lush
to austere.

However there is one oasis on this somber seaward slope. Green
Gulch, to the left of the curving road and at times almost straight
down, was purchased in the 1960's by cattleman George Wheelwright. Irrigation turned dry meadows into deep green pastures
for his prize Hereford bulls. At Wheelwright's initiative, his ranch
became the first agricultural preserve under a new state law to
protect farmlands. In 1971, he philanthropically donated most
of the ranch to the Nature Conservancy, to be preserved for future
generations.

At the bottom of Green Gulch, where it merges with Franks
Valley, is the hamlet of Muir Beach. Redwood Creek, flowing
down from Muir Woods National Monument, forms a brackish
lagoon behind the beach. On extreme high tides, waves wash into
the lagoon, and after winter storms the creek rises high enough
to break through to the ocean, allowing salmon and steelhead to
swim up into Muir Woods to spawn. Muir Beach is protected from
the powerful northwest winds by a high ridge, which Highway 1
climbs in a series of switchbacks. At the summit of the ridge you
are simultaneously struck by a startling panorama of the rugged
coastline and by the wind, which often blows over the ridge with
such force that horse-and-buggy riders in the old days used to
call this point "Cape Horn."

RELICS OF A VANISHED LAND

From the ridge a quarter mile beyond Cape Horn you look out on the magnificent sweep of the Gulf of the Farallones, probably the finest view along the entire highway. On a clear day the craggy rocks of the Southeast Farallon, surmounted by a lighthouse, are visible twenty-five miles offshore; and farther north you can see the even more barren, uninhabited Northwest Farallon. Up the coast Duxbury Point juts seaward, and just beyond it is the greater headland of Point Reyes.

Here, as on Mount Diablo, you peer into the geologic past. The Farallones and Point Reyes, unlike any other visible feature on this shoreline, are composed principally of granite, a clue to their origin. In past geologic epochs, when this coast had not yet risen from the ocean, that granite terrain was part of an ancient land mass known as Salinia, hundreds of miles long. Over the epochs Salinia was eroded away by rain and wind until there was nothing left but these headlands and bleak rocks in the sea, relics of a vanished landscape. These hills on which you stand are much younger and were elevated above sea level at a time when Salinia was already old and eroded.

On the floor of the ocean in front of you, a couple of miles seaward of the surf-lashed cliffs below, is an ocean-floor segment of the San Andreas Fault. The San Andreas' mighty lurch on the morning of April 18, 1906, was merely the latest of hundreds of major jolts along this crack that extends north and south for at least six hundred miles from Cape Mendocino to the Gulf of California. The crust of the earth is in motion here between earthquakes as well. The lands you see beyond the fault—the Farallones, Duxbury Point, Inverness Ridge, and Point Reyes—are all moving ponderously northward. Don't expect to see them move; the average rate is about two inches a year. But many geologists believe that this motion is building up strains in the rock that will someday—tomorrow or a century from now—fracture with another such jolt as that of 1906.

THE RISING MESA

Highway 1 continues along the steep western flank of Mount Tamalpais, several hundred feet above the sea cliffs and rocky shore, turning sharply inland at two points where creeks have carved deep canyons into the mountainside. One is Cold Stream, the other Lone Tree Gulch, once a horseback route down the mountain. For several miles the road traverses the "melange"—that jumble of rocks crushed and mixed by friction where the tectonic plates of the ocean and the continent meet and grind against each other. A mile beyond Lone Tree Gulch, the road cuts through some veins of serpentine, a shiny gray-green rock in some places the color of jade. Just beyond the serpentine the road crosses Steep Ravine; up the canyon to the right, sheltered from the coastal winds, redwoods grow alongside a cascading creek, the only place in Marin and one of the few places along the California coast where the big trees come down close to the ocean.

A trail leads from here up through splendid groves, past ferny dells and waterfalls to Pantoll Camp. Steep Ravine is probably the route followed in 1793 by the first explorer of this region, Lieutenant Felipe de Goycoechea, who thought the redwoods were pines and regarded the groves with some disgust as an obstacle to his explorations.

Before the road drops down to sea level at Stinson Beach, it affords views of the shoreline, Bolinas Lagoon and Duxbury Point. The long sandspit curving north from Stinson Beach, separating Bolinas Lagoon from the ocean, is a prime example of the way the ocean tends to dam off the mouths of bays and inlets. The waves, perennially assaulting the cliffs, batter the rocks and grind them into sand, which is transported along the coast and deposited as beaches. Rather than following the indentations of the shoreline, the beaches continue in the general direction of the coast, and the waves deposit them offshore there, grain by grain, creating sand spits. At the far end of the Stinson spit, the waters of Bolinas Lagoon continue to flow in and out on the tides like a river, keeping the channel open.

Just beyond the channel you can see the village of Bolinas and above and behind it the flat expanse of Bolinas Mesa, which also tells a story of the geologic past. The mesa was created by wave action at a time when the sea was higher or the land was lower. The battering surf always tends to plane off the land, carving a flat terrace below the sea cliffs. Since the crust of the earth is sporadically rising and falling in response to pressures far below, the rising of a section of the coastline elevates the terrace above sea level and leaves it high and dry. At the upper end of Bolinas Mesa, where it meets the rising terrain of Inverness Ridge, you can see the steep slopes that were once sea cliffs, now partially broken down by centuries of erosion. The mesa itself has been eroded by streams, and runoff from the hills has deposited sediment on top of it, so that it is no longer entirely level.

FIRE IN THE SURF

Below the seaward edge of the mesa you can see a half-mile stretch of rough water at high tide and exposed rocks at low tide. This is Duxbury Reef, where the ship *Duxbury* piled up in 1849. The gravelly reef is a wave terrace, in the process of formation, and someday may be elevated above the sea to form another flat land like the mesa above. Oil wells were drilled in this vicinity around the turn of the century but later abandoned as unproductive. For many years a jet of natural gas spouted from the reef, and fishermen would light it, according to legend, to cook their meals by the flame, which would blaze until extinguished by high tide. No trace of it can be found today.

The view from this section of the road above Stinson Beach is one that seems to be different each time you drive by. The surf may be high or low, forming a white fringe to the long curving spit. The water offshore may be several colors simultaneously, ranging from aquamarine indicating clear deep water to a milky brown where the outflowing waters of the lagoon stain the surface with collected sediments and effluents from the land. Offshore the swells sweep around Duxbury Point and bend shoreward in admirable refracted curves, as light is curved by a lens. At other times the scene below may be hidden in swirling vapors which move aside in places to reveal tantalizing glimpses of surf, beach, and lagoon. Sometimes, when the fog along the entire coast is low, you can drive the length of this road looking down on the white roof of a sea of vapor as if you were in a plane above a layer of clouds.

Beyond Stinson Beach, Highway 1 follows the edge of Bolinas Lagoon, winding in and out barely above high-tide level. The road was even lower when Jack London made his trip in 1911; he noted that the wheels of his rig were sloshing through the water a good part of the time. From the lagoon the rolling slopes of Bolinas Ridge rise nearly two thousand feet into the sky.

At the level mouths of some of the canyons leading back to the ridge are neat white farmhouses, including the one at Audubon Canyon Ranch. Ranchers have run cattle on these hills for generations. The tidal flats of Bolinas Lagoon are ideal habitats for shore birds and water birds, and if you drive by here on an ebb tide you can see—along with the egrets and great blue herons—sanderlings and willets, curlews and godwits, moving in graceful patterns of flight or probing the sand for succulent crustaceans, ducks of many varieties, geese, cormorants, gulls, and big brown pelicans.

THE LEGEND OF THE LIME KILNS

Near the head of the lagoon two roads come in, one from either side, the Bolinas Ridge road on the right (often closed) and the road to the town of Bolinas on the left. The highway, continuing north, leaves the lagoon here and enters the long, narrow Olema Valley, a lush region of hills and swales, woods, meadows, and an occasional dairy farm. The valley was created over the eons by erosion along the San Andreas Fault, which emerges from Bolinas Lagoon and crosses the land to Tomales Bay.

A quarter mile beyond the intersection, at the mouth of a small canyon on the right, is the site of vanished Woodville (once known as Dogtown), a center of lumber activity in the 1850's, when the surrounding hills and valleys were logged off to supply wood for the burgeoning city of San Francisco. Woodville was also a mining town; up the canyon behind it a mile-long road led to a copper mine dating from 1863. The mine never produced enough to be commercially profitable, although some ore was taken out as late as 1918. On the left of the highway at the site of Woodville is a eucalyptus grove containing a line of trees that is offset thirteen and a half feet as a result of the big shake in 1906.

Among other signs of the San Andreas farther up the valley are "sag ponds," where depressions created by earthquakes collect runoff water, and two streams flowing in opposite directions on either side of the road. To the right, Olema Creek flows north to Tomales Bay and to the left Pine Gulch Creek flows south to Bolinas Lagoon. Both creeks follow old rifts in the fault zone.

About five miles beyond the head of the lagoon, at a point where the road crosses Olema Creek, you pass on the left three big lime kilns, out of sight on private property. For many years these kilns, long abandoned and disintegrating, were the subject of speculative legends. It was believed that they had been built by the Russians, who had an outpost at nearby Bodega around 1812. Major pieces of evidence were two big Douglas firs growing out of the kilns, obviously from seed deposited since the kilns were abandoned. An accurate count of the tree rings a few years ago, however, indicated that they began growing about 1869, and historical research turned up the fact that the kilns had been built by Americans around 1850.

ICE AGE BAY

Just beyond the village of Olema a turnoff to the left leads to the Bear Valley Ranch, now headquarters of the Point Reyes National Seashore. The road crosses the rumpled-up landscape of the fault zone, and just opposite the park headquarters are four concrete markers set up after 1906 to measure movement of the land. A well-posted trail from here displays other signs of the fault. The ranch immediately south of Bear Valley is the site of one of the most famous legends of 1906; a cow is said to have fallen into a crack which opened up in the ground, then closed, leaving only the tail protruding.

The Point Reyes National Seashore will eventually include most of the land west of Highway 1. There is an excellent public trail from through Bear Valley to the ocean and back along a high ridge. Beyond park headquarters, this side road joins Sir Francis Drake Highway, leading along the west shore of Tomales Bay to the village of Inverness among a forest of bishop pines, to Tomales Bay State Park, across a treeless rolling moorland brilliant with flowers in the spring, to the lighthouse at Point Reyes, and to a beach at Drakes Bay where the swashbuckling English sea captain is believed to have landed on his voyage around the world in 1579, two centuries before the first Spanish settlements in California.

Along Highway 1, two miles beyond the Bear Valley turnoff, Sir Francis Drake Highway branches off to the left, and it is on this stretch of road at the head of Tomales Bay that the greatest displacement was measured in the 1906 earthquake, when the road was offset by twenty feet. Tomales Bay, fourteen miles long and only a mile wide, is itself a continuation of the San Andreas Fault zone. The bay was created when part of the fault zone was invaded by rising sea level at the end of the last ice age.

Highway 1, passing Point Reyes Station, traverses a broad shelf of land with the bay on one side and the rugged peak of Black Mountain and Bolinas Ridge on the other. Like Bolinas Mesa, this shelf is a marine terrace, carved out by waves before the land rose and left it dry. The Northern Pacific Railroad, built in the 1870's, once provided the only transportation between the ranches and villages of this coast and San Francisco. It has been abandoned for many decades, but you can see the old railroad embankment along the shore below, cutting across the mouth of the bays and inlets.

THE PINES OF SALINIA

Like Bolinas Lagoon, the marshes and shores of Tomales Bay are a prime bird habitat—egrets, herons, terns, gulls, pelicans, sandpipers of a dozen species. Hawks and buzzards hover overhead; you may catch a glimpse of an eagle; and the fields in spring are full of robins, redwing blackbirds, and meadowlarks. In a national Audubon bird count a few years ago the region centering on this bay was second in the nation in the number of bird species tallied.

Mammals are abundant here too, including the usual squirrels and rabbits and an occasional deer, and if you keep your eyes on the bay you may glimpse a seal or porpoise breaking the surface. Long rows of stakes in the water mark the location of commercial oyster beds and act as fences protecting them from predators, mainly skates and rays. The oysters seeding the beds are imported from Japan.

Across the bay, sometimes half hidden by wraiths of fog from the ocean, are intriguing coves, white sandy beaches, and pine forests climbing to the ridge of the peninsula. The San Andreas Fault marks a botanical as well as a geological boundary. The trees in the hills to the east are principally redwoods; west of the fault the forests are composed of Douglas fir and here along Tomales Bay the relatively rare bishop pines, which grow only on the gigantic soil of areas that were once part of the "lost continent" of Salinia.

A few miles beyond the town of Marshall, Highway 1 leaves Tomales Bay and follows Keyes Creek, which seems to be surprisingly voluminous until you realize this is tide water; over the millenniums rising sea level (and possibly the subsidence of the land) has inundated several miles of the canyon carved out by the creek in earlier times. Beyond the town of Tomales the highway follows low barren hills, bright with lupine and poppies in the spring, and the valleys of several tidal streams. Through this low *estero* country, summer sea breezes enter the inland regions tributary to San Francisco Bay, lowering midsummer temperatures around Petaluma. The last of these drowned valleys contains the Estero Americano, where American fur traders occasionally anchored in the early 1800's. The *estero* is the boundary between Marin and Sonoma counties. Here the road makes a sharp turn to the left and goes through the village of Valley Ford, where travelers of the 1860's forded the *estero*.

DRAKE AT BODEGA: PRO AND CON

Seven miles west of Valley Ford, Highway 1 rounds a bend and you suddenly confront a shoreline that is purely and utterly classical. There ahead of you shining in the sun is a habor that Sophocles might have seen long ago on the Aegean. A long white sandspit with a curve like a gull's wing encloses a mile-long bay and sweeps seaward toward the great looming eminence of Bodega Head. Fishing boats are moored off the village of Bodega Bay and pass through the channel below the head to the open ocean.

In October of 1775, Juan Francisco Bodega y Cuadra anchored under this head in his vessel the *Sonora.* He was evidently so delighted to find this snug harbor on the rugged northern coastline that he named it for himself, violating Spanish precedent that required the naming of geographical features for saints or holy days. Conceivably, however, he was not the first European to see this place. Historian Henry Raup Wagner was convinced that Bodega Bay was the controversial "lost harbor" of Francis Drake. Although most historians believe that Drake's harbor was not here but at Drakes Bay under Point Reyes, Wagner's argument has a certain logic: Drake was sailing south along the coast, seeking a snug harbor to repair his ship, the *Golden Hind,* for the long voyage home across the Pacific. Having found this harbor, why would he have gone farther?

This place has changed little since the days of Bodega—or Drake. In the spring the meadowlarks call across the green rolling hills behind the bay; the wild surf still breaks on the cliffs of the massive headland and on Bodega Rock just offshore; the combers roll in long curves to the sandspit; and today's clam diggers probe the sand flats at low tide, as did the Coast Miwok Indians whose discarded shells are still abundant along the beach.

RUSSIAN OUTPOST

If you have time, explore the coast north of Bodega, where the road again traverses the old marine terrace. Below it on the shoreline at intervals are the cliffs and beaches of Sonoma Coast State Park. Six miles beyond Bodega the shelf broadens, and you can see remnants of ancient geologic epochs—big rock outcrops jutting incongruously from the flat shelf, old sea stacks carved by the surf before the land rose and left them high and dry. Then over a rise you suddenly look down into a deep canyon, the most dramatic meeting of river and ocean on this coast. The Russian River has cut this cleft in the Coast Range, maintaining its course through the slowly rising mountains over a period of a million years.

Thirteen miles to the north on this road is Fort Ross, once the outpost of the empire from which the river took its name. There the czars had a foothold in the New World early in the last century and hoped to extend their domain down the coast. Fortunately for Americans, the Russian empire was on the decline and badly overextended. Six years before the discovery of gold at Sutter's Mill in the Sierra foothills, the Russians sold Fort Ross to John Sutter and relinquished all claims to California.

On Highway 1 you drive through history as well as past geologic epochs. Such time spans oblige you to ponder the past and wonder about the future. Will this wild coast become another extension of suburbia, as the metropolis around San Francisco Bay spills over the Coast Range to the ocean? Will Highway 1 become a six- or eight-land freeway where you no longer are forced to steer slowly around the curves but can hurtle down the concrete at seventy-five miles an hour past a continuous strip of gas stations, motels, tract houses, and parking lots?

If so, it will still be possible to take comfort in the thought that ultimately nature always prevails. In geologic time the coast may rise again, exposing a new marine terrace as beautiful as this one is today, or it may sink below sea level, inundating all signs of man's depredations. It is even conceivable that men will somehow acquire the wisdom to preserve this superb shoreline as it is. But the time span avilable for attaining that wisdom is very, very short.

8

The March of the Monarchs

WE SAW the first migrating monarchs of the season at the autumnal equinox from the cliff over the ocean at Bolinas. The big butterflies were flying along the cliff top between two eucalyptus trees, singly and in pairs, orange-brown flecks like bright pieces of autumn sunshine against the dark green of the eucalyptus. Below the cliff a blaze of afternoon light welled up from the ocean as the tide ebbed from the rocks, revealing the broad terrace carved by the waves over the millenniums.

In the sky as in the ocean the tides were flowing—tides of life moving south with the sun. This was the season of the winged migrations, and to observe the great flights of waterfowl, of insects, of land birds moving down the autumn sky is to feel the pull of an ancestral tide in the bloodstream as well. Until very recently in the history of the human race, the doings of man were regulated by the same seasonal influences that govern the annual southward movements of the flocks—the coolness in the air, the falling of the leaves, the lengthening shadows at noon.

Of all the mass movements of life taking place at this season, none is more remarkable than the flight of the monarch butterflies —one of the great shows of the autumn. As we watched the spectacle from the cliff at Bolinas, it was taking place simultaneously all over the woods and fields of Marin County and along the California coast. Trees and chaparral were alive with flashes of color and motion as thousands of monarchs stopped en route to drink the nectar of the fall flowers.

The flight had begun a month or two earlier at some unknown place far to the northeast, perhaps hundreds of miles away. A drop in temperature to around fifty-five had given the monarchs the first sign of coming winter, and the advance guard had set out to the southwest, followed by increasing numbers every day. They come to the California coast with the autumnal smells—the damp aroma of the earth drying in the sun after the first rains, the alternate odors of salt and sage as the breezes shift from landward to seaward and back again.

THE LONG FLIGHT HOME

Unlike the strong-winged birds that beat their way purposefully southward at this season, the fragile-looking butterflies flit in zigzag patterns, rising and falling through the air, as if they would be swept miles off course by a slight breeze. Yet they seem to know exactly where they are going. The monarchs we saw at Bolinas had almost reached their destination. They followed a regular route along the cliff between the two trees. A few hundred yards farther they entered a circle of eucalyptus, the ultimate goal of their long trek: There, clinging to the leaves of the trees in long festoons, were hundreds of thousands of monarchs who had arrived earlier, hanging in such numbers that the limbs were bowed down with their weight.

For as long as anyone can remember, the butterflies have come to Bolinas—and other locations along the coast—at this season. How they find their way to these precise trees is one of the greatest mysteries of animal migration. Unlike migrating birds, which could conceivably navigate from memory, having followed the flock south in previous years, none of the monarchs has ever been over their migratory route. The life span of the monarch is scarcely a year, and each autumn a completely new generation follows the trail of its ancestors down the continent to gather in this ancient rendezvous.

Conceivably the butterflies have a built-in sensitivity to certain kinds of light, causing them to fly in a general southwesterly direction in the fall. But what landmarks they use to follow a route they have never seen to the identical trees where the previous generations spent the winter—this is a mystery on which scientists can only speculate.

Mrs. Lewis Pepper, member of a pioneer Bolinas family, recalls that the butterflies once roosted in the Monterey cypress trees around her house near the center of town, but for the past decade or so have inexplicably abandoned the cypresses and occupied the eucalyptuses a few hundred yards away, closer to the ocean.

They rest for the winter, semidormant, rousing only on warm

days to gorge themselves with nectar in nearby gardens. Hanging on the trees upside down, they form well-camouflaged gray-brown clusters, resembling dead leaves. In relatively warm weather they spread out on the branches; in cold weather they huddle closer. Rain has little effect on them, but gale-force winds can tear them from the trees, to which they return when the wind dies. In extremely cold weather some of them freeze and fall to the ground.

THE BUTTERFLY PARADE

The same phenomenon has been observed at some thirty other locations along the California coast at Bodega Bay, for example, Stinson Beach, Mill Valley, Big Sur, and particularly in Pacific Grove on the Monterey Peninsula, where the "Butterfly Trees" are a major tourist attraction. The city of Pacific Grove has an ordinance providing a five-hundred-dollar fine or six months in jail—or both—for any person who may "molest or interfere with in any way the peaceful occupancy of the Monarch Butterflies on their annual visit to the City of Pacific Grove . . . in whatever spot they may choose to stop in."

Although the Pacific Grove butterflies have seldom been deliberately molested, the increasing cutting of nearby trees for construction purposes may remove the natural windbreak and have harmful effects on the colony. The arrival of the monarchs each year is an event in Pacific Grove hailed by community festivities, and school children stage an annual butterfly parade. Flying south down the California coast, the monarchs reach Santa Cruz and face the open water of Monterey Bay. Rather than take the long route around the shore of the bay, they instinctively launch out across miles of water, heading directly for Point Piños at Pacific Grove.

In case there is fog on the water, they cannily wait on the shore. Meanwhile reinforcements arrive from the north. By the time the fog lifts, they have accumulated in great flocks which then head south, flying low on the water. Fishermen miles from shore have sometimes been surrounded by a cloud of the brown and orange insects.

The monarchs usually pass Point Piños late in the afternoon and head for the traditional roosting places. When they arrive in the vicinity they are guided to the exact trees by a signal from the earlier arrivals, who flutter their wings to welcome the newcomers. Others arrive from the south, perhaps having reached the coast via the Carmel Valley. By late November the total number on the trees may reach two million.

Although some residents of Pacific Grove believe the monarchs make their way over the mountains and prairies for a thousand miles or more because of the salubrious climate of that community, actually many of the butterflies head farther south to Southern California and Mexico, where the weather is so warm they do not even bother to cluster in the trees but fly freely all winter.

There is little reliable evidence as to where the hibernating butterflies come from. Monarchs tagged in Toronto, Canada, have been found in the Gulf States and northern Mexico, some two thousand miles away. However, they need moist climates, and it is doubtful that they would normally cross the hot, dry basins between the Rockies and the Sierra.

WANDERER FROM THE TROPICS

The world's champion monarch-tagger is probably Robert Brownlee of San Jose, a specialist in insect chemistry. He has placed white tags, requesting return by finders, on the wings of some tens of thousands of the big insects. Most of Brownlee's work takes place in the butterfly trees at Natural Bridges State Park north of Santa Cruz. About one hundred tagged monarchs have been caught and returned. The most distant capture point was Santa Barbara.

Brownlee is convinced that the monarchs do not necessarily roost in the same trees all winter. An individual may stay in one colony for a couple of weeks, then during moderate weather flutter on to other colonies. How do they find the same trees year after year? Brownlee believes that they pick the trees that offer the most hospitable locations—near the ocean for moderate temperatures and high humidity but sheltered from strong winds.

"Nearly any large eucalyptus grove along the coast with those conditions will have a monarch colony," he says, "although they also roost in Monterey pines and Monterey cypresses. It may be that some of their floral odor—a sex attractant left by the male —remains on the trees from year to year, attracting the next generation."

Brownlee points out that the monarch is a relatively recent immigrant from the tropics. It is habitually a wanderer and during the millenniums since the Ice Age has spread throughout the continent. It still is unable to endure cold northern temperatures, however, and comes south and west in the fall to find the warmest climates, clustering in colonies for further warmth.

In early spring, the warmth of the northward-moving sun begins to have its effect on the monarchs. Those wintering in Mexico may begin to move in January, only a few days after the winter solstice. The semidormant monarchs roosting in Northern California begin to stir with the first warmth of spring. Unusually warm weather will rouse them as early as the end of February, but normally the awakening comes with the warm days of March. The females leave first, hastening north to deposit their eggs on the leaves of the milkweed plant.

Then, having given birth to another generation, the adults fade and die by the end of June. By late September the autumn air over the tawny hills of the Coast Range is again illuminated with flashes of orange-brown color as the migratory march of the monarchs is set off by the southward movement of the sun, the chill in the air, the falling of the leaves at the equinox. Stand on the cliff at Bolinas then, above the ocean, and participate in the tides of migration, as the planet tilts away from the sun and the shadows lengthen day by day toward the winter solstice.

9

South from San Francisco: The Suburban Range

THE HILLS of San Francisco are the northernmost extension of the Santa Cruz Mountains, a remarkable region of rumpled earth extending for seventy-five miles south to Monterey Bay. Drive down Skyline Boulevard along the crest of the range and you will be reminded of the Blue Ridge Skyline Drive in Virginia or the Taconic State Parkway of New York. A dozen miles south of San Francisco you leave the suburbs and skirt the long lakes of San Andreas and Crystal Springs, where afternoon sunlight scintillates from the dark water and dense forests of Douglas fir and redwood rise from the far shores. Farther south there are lookout points where the bay and its cities are visible below for fifty miles like a vision of the promised land from Mount Pisgah.

Gaze westward on a summer afternoon and you may see the ocean fog moving like a white flood through the canyons below. Turn west at Saratoga Gap and you descend into the ferny redwood canyons of Big Basin and the steep valley of the San Lorenzo River where a creek flows through the dining room at Brookdale Lodge and summer cabins cluster around the towns of Boulder Creek and Ben Lomond and Felton.

Take Highway 1, paralleling Skyline down the coast, and you get a different view of the range, beginning with the ridge south of Daly City where you can look for miles down the coast past headlands, cliffs, beaches, and white breakers extending south to Pedro Point. Below Pacifica you edge cautiously along the cliff-bound stretch of road at the Devil's Slide, peering several hundred feet down to the roaring surf. Then comes Half Moon Bay, the sweeping curve of San Gregorio Creek where it flows through rolling dunes to the ocean, the long rhythmic rows of artichokes and Brussels sprouts in the fields down the long, flat shoreline terraces, the views back into the mountains where farms are bordered by steep canyon walls and forests of redwood. Another aspect of the range is visible from the east; from Bayshore Freeway late on summer afternoons you can see colossal combers of fog rolling over the fir-tufted ridges, backlighted by the lowering sun.

EL CAMINO REAL

Since the days of the explorers, who came northward up the coast, this range has been the southern gateway to the Bay Area. Portolá and his scurvy-racked men in October of 1769 took several days to trudge up the coastal slopes of the range to San Pedro Valley (in today's Pacifica), where they camped and next day discovered San Francisco Bay.

En route he had named a creek for the Holy Cross, Arroyo de Santa Cruz; the name was later applied to the mission established at the southern end of the mountains and eventually to the range itself. The year after Portolá's trek, his assistant, Pedro Fages, decided to probe the Bay Area again; this time he found a route easier than the hard scramble along the coast. He skirted the east side of the range, up the Santa Clara Valley. Captain Fernando Rivera in 1774 followed part of the same route, but, to avoid the sloughs of the bay, he pushed into the mountains and up the long valley he named San Andreas, now partly filled by the San Andreas and Crystal Springs reservoirs. (It was here a little more than a century later that geologist Andrew Lawson discovered traces of the earthquake fault and named it for the valley). When Captain Juan Bautista de Anza scouted the region in 1776 seeking a site for the planned mission and presidio of San Francisco, he stayed along the eastern foot of the range, and today's El Camino Real follows his trail into the city. Similarly, the four main routes across the range from east to west follow the Spanish trails used during the mission era over the mountains to Half Moon Bay, San Gregorio, Pescadero, and Santa Cruz.

The enterprising Americans found wealth in the range—timber in the forests and limestone for cement. They found another kind of wealth as well—scenery. Down the easily accessible eastern foothills the bonanza millionaires built their palaces, such as Ralston's mansion at Belmont, now the College of Notre Dame. Back in the mountains on the old land-grant ranches San Franciscans built vacation cabins in the redwoods, particularly in the valley of the San Lorenzo River. For more than a century city residents have escaped summer fogs and urban tensions by retreating to sanctuaries in these folded mountains.

Above the redwoods in the protected canyons are forests of Douglas fir, blanketing the upper slopes. On high sandy tracts that were once beaches (before the elevation of the range) grow stands of ponderosa pine. In the entire range there are only four small groves of the rare Santa Cruz cypress. Like the equally scarce Monterey cypress, which grows only at Carmel, this tree is a vestige of forests that once extended over far greater areas.

THE MOVING MOUNTAINS

Geologically, the region has at various times in the past been sea bottom, an island, and a peninsula of varying shapes—all stages readily visible to the geologist in the rocks protruding from the surface. A great portion of the range's bedrock is sandstone and shale laid down as sand and mud on the bottom of ancient seas and lifted when the mountains rose above sea level. But over large areas, such as Montara Mountain in the north and Ben Lomond Mountain in the south, the bedrock is granite. It tells a surprising story.

The granite is all west of the San Andreas Fault, which slices along the eastern slopes. Along this rift the range is splitting asunder. Just as it is doing north of the Golden Gate, the land west of the fault is moving ponderously northward about two inches a year. This motion has been going on for many millions of years. One clue to the time scale is the granite, which does not appear anywhere along the east side of the fault except in the Tehachapi Range, about three hundred miles to the south. Some scientists, matching up the granite on both sides, maintain that this land has drifted up from Southern California and in time will move on toward Alaska.

During the latter part of this northward drift, the range has evidently continued to rise, and evidence of previous landscapes, developed when the range was lower, are clearly visible. The most obvious is the same marine terrace encountered north of the Golden Gate, that flat coastal strip where Highway 1 and towns and farms are located along many parts of the California shoreline. Traces of the old sea cliff carved by the waves appear above the terrace east of the highway. If you look closely up the ridges at certain points along the coast, you will see signs of even earlier terraces in giant stairsteps, each created by the waves at periods when the range paused a while in its upward growth and the ocean had time to gouge away the edge of the land.

Higher up in the mountains, where you might expect sharp ridges and peaks, there oddly appear nearly flat expanses of forest and meadow. These are old erosion surfaces formed at a time when the mountains were much lower; the land was almost level, tending toward a peneplain, then was lifted when the mountains rose. The largest of these ancient landscapes is around Bonny Doon about twelve hundred feet above the sea, some eight miles northwest of Santa Cruz.

BIG BASIN

In terms of human time, the future of the range is uncertain. If it had been possible to act some years ago, this entire range might have been a national park, like the Great Smokies, which it resembles in many ways. But more and larger state parks, plus open-space zoning for the agricultural lands, could still save a large portion of the range from the kind of destructive development that has mutilated other ranges near large urban areas.

The best-known of the state parks is Big Basin, the oldest unit of California's park system. In 1900 an artist named Andrew P. Hill, commissioned by an English magazine to photograph some of California's big trees, became alarmed at the depredations of the loggers throughout the Santa Cruz Range. In May of that year he led thirty people over a logging road to Slippery Rock at the edge of the valley known as Big Basin, where they explored for three days and watched the loggers moving toward the floor of the valley. Camping under the redwoods, they formed the Sempervirens Club and planned a campaign to save the trees by state purchase. That was the beginning of the first save-the-redwood effort anywhere and the first attempt to induce the state to buy large areas of private land for public purposes. The result was to make Californians aware of their redwood heritage and the threat to its existence. After a hard-fought two-and-a-half-year campaign, the state bought the first block of 3800 acres from the Big Basin Lumber Company for $250,000. And so began California's unprecedented state park system.

THE REAL ESTATE INVASION

Over the decades Big Basin, now twelve thousand acres, has become the most popular of California's Redwood State parks—too popular for its own good. More than half-a-million people annually visit the park, staring at such giants as the Santa Clara Tree, listed as the largest-diameter redwood in the world. But intensively used campgrounds in the groves and large areas of blacktop for roads and parking have caused the big trees to deteriorate. And the park has never been completed. Large areas of the basin, including prime virgin groves and upstream areas vital for protection, remain outside the boundaries, susceptible to logging. The boundaries should be extended to include these areas and down the lush valley of Waddell Creek to the ocean. Parking lots, campgrounds, and other visitor facilities could be moved out of the major groves and dispersed into these and other areas.

A few miles away from this oldest state park is one of the newest, Castle Rock, at the crest of the range 3200 feet above sea level, a labyrinthine outcrop of Chico sandstone where amateur rock climbers practice belays and delighted youngsters scramble through the honeycombed aeolian caves. Massive contorted trunks of madroño and oak grip the rock, and it is surrounded by a prime mixed forest.

There are other state parks in the range—Portola, Butano, Cowell, some state beaches and a few county parks. These, however, are but patches of land compared to the whole magnificent range, and real estate developments are moving rapidly into the mountains from all sides. A proposed dam on Pescadero Creek and planned freeways down and across the range would make urbanization inevitable. It is too late to make the range a national park, but there are other ways of preventing its destruction, given the will to do so. Meantime it remains one of the finest natural areas in any American metropolitan region, inviting exploration and enjoyment of its forests and canyons, its rolling grasslands and meadows, its streams and lakes and long, wild shoreline.

10

The Western Shore

MORE THAN any other American metropolis, San Francisco is a city of the sea. Other Pacific Coast cities are sheltered from the full impact of the ocean by peninsulas or islands or shoreline indentations. East Coast cities, owing to the motion of the great air masses from west to east in these latitudes, are climatically influenced far more by the continent than by the Atlantic. But in San Francisco not only are the ships of the world visible from its hills; the currents of the ocean and bay flow past it on three sides; the salt winds and fogs sweep through its streets; the long Pacific combers perennially pound its western boundary.

The San Francisco experience must be in some degree an experience of the ocean. In order to know the city fully and the influences that have acted on it throughout its history, it is necessary to confront the Pacific face to face, not only at Ocean Beach south of the Golden Gate, but at representative places along the Bay Area coastline from the Russian River to Santa Cruz. It is necessary to know this shore not merely from the highway but directly, in an intimate personal relationship unavailable from the car or from the windows of buildings with an ocean view. You have to get out and explore on foot the cliffs and headlands and coves, feeling the sand between your toes and the spray of the surf on your face and even the power of the waves on your body.

IN THE BEGINNING

Sleeping near the ocean, you are dimly aware, at intervals through the night, of the rhythmic rising and falling roar of the surf, surely the most primeval sound on this planet, taking you back to all the beginnings, and the beginnings before the beginnings. In the morning you emerge slowly from the ocean of sleep, coming gradually to consciousness, blinking and doubtful, like the first form of life that ventured from the dim regions of the sea into a clear bright morning on some ancient shoreline.

Eastward on this spring morning, the sun is rising over a rocky chaparral-covered ridge of the Coast Range, and the fresh salt air is flavored with the scent of sage and lupine. Below the sea cliff the margin of the ocean is still in shadow, but a wave wells up from the darkness and catches the first morning light; a rim of white appears on the crest and breaks into a sunlit line of driven foam.

Extending into the ocean from the shoreline are broad surface streaks where the water seems brighter, wide avenues that stretch sinuously toward the horizon through the darker fields of the sea, twisted and curved by the winds and flowing currents. On the horizon you see the occasional silhouette of a ship, standing down the coast or bound for the sea lanes of the far Pacific. Several miles offshore a few boats hover over invisible schools of salmon. In the cove directly below you, a seal pokes its head through the surface and peers around. Swift-winged black cormorants skim the water in purposeful, hurried flight.

Behind the sea cliff, rising to the base of the high eastern ridge, are rolling downs and hillocks and swales, meadows above the sea, covered now in May, after the long rains, with lush green grasses and the most spectacular display of wild flowers in memory. Above the continual sound of the surf, the air over the meadows is full of bird calls—the musical twang of the redwings, the chattering of the finches, the startled alarm of the quail, the cawings of gulls, the liquid melody of a thrush, a thousand unidentified twitterings and whistlings. Quick swallows dart over a pond in a hollow and occasionally break the water to skim up an insect.

COPA DE ORO

You walk to the head of a draw where a brook is flowing over low outcrops in a series of small waterfalls and pools. All around you are the bush lupine, standing three and four and occasionally five feet high, with huge spikes of flowers rising like elaborate candelabra, glistening with dew in the morning sun. They appear in an immense variety of sizes and colors—purples and blues and lavenders and pinks.

Below the lupine are the California poppies, spreading bright gold across the meadow, in some places so thick that you can scarcely avoid treading on them. Some of them are pure gold—the Spaniards called them *copa de oro*—others are lighter, with a pale yellow rim. As the morning advances and the warmth of the sun opens the blossoms, their color intensifies until they seem to be incandescent.

Below the lupine and the poppies is an understory of smaller flowers, scarcely larger than a pencil head—reds and purples and blues. In some of the steeper areas the blossoms of the "ice plant" glow in purple and mauve and yellow. Across the meadows are purple nightshades and yellow monkey flowers and pastel morning-glories. Individually, each blossom is worth an hour's study, directly and through the hand lens, which reveals new splendors. In the mass they present an overwhelming excess of beauty you find it impossible to assimilate. And always just beyond them is the brilliant aqua-marine expanse of ocean; its muted roar penetrates every dale and glade. These meadows at the edge of the sea are themselves in-comparable poetry of color and form and sound.

This is an experience of natural art that transcends the art of the museums and the concert halls; it is not someone's interpreta-tion but a firsthand experience of the life force at a vernal peak of exuberance. These wild gardens on the seaward slopes at this sea-son, after the long late rains, are the quintessence of spring, the time of new life, of hope and promise and unbounded prospects.

WAR, PEACE, AND SPRING

It is not only the abundant rains that have given this experience a special intensity this year; it is the incredible contrast between this scene and the continuing human tragedy that cannot be wholly forgotten by anyone who is fully alive. Doubtless some of those ships on the horizon are bound for the holocaust on the far shore, and here at the edge of the continent in the fullness of the spring, the enormity of that war becomes clearer than ever.

In these fields above the ocean every square yard of the flowering earth is an affirmation of life—the ultimate answer to the bulletins from Washington, with their death counts, their tallies of success in the number of bodies on a battlefield, their official regrets for the children maimed and killed. Here, on this coast in the sun at this season of hope and rebirth, is manifest the irresistible sense of life that must somehow overcome the prophets of death, that must spread abroad into all our doings, all our business, all our politics, all our diplomacy, a declaration of life's renewal and triumph.

At the end of the day the lowering sun illuminates a glowing goldbar of cloud over the ocean, then throws flaring red lights on feathery cirrus plumes that rise above, great sweeping swirls and banners and veils of sky vapor like thin fibrous sheets of spindrift flying from an ocean comber. The corrugated ocean surface transmutes the evening colors like a reflecting gem.

In the spreading darkness a pungent zephyr of dry mountain air comes down from the hills. The haunting call of an owl is answered by the mournful tone of a whistle buoy offshore and by the rushing of waves over the sea-worn gravel and cobble of the beach below the cliff. The sphere of Venus burns over the ocean like a point of white fire. The disk of Jupiter is overhead, near the zenith, and in the east appears the red pinpoint light of Mars. A bright star near the southwestern horizon flitters and gleams with all the colors of the spectrum—flashing with dark reds and purples and midnight blues and fiery greens.

You watch as the eastern ridge imperceptibly rolls back with the turning of the earth, revealing new zones of the heavens; and, finally, to the hypnotic rhythms of the ocean, you are absorbed again in sleep.

THE WARM POOL

On a midsummer morning as you walk down to the cove, an extraordinarily low tide has exposed an area of wet sand the size of a polo field. Early morning sunlight, slanting down the steep Coast Range hillside, glistens from the tidal flats, from the white charging surf, from the waves battering the headlands beyond the cove. Far out over the ocean, perhaps ten miles offshore, is a river of fog, moving imperceptibly southward, formed by the oceanic winds as they come into contact with the deep currents of frigid water welling up from the bottom.

The hard wet sand is resilient underfoot. The salt air, the morning light, and the heady excitement of the booming surf are so exhilarating that you involuntarily break into a run, jogging down the exposed sea floor which only a few hours earlier was under eight feet of water. You are drawn irresistibly to the surf, plunge into a headlong comber, and ride several waves before the icy water begins to chill you to the marrow. As you emerge blue and benumbed from the ocean, your eye is caught by a peculiar phenomenon: At the far end of the exposed beach, wisps of vapor seem to rise from the wet sand drift along the surface.

Walking to that area, you note that the vapor is steam and the wet sand is warm to the feet. Evidently this is a hot spring that normally is covered by the ocean but is exposed at times of very low tide. Next to a half-buried boulder is a shallow, warm pool from which rise wisps of steam and a faint smell of sulfur. You lie down in the water, stretching out full length, instantly and gratefully absorbing its warmth. Slowly the heat penetrates inward, thawing your frozen bones. No Roman emperor in his baths ever lolled in greater luxury—or had half so magnificent a view.

The morning sun, just above the steep ridge behind the cove, backlights the brown-gray-green chaparral on the hillside, shining through every translucent leaf of sage and manzanita, illuminating the wild flowers—golden poppies and yellow lupine and red paintbrush. Waves assaulting the rocks of the far point rise in white slow-motion explosions, sending up arching jets that seem to pause imperceptibly at the high point of their trajectory, then shatter and fall like the flowing jewels of light from a dying Roman candle.

At intervals, above the roar of the surf, you hear a puzzling far-off deep moan. You imagine that it might be the call of some ancient brontosaurus that once haunted this flat margin of the land when sea level was lower and returns at these times of rare low tide. Although the moan is audible sporadically, the monster fails to appear, and you totally relax in the sulfurous waters, stretching out fingers and toes to feel the blessed warmth on every square inch of your body.

THE HEAT OF THE EARTH

The steam rises around you in thin veils, and you can feel the sand and water beneath you bubbling pleasantly with the escaping vapors. It occurs to you that you are experiencing, for the first time in your life, the physical heat of the earth itself. Other sources of heat—the heat in buildings, the warmth of direct sunlight, the heat of the dry sand, all are the direct or indirect warmth of that blazing star ninety million miles out in space. But here, in this pool at the edge of the land, the heat from the innards of the earth warms your own innards, and your relationship with the planet is direct and personal.

You recall the only experience you have had which was remotely similar: a hike across the active crater of the volcano Kilauea on the island of Hawaii, as jets of steam rose from volcanic vents in the hardened lava beds around you. Here on this beach, however, you are more than a spectator watching surface manifestations of the inner heat boiling up from the depths of the planet; you are a participant, immersed in it, feeling a direct change in your physical constitution as the earth transmits its heat to your body after the cold swim.

Never before have you felt so close to the earth, never so intimately related to this big rolling sphere that gave birth to all life. As you lie there, absorbing the warmth of the inner earth, it occurs to you that this water is rising from the hot layers thousands of feet below, rock masses that have not cooled off since the entire surface of the planet was a steaming mass of inert matter, totally lifeless.

The primordial rocks that once covered the surface, cooled, produced an atmosphere, somehow gave birth to primitive plant life that in time enriched the atmosphere with its own exhalations. After countless eons, the planet's surface and atmosphere reached the precise balance of elements that created animal life—and ultimately human life.

Now, you reflect, man is releasing new combinations of substances that alter the earth and its air and waters in unknown ways, recklessly tampering with the delicate equilibrium that makes life possible. If in his ignorance he should succeed in upsetting that equilibrium and banishing life from this sphere, would the earth ever again be able to re-establish the balance and cause life to reappear? Or was the creation of life dependent on the exact sequence of events that brought it about—a sequence that will never recur as the earth cools further and even the hot strata that heat this water will grow cold?

Suddenly your reverie is ended as a wave from the surf spreads across the flat sand and spills into your pool, turning it cold. The tide is rising, and your Roman bath is over. Climbing the hillside behind the beach, you hear the low-pitched moan again. Gazing out to sea, you find the source several miles offshore—a giant aircraft carrier moving slowly northward. From below on the beach it had been invisible, hidden by the curvature of the earth—or the curvature of the sea. As you watch, the modern brontosaurus slowly turns seaward and disappears into the fog bank.

AUTUMNAL EQUINOX

Looking out over the ocean on a September afternoon, you are surprised to see two eloquent signs of fall—a monarch butterfly and a Mexican sky. The monarch flutters by in a quick flash of brown and orange, beating an erratic course along the top of the sea cliff, evidently heading for the ancestral wintering place in a nearby grove of eucalyptus. The sky over the ocean and coastal hills is unmistakably autumnal. After the winds and fogs of summer, the upper air now is streaked with white vapors for the first time since spring—thin feathery cirrus clouds from the south, very high, followed by wisps and clusters of lower altocumulus, some of it combed and silky, some thick and woolly.

Slowly, as you watch, the cloud patterns move from the south across the sky in spreading masses and long salients like meteors trailing billowing veils of vapor. This is the visible front of a warm, humid air mass from the seas of Mexico, perhaps from the gulf off Vera Cruz or the Pacific off Puerto Vallarta or possibly even from subtropic seas off the isthmus of Tuantepec.

All summer the prevailing westerlies—pushed onshore by the Pacific High, sucked inland by the low-pressure heat of the California's Central Valley—have assaulted this coast, bringing low fogs or cool clear marine air, totally dominating the coastal weather system. But now, near the time of the equinox, the Pacific High is moving south with the sun to a position perhaps beyond Oahu and Kauai, and the Central Valley is cooling off as the nights grow longer. So the westerlies have subsided, at least temporarily, allowing the warm tropical air to move in from the south.

The sky is pure Mexico, growing more ornate all afternoon. The perfectly level line of stratus that hangs off the coast all summer, or closes in as fog, has now been replaced by wild zigzags of dark vapor that swoop low over the ocean, then soar for the empyrean. The spectacle changes by the minute as the sky grows darker. Sea birds dart nervously overhead, as if anticipating major atmospheric upheavals. You notice that three of the birds overhead are terns, swifter, slimmer, whiter, more angular than gulls, evidently headed southward on their long migrations from the arctic to the tropics.

WAR IN THE SKY

To see the atmospheric show from another vantage point, you turn your back on the ocean and climb into the hills, walking through sun-bleached grasses now golden in the late, cloud-filtered light. The curvaceous forms of the land seem to glow preternaturally in the mellow autumnal atmosphere. Up ahead on the ridge tops, the same light deepens the contrasting rich greens in the walls of Douglas fir and redwood. Low white mists now hang over the ocean and creep up the canyons, vague and translucent, obscuring the sharp edges of rocks and trees, ridges and groves, reminding you of the floating landscapes of Chinese paintings.

As you climb the steep valleys and ridges over the ocean, you can feel on your face the signs of a conflict in the atmosphere. Cool zephyrs off the water alternate with warm air masses from inland. The aromas of salt and kelp are momentarily replaced by the warm smells of sage and laurel and dry grasses.

Climbing over a rise, you can see, far off to the southeast beyond successive ridges, the top of the Golden Gate Bridge and beyond it a sector of the city, rising out of the milky mists like the towers of Camelot. Shafts of sunlight penetrating the cloud canopy illuminate arcs of blue bay and the Berkeley Hills along the eastern shore. Beyond the far hills, the upper slopes of Mount Diablo rise from the haze into an intermediate layer of clear air.

Walking back down the steep slope of the Coast Range, you face the ocean, now nearly white in the blacklighted mists. The line between sea and sky is obscured, and a single fishing boat moves slowly across the merged mass like an ant crossing a blank movie screen, alone and somehow heroic against the vast aqueous backdrop.

As you descend the long winding trail to the cliff top, there is a sudden change in the atmospheric forces. The conflict between cool sea air and warm land breeze swiftly escalates into war. Great gusts of hot wind roar down from the mountain, stirring up swirls of dust and leaves, bending the dry grasses and chaparral in ripples and waves. Over the cliffs the gulls ride the roller-coaster air currents with zest, rising on invisible thermal elevators and sliding down again in nearly vertical dives.

TWILIGHT OF A RACE

Suddenly against the dark sky to the south, over the Golden Gate, lightning crackles out of a cloud, blue and prickly. There is a spatter of rain, then a second flash much closer, and the hills and sea cliffs resound with volleys of thunderbolts. Even more startling than the lightning is a sight straight overhead. A dozen huge pelicans, spread-winged, sail across the zenith at an altitude of several hundred feet. They circle slowly, change from a ragged-V formation to a straight file and back again, moving gradually northwestward along the coast and over the ocean, taking advantage of every air current. Then from over a ridge behind you comes another flight of the giant birds, followed in a few moments by two more squadrons until perhaps fifty birds are in view.

They glide leisurely toward the ocean through the storm, moving their wings occasionally, dipping, rising and and falling in a fantastic slow-motion ballet. At intervals four or five individuals sail off from the flight on a tangent of their own, going through some intricate, specialized maneuvers that bring them back eventually to the main group. As they soar against the wild sky, unperturbed by the Wagnerian flashes of lightning and thunderclaps, you recall that they may be the last of their race, a final heroic generation without progeny, the last survivors of a species, victims of accidental extermination by man's ravaging poisons. Is this magnificent aerial exhibition a symbolic ceremony, the *Götterdämmerung* of a race, the stormy finale of a million-year drama?

A zigzag flash of blue-white light explodes with an ear-ringing impact over the nearest ridge. The stray raindrops turn to a pelting downpour. The squadrons of big birds disappear over the far headland as the lowering sun sets long cloud strata ablaze with orange fire, edged with crimson and purple. In a few minutes the spectacle is over. The sky is gray; the wind dies; the rain stops. Far off to the south, perhaps over Monterey Bay, there are still some glimmerings of light playing among the cloud curtains of dying thunderheads.

Waves swirling into foam around the rocks below the sea cliff appear oddly luminous in the gathering dark, as if they were belatedly reflecting the departed fires in the sky. Here is another sign of the coming equinox—the fall flowering of the dinoflagellates, minute planktonic life sometimes proliferating so abundantly that the ocean is stained rust red by day and radiates a ghostly glow at night. These are the ominous red tides the Indians wisely regarded as signs that shellfish may be poisonous. Unlike the poisons that the Indians' successors are pouring into these waters, the red tide will disappear in a few days.

Tomorrow the westerlies may resume, but with decreased force. In the days to come, the fog will move in again intermittently, flowing with autumnal slowness, clinging to the contours of the land, diminishing steadily day by day, as the sun passes over the equator, the earth tilts on its axis, and the Northern Hemisphere begins its journey into the season of darkness.

Finale: Camelot in Crisis

WHEN ONE of San Francisco's contemporary supervisors was asked to participate in a symposium on "The City in Crisis," he commented wearily that the title was redundant. These days, he pointed out, the city—any city—is a veritable synonym for crisis. Nearly every American metropolis is precariously close to bankruptcy, and the ritual recital of accelerating decadence is too familiar—crime in the streets, traffic congestion, smog, water pollution, urban sprawl, ghettos, impoverished schools, discrimination, unemployment—the list is long and dismal. San Francisco and the regional metropolis of which it is the center are not immune to these urban viruses. However, we will make no detailed attempt here to analyze the city's social problems. Such a task would require a book in itself—and that book has already been written many times. The story has been told in dozens of volumes about America's urban travail, which does not differ greatly from city to city.

However, this city and its environs face one major threat not present to the same degree in any other U.S. urban region. The Bay Area metropolis is the only American conurbation resting directly on an earthquake fault system of the first magnitude. The San Andreas Fault—probably the greatest continental rift on earth, extending for hundreds of miles through California—slices across Marin County between Tomales and Bolinas bays, runs along the ocean shore off the Golden Gate, and strikes land again just south of the San Francisco-Daly City boundary. It proceeds south down the Peninsula, where hundreds of homes have been built directly on the broad fault zone. East of the bay, the Hayward Fault, a major branch of the San Andreas, runs along the foot of the Berkeley Hills and has also been covered with buildings. Besides these two major breaks, the surface of the entire region is cobwebbed with minor or inactive faults, including two within San Francisco itself. It should be remembered that the Southern California quake of February 1971, which took sixty-four lives and destroyed one billion dollars worth of property, took place along a minor fault which had been considered inactive.

Within historic times, the San Andreas and Hayward faults have heaved disastrously, causing serious damage, long before the fault zones were covered with houses. There have been major quakes in 1836 (Hayward), 1838 (San Andreas), 1865 (San Andreas), 1868 (Hayward), and 1906 (San Andreas). The last mentioned directly and indirectly killed about one thousand people. The long quiescence since 1906, except for some unimportant tremors, is highly ominous. Intolerable strains are building up deep in the earth and may be released at any time in a great quake comparable to that of 1906.

THE OSTRICH POSE

Despite this clear and present danger, Bay Area residents, like most other Californians, prefer to pretend that the earthquake threat does not exist. If adequate precautions were taken, even in another 1906-sized jolt most of the potential casualties and property damage could be prevented. Yet "earthquake" is a taboo word in the Bay Area, and officials are afraid to mention it. The most widespread danger in the next quake would be in downtown areas, where falling cornices, parapets, bricks, and glass would hurtle down into the street. In 1969 San Francisco's supervisors, jogged by earthquake experts, belatedly passed a "parapet ordinance" requiring removal of potentially lethal ornamentation on large buildings. But for three years they failed to appropriate any money for inspectors to enforce the law. Since many years would be required for full enforcement, the lost time could mean thousands of unnecessary casualties.

A parapet ordinance, however, is only the first step. There should be a detailed inspection of every building in the city to find what strengthening is necessary; prohibition of all building on faults and on unstable steep slopes; education of householders to earthquake precautions around the home; repair or rebuilding of unsafe school and public buildings. About one-third of San Francisco's schools do not measure up to legal earthquake standards.

It is not only only old buildings that are dangerous. Some modern skyscrapers, structural engineers believe, can be expected to collapse on their occupants in a 1906-scale quake. Yet there is no program even to identify these buildings. On the other hand, most frame houses will probably come through a maximum shake without important damage, provided they are built on solid ground and bolted to the foundations. Most brick or adobe houses are a bad bet, as are many houses on steep slopes or poorly filled ground.

When the inevitable quake comes, anyone in an area of large buildings would be well advised not to rush out into the street but to get away from windows and take refuge in a doorway or under a table—and remember that it will all be over in less than a minute. In order to make a home secure in advance of a shake, it would be prudent to remove heavy pictures and mirrors from locations above beds and chairs, be sure the water heater is well braced, check loose roof tiles, and learn where to turn off the gas, water, and electricity in case of breaks in the lines. Above all, it would be wise to elect officials who do not have their heads in the sand when it comes to earthquakes. Nearly all incumbents do.

THE FREEWAY JUGGERNAUT

Earthquakes aside, there are signs that the residents of this region are capable of meeting contemporary urban dilemmas with some of the individualism, ingenuity, and vitality that have been characteristic of San Francisco since the Gold Rush. On notable occasions they have refused to prostrate themselves before the bulldozers that are relentlessly paving over, besmogging, and homogenizing every American city in the name of progress.

San Francisco was the first large city to resist successfully the efforts of the freeway builders. In the late 1950's and early '60's, federal, state, and city governments were determined to interconnect the various bridges and freeways coming into the city with a network of cross-town freeways that would have invaded Golden Gate Park, several neighborhoods, and the northern waterfront. Residents rose up in the great freeway revolt, deluged the City Hall with petitions and protests, and forced abandonment of the scheme. The chief source of their inspiration—or desperation—was the monstrous Embarcadero Freeway, which some years earlier had been built halfway along the eastern waterfront and in front of the hallowed Ferry Building before anyone realized what was happening. A campaign to demolish it has not yet been successful, but at least its extension along the northern shore was stopped cold at the stub ends.

As a consequence of San Francisco's victory, several other cities, including New Orleans and Boston, have found it possible to resist the freeway juggernaut, and substantial highway reforms were incorporated in the act of Congress establishing the U. S. Department of Transportation. Doubtless the cross-city freeway proposal will come up again, however, testing San Francisco's will to resist.

In order to clear up the chaos of urban transportation, it is not enough to resist the construction of new freeways. Accordingly, the voters of the region in 1962 approved the first-stage construction of the Bay Area Rapid Transit system (BART), a network of electric trains to link various parts of the region with the central city, including a tube under the bay. Despite financial difficulties during construction, BART is to be the nation's first large modern public transportation system—the only rational alternative to submitting to the insatiable demands of the automobile.

MANHATTAN BY THE GATE

Another menacing face of progress is the ongoing Manhattanization of San Francisco. In the 1960's a score of high-rise buildings drastically altered the city's skyline, some of them twice the height of the thirty-one-story Russ Building, which has been the city's tallest for forty years. San Francisco's hills and views of the bay have always been its greatest physical assets. Yet increasingly they are being surrounded by walls of concrete that have already turned some downtown streets into dismal canyons where the sun never penetrates.

The city's first successful efforts to resist high-rise blight took place before World War II, when some foresighted residents of Telegraph Hill were able to preserve the special quality of that enclave by obtaining a forty-foot height limit on buildings there. In the mid-1960's the twin slabs of the high-rise Fontana Apartments walled off a portion of Russian Hill from the bay and so enraged residents that they succeeded in obtaining a forty-foot limit for most of the rest of the northern waterfront. The consequence was not only to preserve the city's views northward but to save the old Ghirardelli Chocolate Factory, which would have been replaced by a skyscraper. Instead, the old buildings were remodeled and supplemented; the resulting shops, plazas, terraces, and restaurants of Ghirardelli Square, overlooking the bay, are now one of the city's brightest attractions—as is the nearby Cannery, where a similar rehabilitation took place. Both are infinitely more valuable—and more San Franciscan—than the high-rise structures that would have been built there.

But still the monoliths continued to rise in the Financial District and immediately south of Telegraph Hill, including the pointed Transamerica "pyramid," which resembles a space rocket. Lewis Mumford has described it as exhibiting "the essentially archaic and regressive nature of the science-fiction mind." Such urban dinosaurs as these, including a proposed office building on the waterfront just south of the Ferry Building, to be as high as the towers of the Bay Bridge, provoked another revolt. In 1971 dressmaker Alvin Duskin sponsored a petition campaign to require that any planned building higher than six stories be submitted to the voters for approval. Practical or not, the proposal dramatized the high-rise issue and put pressure on city officials to take action against chronic Manhattanization. At about the same time, the city adopted the new Urban Design Plan, which would mitigate but not eliminate further high-rise blight.

SAVE THE BAY: SAVE THE LAND

The walling of the hills has been accompanied by another incursion of progress, the filling of the bay. By the mid-1960's vast areas of the bay had been replaced by subdivisions, airports, commercial centers, freeways, and garbage dumps. The resulting citizens' uprising was stimulated by accumulated resentment against the continued degradation of the environment in the name of "development." The remarkable grass-roots save-the-bay campaign involved thousands of people and in 1969 resulted in state legislation setting up a permanent Bay Conservation and Development Commission. BCDC's job is to hold the line on filling and carry out a plan for enhancing the bay and its shores for public use. The remarkable success of the save-the-bay crusade offered heartening evidence that it is possible for ordinary citizens to triumph over the well-financed and highly organized strength of politically powerful developers. Degradation of the environment, it seems, is not inevitable.

The save-the-bay victory set the stage for a similar campaign to save the land. As in the case of the Embarcadero Freeway, the skyscrapers, and the bay fills, there was a "horrible example" to stimulate citizen action. For generations the broad Santa Clara Valley at the southern end of the bay was filled with orchards producing great quantities of pears, apricots, prunes, and cherries. To walk or drive through the valley was an unsurpassed experience in rural beauty, particularly at blossom time in March. After World War II, however, the orchards began to be ripped up for subdivisions, and the process was accelerated until the entire valley, centering on San Jose, became a prime example of urban sprawl— mile after mile of housing tracts, used-car lots, gas stations, shopping centers, factories, billboards, parking lots, congested traffic, and smog.

Residents of the Napa Valley, at the north end of the bay, watching subdivisions invade their famed vineyards, organized a save-the-vineyards campaign. In 1970 they succeeded in setting up an agricultural preserve in which subdivision into less than twenty-acre holdings was prohibited. The result was to halt the bulldozers. In the same year Bay Area conservation organizations—notably People for Open Space—launched a major effort for an open-space commission modeled on BCDC to save a large proportion of the remaining hills and valleys as the bay had been saved. In 1971 the goal was modified to embrace a comprehensive regional agency with jurisdiction over open space, transportation, and other environmental matters.

END OF THE GROWTH CULT

Central to the environmental crisis in this region as elsewhere is the entire problem of growth. How long can constantly increasing automobile traffic be accommodated by additional freeways? How far should communities "grow" into the bay or into the sky, or into the countryside? Is there a limit to the number of people who can be accommodated in a city or region? There are still powerful champions of unlimited growth in the Bay Area, but they are increasingly being questioned and challenged. Perhaps the crowning symbol of the new viewpoint came in 1971 when the director of the hyperthyroid Santa Clara County Chamber of Commerce resigned, indicating that he had had a change of heart. The unlimited growth the chamber had promoted so successfully had brought innumerable troubles to the Santa Clara Valley. San Jose's strenuous effort to become the most populous city in the Bay Region began to seem anachronistic in the 1970's. But for the once-verdant valley at the southern end of the bay it was too late.

It was not too late, however, for other valleys, for Napa and Sonoma, the example; for the hills of West Marin, for the coast side of San Mateo County, for Santa Cruz County—all still largely rural, agriculturally productive, and scenically magnificent. To maintain most of these green regions as breathing spaces for the increasingly crowded metropolis around the bay would be to preserve a vital element of the special quality of life that has always been distinctively San Franciscan. The alternative is the kind of homogeneous sea of tract houses, asphalt, smog, and pollution that is engulfing metropolitan regions elsewhere.

THE COST OF QUALITY

It is easy, of course, to decide to save the open valleys, hills, streams, and canyons; it is something else to devise the ways and means. Who is to pay for preserving open space? Is the land to be purchased from the owners? Or if it is simply zoned for open space, are the owners to be compensated for the resulting diminished value of their property? To answer these questions will tax the ingenuity of the planners and economists. However, certain guiding principles are evident. Economic studies indicate that it can be less expensive in the long haul for a community to buy open land on the periphery than to pay the expenses of servicing the new subdivisions that would be built there. To provide streets, utilities, police and fire protection, and schools would in many cases cost more than to purchase the land and leave it open.

When funds are needed for parks, open spaces and other amenities, the bill should not be sent to the homeowner but to the speculators who are making fortunes as a result of socially increased land values. If cities and urban regions are near bankruptcy, the reason is the failure of the tax system to tap these sources of unearned wealth. A case in point is BART. Experience elsewhere indicates that land around BART stations will increase in value up to ten times. The fortunate owners, through no effort of their own, will reap most of the benefit. Why shouldn't the public recover its investment in BART with a tax on the increased value? Estimates indicate that the increase in value would roughly equal the total cost of building the system.

BART is the most obvious example, but other public actions also cause the value of land to skyrocket—roads, aqueducts, schools, population growth. A tax on this increased value, payable at time of sale or change in use, would retrieve the public investment and enable communities and regions to purchase the land necessary for public purposes. In 1971, as a result of unofficial recommendations from San Francisco, a committee of the legislature for the first time proposed a special tax on increased land values resulting from public projects. Perhaps local-government bankruptcy, like environmental degradation, is not inevitable after all. And perhaps the Bay Area can again show the way.

THE HERITAGE OF GOLD

My own first residence in the Bay Area was International House in Berkeley, during my student days long ago. From there, at the foot of the Berkeley Hills, I could look down the sloping plain to the bay glittering in the sunlight, to the white towers of the city rising on the far shore like some modern Camelot. I watched the sun set behind the Golden Gate or the purple ridge of Tamalpais and saw the lights come on in the cities around the shores—a prospect to send the blood racing and to fire the imagination with untold possibilities. I wondered, then, about the people living in this metropolis. Did this superlative environment produce superlative individuals? Did it inspire them to brilliant insights and heroic achievements?

Later, to sober analysis, the question appeared unduly romantic. On the average, people everywhere seemed very similar in their range of talents and achievements, regardless of the environment. And at times San Francisco even seemed less dynamic, more preoccupied with the past, less progressive than the residents of booming Los Angeles, for example.

Now, however, three decades later, I am inclined to believe that my first impulsive reaction may have had more than a modicum of validity. The reasons may be historical as well as geographical. San Francisco did not grow slowly into cityhood but fairly exploded into existence with the Gold Rush. Its population was composed to a high degree of reckless individualists who endured grueling hardships to come here from various parts of the globe. San Francisco attracted people temperamentally bold and innovative; they took high risks for high stakes. Many gambled and lost, but altogether they possessed extraordinary vitality and ingenuity. With crude impatience they brushed aside custom and convention for new approaches and unorthodox methods. Their vitality took many directions, not all socially beneficial, but it set the tone and style of the city for generations to come. These extraordinary people came to an extraordinary environment—a place which explorers for nearly two centuries had predicted would be the site of an "imperial city."

THE ENVIRONMENTAL REVOLUTION

I have a feeling that something of the heritage of energy and innovation remains, continually recharged by the special quality of this land around the bay. Appropriately, the heritage nowadays takes new shapes. It is no longer primarily concerned with empire building and booming growth but with the quality and style of life. Consider the innovations in architecture, for example, (Bay Region Modern); in painting (the "San Francisco School"); in music (rock groups); in avant garde cultural movements (the beat generation, the "San Francisco Renaissance," the hippies); in student activism (Berkeley and San Francisco State College); in the entire counterculture, that widespread challenge to American complacency in the early 1970's. For better or for worse, these are not indications of a smug or stagnant society; they are signs of ferment and challenge, a modern counterpart of the vital turbulence of the Gold Rush era.

Perhaps the most emphatic evidence of this innovative activity related to the quality of life has been the region's leadership in preservation of the human environment. The freeway revolt, the save-the-bay victory, the anti-Manhattanization campaign, the open-space effort must be seen against the background of a region where the natural environment has been a matter of urgent concern since John Muir founded the Sierra Club here in 1892 and began the modern conservation movement. Long before the contemporary excitement over ecology swept the nation, a Bay Area organization called Ecology Action was holding demonstrations against pollution, and the first Ecology Center was established in Berkeley in 1969. Within two years there were more than one hundred Ecology Centers throughout the U.S. A major recognition of San Francisco's pre-eminence in this field came when it was chosen in 1969 as the site of the national UNESCO Conference on Man and His Environment. In the face of a tyrannical technology that would submerge every American city in concrete, asphalt, and sterile uniformity, the San Francisco region has provided resistance and leadership, much as Boston was the initial center of resistance to another kind of tyranny two hundred years ago.

Are these vital currents of thought and action a consequence of geography as well as history? Do they arise inevitably out of this superlative environment, as the distinctive qualities of Hellenic culture rose from the shores of the eastern Mediterranean?

The question, of course, cannot be answered simply or definitively, and possibly it cannot be answered at all. But go to any of the heights around these shores, gaze out at the great bay, watch the light scintillate from the cobalt surface, from the surrounding constellations of cities and the far rim of mountains, feel the cool sea wind here at the continent's end, and ask yourself the same question. The attempt to answer it is an indispensable part of the San Francisco experience.

Epilogue

LISTEN, FIRST, to the foghorn chorus.

This is the sound San Franciscans hear on many mornings before dawn, through the curtain of sleep. These are the voices of the deep, chanting, in their own solemn language, a warning to navigators who sail the bay through the gloom of the thick mists that hang over the waters in this dark hour like a shroud.

They warn of danger, of rocks and shoals, of sea walls and cliffs where many a ship has met disaster. Out in the Golden Gate, the pilot of an incoming freighter listens attentively and guides his ship between the cliffs of the strait.

There are other sounds in the black of early morning, while the city still sleeps, down along the waterfront at Fisherman's Wharf. Out behind the darkened restaurants, along the wharves where the long rows of boats are moored, fishermen's voices are heard across the water in Italian. One-cylinder engines sputter tentatively, then begin a rhythmic chug-chug as they move out through the fog to gather the harvest of big succulent crabs from the ocean floor.

At the Islais Creek Produce Terminal, in the southeastern corner of the city, the noises are the roar of diesel trucks with food for the city's markets; the yells of the drivers, jockeying the big diesels into position; the voices of the clerks tallying the crates and cartons of fruit from the orchards of the Sacramento Valley, lettuce from the fields on the Salinas, asparagus from the rich peat islands of the Delta.

As the gray light of morning appears through the fog, diffuse and directionless, the sleepers of the city begin to stir in the warmth of their beds, and many of them hear another sound as they rouse to wakefulness—the click and hum of the long cables in the slots beneath the street, adding their running flow, like the sound of a river, to the rhythms of the city. Then, as the sleepers awaken, come the sounds of the cars themselves, first the familiar tattoo of the gripman clanging his bell, then the rumble of the car on the tracks and a grinding clash as the conductor tightens the wooden shoe brakes on a downhill grade.

From several directions now come the sounds of a flood tide of workers flowing into the city—the distinctive hum of automobiles and trucks and buses on the top deck of the Bay Bridge; the rumble of cars on the fogbound span at the Golden Gate, as the foghorn beneath the deck gives a loud blast; the whistles of locomotives, the rumble of the railroad cars, the click of the wheels on the rails as the commuter trains roll in from the Peninsula and grind to a stop at the Southern Pacific depot. On Market Street the din of traffic reaches a peak at eight o'clock as the Ferry Building siren sends its wail out across the city, signaling the start of the working day. From schoolyards in every neighborhood come the voices of hordes of energetic youngsters screaming exuberantly, then the bell, bringing silence, and the solemn high-pitched chant: "I pledge allegiance to the flag . . ."

The sounds of San Francisco now are the sounds of a city at work. From the factories and foundries south of Market comes the roar of engines and forges and presses; from Montgomery Street and the business district the clack of typewriters, the whir of calculators, the click of the tickers at the Stock Exchange.

From the bay comes the whistle signal of a freighter—one long blast, three short, one long—the call for a Redstack tug; and the higher-pitched whistle of a tug echoes the call. To the ear of the initiate along the waterfront, the tone of a whistle may reveal a ship's identity—the gravelly bass of the *China Bear,* the resounding baritone of the *President Cleveland,* the soprano toot of the Santa Fe tug, the reverberating blast of the P & O liners from London.

From the docks where the ships are loading come the yells of longshoremen, the creak and rattle of winches, the clatter of sling loads lowered to the piers. Along the Embarcadero is the sound of an insistent bell, the whine of an electric locomotive, the banging of freight cars together as the Belt Line Railroad shunts the cars to and from the docks.

At noon the Ferry Building siren is joined by an ensemble of factory whistles and a paean of bells from a score of church towers, from Grace Cathedral on Nob Hill, from Saints Peter and Paul in

North Beach, from Old Saint Mary's at the edge of Chinatown. From the restaurants and grills and cafeterias come the clank of silver and the rattle of dishes and the babble of voices ordering lunch.

In the afternoon, if the fog burns off, the people gather in the parks or stand on street corners in the sun and pass the time of day in a score of languages, and you know with a reasonable certainty where you are by hearing the dialect. Italian: North Beach. Cantonese: Grant Avenue. Russian: Potrero Hill or the Richmond. Spanish, the Filipino colony on Kearny or the Latin American colony in the Mission.

The sounds of the city in the afternoon are the shrill, urgent squawk of a turning Muni bus like bleating sheep led to the slaughter; the straining of an automobile engine rising Nob Hill and the thud of brakes as the car ahead stops suddenly at the crest; the calliope of the merry-go-round at Playland; the laughing dummy in the Fun House.

The sounds of an afternoon in San Francisco are the primeval barking of the sea lions on Seal Rocks, the minor-keyed cries of the gulls riding the air currents at Land's End, the shattering impact of giant combers on the rocks below the Cliff House like the rumble of distant artillery. The same wind that blows from the ocean and rips the tops off the breaking waves also funnels through the narrows of the Golden Gate, plucks the cables of the bridge and hums through the girders until the steel colossus sings like an aeolian harp.

San Francisco is a city where the sounds are music and fragments of music weave a pattern of meaningful sound. Wander through the streets at night and listen—a high-pitched chant from a Chinatown phonograph; the sound of an accordion on the lower slopes of Telegraph Hill; from the Opera House on Van Ness the tympanic thunder of a Wagnerian overture; from Longshoremen's Hall the electronic din of a rock concert. Along Broadway in North Beach the doors of the bars swing open, spilling into the street the operatic anguish of a Pagliaccian tenor, the sad sweet lilt of an Italian folk song, the off-key bellows of a bibulous crowd singing "Daisy, Daisy, give me your answer, do . . ."

Some time after midnight, as the theaters grow dark, the neon flickers off, and the bars are emptied, quiet settles over the city, broken only by a few sounds—the clink of coffee cups in all-night eateries, the dismal wail of an ambulance siren, the grinding of winch engines at the wharves where longshoremen work perishable cargoes and the Belt Line Railroad continues to clang along the Embarcadero.

In the offices of the morning paper the bulletins clatter in on the teletypes; the night city editor listens with one ear to the police radio; and down in the basement with an impenetrable din the presses roll out a thousand papers a minute for a half million breakfast tables.

Through the dark deserted streets the fog rolls in thick damp billows, and from far out over the cold black surface of the bay and the hidden cliffs of the Golden Gate come the voices of the deep, once more in a solemn chorus chanting the rhythms of the sea and of the vapors that rise from the waters . . . as the city sleeps.

Index